The Relaxation &
Stress Reduction
Workbook

by Martha Davis, Ph.D.
Elizabeth Robbins Eshelman, M.S.W.
Matthew McKay, Ph.D.

Illustrations by Valerie Winemiller

Significant contributions to the third edition were made by writers Susan Johnson and Mary Hills Hoffman.

Publisher's Note
This publication is designed to provide accurate and authoritative information in regard to the subject matter covered. It is sold with the understanding that the publisher is not engaged in rendering psychological, financial, legal, or other professional services. If expert assistance or counseling is needed, the services of a competent professional should be sought.

Copyright © 1988 by **New Harbinger Publications, Inc.**

5674 Shattuck Avenue

Oakland, CA 94609

All rights reserved

Printed in the United States of America

FIRST EDITION

First printing May 1980, 1,000 copies
Second printing November 1980, 9,000 copies
Third printing April 1981, 10,000 copies
Fourth printing October 1981, 10,500 copies

SECOND EDITION

First printing April 1982, 20,000 copies
Second printing February 1983, 10,500 copies
Third printing November 1983, 12,000 copies
Fourth printing July 1984, 15,000 copies
Fifth printing February 1985, 15,000 copies
Sixth printing October 1985, 15,000 copies
Seventh printing September 1986, 10,000 copies
Eighth printing April 1987, 10,000 copies
Ninth printing September 1987, 10,000 copies

THIRD EDITION

First printing September 1988 , 10,000 copies
Second printing February 1989, 20,000 copies
Third printing July 1989, 10,000 copies
Fourth printing November 1989, 5,000 copies
Fifth printing February 1990, 5,000 copies
Sixth printing May 1990, 7,000 copies
Seventh printing August 1990, 10,000
Eighth printing November, 1990, 15,000

Contents

How to Get the Most Out of This Workbook

This workbook can be used effectively without the assistance of a professional therapist or teacher. Ample additional resources are provided as "Further Reading" at the end of each chapter, so that you can seek out additional knowledge or assistance if you need it.

Read chapters one and two first. They are the foundation upon which all the other chapters are built. After you have read the first two chapters, you will know enough about stress and your personal reactions to stress to decide which chapter it will be most beneficial for you to read next.

This book is particularly useful if you work with people who are in stress. Doctors, nurses, therapists, teachers, supervisors and others will find many of the techniques described in this workbook not only of use in their personal lives, but also of help to their patients, students and employees.

A basic premise of this workbook is that the benefits of relaxation and stress reduction techniques can only be fully realized after they have been practiced regularly over a period of time. Intellectual understanding of most techniques is of little value, unless accompanied by first hand experience. Therefore, if you plan to use these techniques in a professional setting to help others who are experiencing stress, first develop personal familiarity with them.

The length of time required each day to practice the relaxation techniques in this workbook varies. We suggest that you spend some time doing the exercises of your choice every day. If doing the exercises seven days a seek seems too much, plan one or two holidays a week—but don't let them just happen! Choose a quiet place where you will not be interrupted to learn the techniques. Since this is a new activity for you, it is wise to explain to the people around you what you are doing. Ask them politely to help you by leaving you alone without any distractions. Family members, fellow office workers and friends tend to be very supportive of these exercises once they understand what you are doing and why.

The purpose of regular practice is twofold. First, it will ensure that you will be able to consciously carry out the exercise instructions anytime you need to, without having to refer to written materials. Secondly, regular practice will develop the habit of relaxing at an unconscious level.

If for some reason you are unable to do your exercises one day, treat this as if you had missed an appointment with a busy doctor. Give yourself the same courtesy that you would give the doctor: immediately set up your next appointment with yourself at a specific time.

If you are not very highly motivated or have a history of vey poor self-discipline, do your exercises with another person. That way you can share your experiences and give and receive encouragement. If you still have trouble accomplishing what you set out to do, turn to Chapter 2(

If your reaction to stress involves physical symptoms such as frequent headaches, stomach problems or high blood pressure, get a checkup first. Tell your doctor that you intend to practice relaxation techniques, and ask him or her to determine whether your physical symptoms are caused entirely by stress, or if there are physiological causes as well. Once you start, consult your physician if you experience any prolonged physical ill effects.

1

How You React To Stress

Stress is an everyday fact of life. You can't avoid it. Stress is any change that you must adjust to. While you usually think of stressful events as being negative, such as injury, illness, or death of a loved one, they can also be positive. For instance, getting a new home or a promotion brings with it the stress of change of status and new responsibilities. Falling in love can be as stressful for some people as falling out of love. All stress is not bad. Stress is not only desirable but essential to life. Whether your stress experience is a result of major life changes or the cumulative effects of minor everyday hassles, it is how you react to stressful experiences that can create a stress response.

You experience stress from three basic sources: your environment, your body, and your thoughts. Your environment bombards you with demands to adjust. You must endure weather, noise, crowding, interpersonal demands, time pressures, performance standards, and various threats to your security and self-esteem.

The second source of stress is physiological. The rapid growth of adolescence, menopause in women, aging, illness, accidents, lack of exercise, poor nutrition, and sleep disturbances all tax the body. Your reaction to environmental threats and changes also produce body changes which are themselves stressful.

The third source of stress is your thoughts. Your brain interprets and translates complex changes in your environment and determines when to push the panic button. How you interpret, perceive, and label your present experience and what you predict for the future can serve either to relax or stress you. Interpreting a sour look from your boss to mean that you are doing an inadequate job is likely to be very anxiety provoking. Interpreting the same look as tiredness or preoccupation with personal problems will not be as frightening. Stress researcher Richard Lazarus has argued that stress begins with your *appraisal* of a situation. You first ask yourself what is happening and why (causality). Then, to determine the situation's significance for your well being, you ask how dangerous it is and what resources you have to cope with it. Anxious, stressed people often decide that (1) an event is dangerous, difficult, or painful and (2) they don't have the resources to cope. This book is designed to help you change your appraisals. The skills you learn here will give you confidence that you can cope.

Fight or Flight Response

The groundwork for the modern meaning of "stress" as a psychological problem was laid by Walter B. Cannon, a physiologist at Harvard around the turn of the century. He was the first to describe the "fight or flight response" as a series of biochemical changes that prepare you to deal with threats. Primitive man needed quick bursts of energy to fight or flee such predators as the saber-toothed tiger. These days, when social custom prevents you from fighting or running away, stress triggers a mobilizing response that is no longer useful. In fact, a chronic fight or flight response can greatly harm you both physically and emotionally.

Hans Selye, the first major researcher on stress, was able to trace exactly what happens in your body during the fight or flight response. He found that any problem, imagined or real, can cause the cerebral cortex (the thinking part of the brain) to send an alarm signal to the hypothalamus (the main switch for the stress response, located in the midbrain). The hypothalamus then stimulates the Sympathetic Nervous System (SNS) to make a series of changes in your body. Your heart rate, blood volume, and blood pressure all go up. You start to perspire. Your hands and feet get cold as blood is directed away from your extremities and digestive system into the larger muscles that can help you fight or run. Your diaphragm and anus lock. Your pupils dilate to sharpen vision and your hearing becomes more acute.

While all this is going on, something else happens that can have long-term negative effects if left unchecked. Your adrenal glands start to secret corticoids (adrenaline, epinephrine, norepinephrine) which inhibit digestion, reproduction, growth and tissue repair, and the immune and the inflammatory responses. In other words, some very important functions that keep you feeling healthy and strong start to shut down.

The same mechanism that turned the stress response on can turn it off. As soon as you decide that a situation is no longer dangerous, your brain stops sending emergency signals to your brain stem, which in turn stops sending panic messages to your nervous systems. The hormones and chemicals that put your body in a state of arousal are quickly metabolized. Three minutes after you stop sending your body danger messages, the fight or flight response burns out and you return to normal. Unfortunately if the message to turn off the fight or flight response does not occur, and if the biochemical and hormonal changes that happen during the fight or flight reponse continue, chronic stress can result.

Chronic Stress and Disease

There are, of course, times when the stress response is still adaptive today: in the face of physical danger or in sports that require fast, rigorous muscle activity. However, if you are experiencing a constant or prolonged stress response, you can be increasing your chances of a stress-related disease.

Researchers have been looking at stress physiology for the past fifty years. Scientists have observed that people suffering from stress-related disorders tend to show hyperactivity in a particular "preferred system," such as the skeletal-muscular, cardiovascular, or gastrointestinal system. For example, the evidence shows that chronic stress can contribute to muscle myopathy (weakness) for some people. For others, elevated blood pressure can develop into stress hypertension, damaging the heart and arteries. Still others develop diseases such as peptic ulcers, colitis, and chronic diarrhea when stress inhibits the body's digestive functions.

Almost every body system can be damaged by stress. Suppression of the reproduction system can cause amenorrhea (suppression of menstruation) and failure to ovulate in women, impotency in men, and loss of libido in both. Stress-triggered changes in the lungs contribute to asthma, bronchitis, and other respiratory conditions. Loss of insulin during the stress response may contribute to the onset of diabetes. Stress suspends tissue repair and remodeling which in turn causes decalcification of the bones, osteoporosis, and susceptibility to fractures. Inhibition of the immune and inflammatory systems makes you more susceptible to disease. In addition, stress has been found to be related to other ailments such as headaches, muscle tension, fatigue, and arthritis. There is some evidence that the continued release and depletion of norepinephrine during a state of chronic stress can contribute to major depression.

The relationship between chronic stress, disease, and aging is another area of research which is of interest to scientists. Aging experts are looking at the changing patterns of disease and the emergence of degenerative disorders. The threat of infectious diseases such as tuberculosis, typhoid, pneumonia, and polio have been replaced with "modern plagues" including cardiovascular disease, cancer, arthritis, respiratory disorders such as asthma and emphysema, and a pervasive incidence of depression. As you age normally, there is an expected and natural slowing down of the body's functioning. However, many of the disorders listed above and found from mid-life to late-life are stress-sensitive diseases. Both researchers and clinicians are now asking how stress accelerates the aging process and what can be done to counteract this process.

Coping With Stress

The cost of health care in the United States is skyrocketing. One of the major reasons for this is that the great majority of Americans do not practice preventive medicine. They don't make an effort to reduce the stresses in their lives.

If your lifestyle and thoughts constantly require your brain to send signals to start up or keep the stress response going, you are not giving your brain a chance to do its primary job—health maintenance. In their book *The Healing Brain,* David

Sobel and Robert Ornstein assert that "Health maintenance is the primary function of the brain, not rational thought, language, or poetry." The very centers of the brain that speed up your biochemical processes when you are alarmed can be called upon to slow these processes down. The relaxation response is the opposite of the alarm response and it returns your body to its natural balanced state. Your pupils, hearing, blood pressure, heart beat, respiration, and circulation return to normal and your muscles relax. The relaxation response has a recuperative effect in that it allows you a respite from external stress of the environment and the internal stress of your thoughts. It keeps you from using up all your vital energy at once as you react, then overreact, and are finally overwhelmed by the stresses in your life. The relaxation response normalizes your physical, mental, and emotional processes. You don't have to remain at the mercy of your fight or flight reaction. You can learn to be aware of your own stress response and then control it. You can learn to relax.

Schedule of Recent Experience

The first step in reducing stress is to become aware of the major sources of stress in your life. Although you are probably aware of the major ongoing environmental stresses in your life, you are likely to underestimate how many stressful changes occur every day to which you are forced to adjust. In order to become aware of the amount of stress you have had in the last year, please fill out and then score the following *Schedule of Recent Experience,* prepared by Thomas Holmes, M.D., at the University of Washington School of Medicine, Seattle, Washington.

Schedule of Recent Experience
Part A

Instructions. Think back on each possible life event listed below, and decide if it happened to you within the last year. If the event did happen, check the box next to it.

	Check here if event happened to you	*Mean value (use for scoring later)*
1. A lot more or a lot less trouble with the boss.	————	————
2. A major change in sleeping habits (sleeping a lot more or a lot less, or change in part of day when asleep).	————	————
3. A major change in eating habits (a lot more or a lot less food intake, or very different meal hours or surroundings).	————	————
4. A revision of personal habits (dress, manners, associations, etc.).	————	————
5. A major change in your usual type and/or amount of recreation.	————	————
6. A major change in your social activities (clubs, dancing, movies, visiting, etc.).	————	————
7. A major change in church activities (a lot more or a lot less than usual).	————	————
8. A major change in number of family get-togethers (a lot more or a lot less than usual).	————	————
9. A major change in financial state (a lot worse off or a lot better off than usual).	————	————
10. In-law troubles.	————	————
11. A major change in the number of arguments with spouse (a lot more or a lot less than usual regarding child-rearing, personal habits, etc.).	————	————
12. Sexual difficulties.	————	————

Schedule of Recent Experience
Part B

Instructions. In the space provided, indicate the *number of times* that each applicable event happened to you within the last two years.

	Number of times	×	Mean value	=	Your score
13. Major personal injury or illness.	_____		_____		_____
14. Death of a close family member (other than spouse).	_____		_____		_____
15. Death of spouse.	_____		_____		_____
16. Death of a close friend.	_____		_____		_____
17. Gaining a new family member (through birth, adoption, oldster moving in, etc.).	_____		_____		_____
18. Major change in the health or behavior of a family member.	_____		_____		_____
19. Change in residence.	_____		_____		_____
20. Detention in jail or other institution.	_____		_____		_____
21. Minor violations of the law (traffic tickets, jaywalking, disturbing the peace, etc.).	_____		_____		_____
22. Major business readjustment (merger, reorganization, bankruptcy, etc.).	_____		_____		_____
23. Marriage.	_____		_____		_____
24. Divorce.	_____		_____		_____
25. Marital separation from spouse.	_____		_____		_____
26. Outstanding personal achievement.	_____		_____		_____
27. Son or daughter leaving home (marriage, attending college, etc.).	_____		_____		_____
28. Retirement from work.	_____		_____		_____
29. Major change in working hours or conditions.	_____		_____		_____

	Number of times	×	Mean value	=	Your score

30. Major change in responsibilities at work (promotion, demotion, lateral transfer).   _____ _____ _____

31. Being fired from work.   _____ _____ _____

32. Major change in living conditions (building a new home, remodeling, deterioration of home or neighborhood).   _____ _____ _____

33. Wife beginning or ceasing work outside the home.   _____ _____ _____

34. Taking on a mortgage greater than $25,000 (purchasing a home, business, etc.).   _____ _____ _____

35. Taking on a mortgage or loan of less than $25,000 (purchasing a car, TV, freezer, etc.).   _____ _____ _____

36. Foreclosure on a mortgage or loan.   _____ _____ _____

37. Vacation.   _____ _____ _____

38. Changing to a new school.   _____ _____ _____

39. Changing to a different line of work.   _____ _____ _____

40. Beginning or ceasing formal schooling.   _____ _____ _____

41. Marital reconciliation with mate.   _____ _____ _____

42. Pregnancy.   _____ _____ _____

Your total score   _____

Scoring

The "Mean values" for each life event are listed below. Write in the mean values for those events that happened to you. For items in Part B, multiply the mean value by the number of times an event happened, and enter the result in "Your score." Add up the mean values in Part A and your scores in Part B to get your total score.

Life event	Mean value	Life event	Mean value	Life event	Mean value
1	23	15	100	29	20
2	16	16	37	30	29
3	15	17	39	31	47
4	24	18	44	32	25
5	19	19	20	33	26
6	18	20	63	34	31
7	19	21	11	35	17
8	15	22	39	36	30
9	38	23	50	37	13
10	29	24	73	38	20
11	35	25	65	39	36
12	39	26	28	40	26
13	53	27	29	41	45
14	63	28	45	42	40

The more change you have, the more likely you are to get sick. Of those people with a score of over 300 for the past year, almost 80 percent get sick in the near future; with a score of 200 to 299, about 50 percent get sick in the near future; and with a score of 150–199, only about 30 percent get sick in the near future. A score of less than 150 indicates that you have a low chance of getting sick. So, the higher your score, the harder you should work to stay well.

Stress can be cumulative. Events from two years ago may still be affecting you now. If you think this applies to you, repeat this test for the events of the preceding year and compare your scores.

Symptoms Checklist

The major objective of this workbook is to help you achieve symptom relief using relaxation and stress reduction techniques. So that you can determine exactly which symptoms you want to work on, complete the following checklist. This symptoms checklist will tell you a great deal about how you respond to stress. Depending on the nature of the stress in your life and your unique response to it, different techniques will be more helpful to you than others.

   After you have used this workbook to master the stress reduction techniques that work best for you, return to this checklist and use it to measure your symptom relief.

Rate your stress-related symptoms below for the degree of discomfort they cause you, using this 10-point scale:

Slight Discomfort			*Moderate Discomfort*				*Extreme Discomfort*		
1	2	3	4	5	6	7	8	9	10

Symptom (Disregard those you don't experience)	*Degree of discomfort (1–10) now*	*Degree of discomfort (1–10) after mastering relaxation & stress reduction techniques*
Anxiety in specific situations		
Tests	_____	_____
Deadlines	_____	_____
Interviews	_____	_____
Other _____	_____	_____
Anxiety in personal relationships		
Spouse	_____	_____
Parents	_____	_____
Children	_____	_____
Other _____	_____	_____
Anxiety, general—regardless of the situation or the people involved	_____	_____
Depression	_____	_____
Hopelessness	_____	_____
Powerlessness	_____	_____
Poor self esteem	_____	_____

Symptom	Degree of discomfort (1–10) now	Degree of discomfort (1–10) after mastering relaxation & stress reduction techniques
Hostility	————	————
Anger	————	————
Irritability	————	————
Resentment	————	————
Phobias	————	————
Fears	————	————
Obsessions, unwanted thoughts	————	————
Muscular tension	————	————
High blood pressure	————	————
Headaches	————	————
Neckaches	————	————
Backaches	————	————
Indigestion	————	————
Irritable bowel	————	————
Ulcers	————	————
Chronic constipation	————	————
Chronic diarrhea	————	————
Muscle spasms	————	————
Tics	————	————
Tremors	————	————
Fatigue	————	————
Insomnia	————	————
Sleeping difficulties	————	————
Obesity	————	————
Physical weakness	————	————
Job stress	————	————
Other ————————	————	————

Important: Physical symptoms may have purely physiological causes. You should have a medical doctor eliminate the possibility of such physical problems before you proceed on the assumption that your symptoms are completely stress-related.

Symptom Effectiveness Chart

Now that you have identified your stress-related symptoms, it is time to choose the one or two that bother you the most, and to select the techniques that you will use to relieve them. Since everyone reacts differently to stress, it is hard to say which stress reduction techniques will be best for you. However, this chart will give you a general idea of what to try first, and where to go from there.

Chapter headings for each stress reduction method are across the top, and typical stress-related symptoms are listed down the side. You may have only one or several of these symptoms.

As you can see, more than one stress reduction technique is indicated as effective in treating most symptoms. The most effective techniques for a particular symptom are marked with a boldface X, while other helpful techniques for that same symptom are indicated by a lighter x.

Techniques

Symptoms	Progressive Relaxation	Breathing	Meditation	Imagination	Self Hypnosis	Autogenics	Thought Stopping
Anxiety in specific situations (tests, deadlines, interviews, etc.)	X	X	x	x	x		X
Anxiety in your personal relationships (spouse, parents, children, etc.)	X	X			x		
Anxiety, general (regardless of the situation or the people involved)	X	X	X	x		x	x
Depression, hopelessness, powerlessness, poor self esteem	x	x	X				X
Hostility, anger, irritablity, resentment		X	x			x	
Phobias, fears	X						X
Obsessions, unwanted thoughts		x	X				X
Muscular tension	X	X		x	x	X	
High blood pressure	X		x			X	
Headaches, neckaches, backaches	X			X	X	x	
Indigestion, irritable bowel, ulcers, chronic constipation	X				X	X	
Muscle spasms, tics, tremors	X			x	x		
Fatigue, tired all the time	x	X			X	x	
Insomnia, sleeping difficulties	X				x	x	X
Obesity							
Physical Weakness							
Job Stress							

Important: Physical symptoms may have purely physiological causes. You should have a medical doctor eliminate the possibility of such physical problems before you proceed on the assumption that your symptoms are completely stress-related.

Also note that the techniques fall roughly into two categories: relaxation techniques that focus on relaxing the body, and stress reduction techniques that condition the mind to handle stress effectively. Your mind, body and emotions are interrelated. In seeking relief from stress, you will probably obtain the best results by using at least one technique from each of these two broad categories. For example, if your most painful symptom of stress is general anxiety, you might practice progressive relaxation and breathing exercises to calm your body, and do exercises from the chapter on refuting irrational ideas to reduce your mental and emotional stress.

Before you move to the chapter on the technique in which you are most interested, read chapter two. Body awareness is the key to everything else in this workbook, and without it you cannot use any of these techniques effectively.

Refuting Irrational Ideas	Coping Skills Training	Assertiveness Training	Time Management	Job Stress Management	Brief Combination Techniques	Biofeedback	Nutrition	Exercise
x	X		x					
		X						
X	x					X		x
X		X					x	x
X						x	x	x
	X					x		
					x	X		X
					x	X	X	x
						X	x	X
					x	x	X	x
						X		x
			X				x	x
						x	x	x
							X	X
								X
	x		x	X	X			

Further Reading

Benson, H. *The Relaxation Response.* New York: Morrow, 1975.

Cousins, Norman. *Anatomy of an Illness.* New York: Bantam Books, 1981.

Lazarus, Richard S. *Psychological Stress and the Coping Process.* New York: McGraw-Hill, 1966.

Lazarus, Richard S., and Folkman, Susan. *Stress Appraisal and Coping.* New York: Springer Publishing Co., 1984.

Orioli, E., Jaffe, D., and Scott, C. *Stress Map.* New York: Newmarket Press, 1987.

Ornstein, R., and Sobel, D. *The Healing Brain.* New York: Simon & Schuster, 1987.

Pelletier, Kenneth. *Holistic Medicine.* New York: Dell Publishing Co., 1979.

Selye, Hans. *Stress Without Distress.* N.Y.: Dutton, 1974.

Selye, Hans. *The Stress of Life.* N.Y.: McGraw-Hill, 1956.

2

Body Awareness

Most people are more aware of the weather, the time of day or their bank balance than they are aware of the tension in their own bodies. Body awareness is the first step in recognizing and reducing stress.

The importance of body states, their effect on consciousness, and their relationship to stress have been emphasized by eastern philosophies such as Zen, Yoga and Sufi for many centuries. During this century, the work of Wilhelm Reich, originally a student of Freud, persuaded western psychiatry to study the body's interaction with emotional conditions. Two modern therapies that concentrate on the body and its relationship to emotional stress are the Gestalt Therapy of Fritz Perls and the Bio-energetic Therapy of Alexander Lowen. Both of these therapies work closely with the mind-body relationship and emphasize the notion that the body registers stress long before the conscious mind does. Muscular tension is your body's way of letting you know you are under stress.

Lowen has found it inevitable that when you experience stress you tense your body. When the stress is removed, the tension will also go away. Chronic muscular tension occurs in people with particular attitudes which tend to tighten specific muscle groups. For example, a woman who believes that it is bad to express anger is likely to have chronic neck tension and pain, or a man experiencing a lot of anxiety about the future may develop chronic stomach problems. This chronic muscular tension restricts digestion, limits self expression and decreases energy. Every contracted muscle blocks movement.

Perls believed in the importance of differentiating between your external awareness and internal awareness in order to separate the world from your physical reaction to it. External awareness includes all stimulation to the five senses from the outside world. Internal awareness refers to any physical sensation, feeling, emotional discomfort or comfort inside your body. Much of the tension in your body isn't felt because most of your awareness is directed to the outside world. In the body inventory, you will experience Gestalt exercises designed to locate and explore your body tension.

Body Inventory

The following exercises promote body awareness, and will help you identify areas of tension.

Awareness

1. First focus your attention on the outside world. Start sentences with, "I am aware of _____." (e.g. "I am aware of the cars going by outside the window, papers moving, the coffee perking, the breeze blowing and the blue carpet.")

2. After you have become aware of everything that is going on around you, shift to focusing your attention on your body and your physical sensations, your internal world (e.g. "I am aware of feeling warm, my stomach gurgling, tension in my neck, nose tickling, and a cramp in my foot.")

3. Shuttle back and forth between internal and external awareness (e.g. "I am aware of the chair pushing into my buttocks, the circle of yellow light from the lamp, my shoulders hunching up, the smell of bacon.")

4. Used at free moments throughout the day, this exercise allows you to separate and appreciate the real difference between your inner and outer worlds.

Body Scanning

Close your eyes . . . Start with your toes and move up your body . . . Ask yourself, "Where am I tense?" . . . Whenever you discover a tense area, exaggerate it slightly so you can become aware of it . . . Be aware of the muscles in your body that are tense . . . Then, for example, say to yourself, "I am tensing my neck muscles . . . I am hurting myself . . . I am creating tension in my body" . . . Note that all muscular tension is self-produced . . . At this point, be aware of any life situation that may be causing the tension in your body and what you could do to change it.

Letting Go of Your Body

Lie down on a rug or a firm bed and get comfortable . . . Pull your feet up until your feet rest flat on the floor . . . Close your eyes . . . Check yourself for comfort . . . This may require shifting your body around . . . Become aware of your breathing . . . Feel the air move into your nose, mouth and down your throat into your lungs . . . Focus on your body and let all of the parts come into your awareness spontaneously . . . What parts of your body come into awareness first? . . . What parts are you less aware of? . . . Become aware of which parts of your body you can easily feel and which parts of your body have little sensation . . . Do you notice any difference between the right and left side of your body? . . . Now become aware of any physical discomfort you are feeling . . . Become aware of this discomfort until you can describe it in detail . . . Focus and be aware of what happens to this discomfort . . . It may change . . . Let your body do whatever it wants to do . . . Continue this for five to ten minutes . . . Allow your body to take over.

Stress Awareness Diary

Some parts of the day are more stressful than others, and some stressful events are more likely to produce physical and emotional symptoms than others. Certain types of stressful events often produce characteristic symptoms. It is useful to keep a record of stressful events as well as symptoms that may have been a stress reaction.

Keep a stress awareness diary for two weeks. Make a note of the time that a stressful event occurs and the time you notice a physical or emotional symptom that could be related to the stress.

The following stress awareness diary is from the Monday of a department store clerk:

Time	Stressful event	Symptom
8:00	Alarm doesn't go off, late, rushing	
9:30		Slight headache
11:00	Customer is rude and insulting	
11:15		Anger, tightness in stomach
3:00	Return of 3 big ticket items, much paper work	
3:15		Depression, slight headache
5:30	Heavy commute traffic	
6:30		Irritable with son
6:35	Wife defends son	Tightness in stomach

As you can see, the diary identifies how particular stresses result in predictable symptoms. Interpersonal confrontations may characteristically be followed by stomach tension. Rushing may be causing vasoconstriction (tightening of the blood vessels) for this individual, and therefore results in irritability and headaches. You can use your stress awareness diary to discover and chart your stressful events and characteristic reactions.

Stress Awareness Diary

Date _____   Day of the week _____

Time	Stressful event	Symptom
_____	_____	_____
_____	_____	_____
_____	_____	_____
_____	_____	_____
_____	_____	_____
_____	_____	_____
_____	_____	_____
_____	_____	_____
_____	_____	_____
_____	_____	_____
_____	_____	_____
_____	_____	_____
_____	_____	_____
_____	_____	_____
_____	_____	_____
_____	_____	_____
_____	_____	_____
_____	_____	_____
_____	_____	_____
_____	_____	_____
_____	_____	_____
_____	_____	_____
_____	_____	_____
_____	_____	_____

After using these body awareness exercises, you will begin to recognize where your body stores muscular tension. When you allow yourself increased awareness, you can find ways to let go of the tension you discover. Along with the release of tension, you will experience increased energy and a sense of well-being.

After your stress awareness diary has helped you identify your reactions to stress, you should continue to record your progress with the other relaxation techniques in this workbook. To keep a convenient record of how you feel before and after your relaxation exercises, use the following record of general tension.

Record of General Tension

Rate yourself on this 10-point scale before and after you do your relaxation exercise.

1	2	3	4	5
totally relaxed no tension	very relaxed	moderately relaxed	fairly relaxed	slightly relaxed

6	7	8	9	10
slightly tense	fairly tense	moderately tense	very tense	extremely tense (the most uncomfortable you could be)

Week of _____	Before session	After session	Comments
Monday			
Tuesday			
Wednesday			
Thursday			
Friday			
Saturday			
Sunday			

Further Reading

Lowen, Alexander. *Bioenergetics*. Cowan, McCann and Georghegan, 1975.

Stevens, John O. *Awareness*. Real People Press, 1971.

Schutz, William C. *Joy*. Grove Press, 1967.

3

Progressive Relaxation

You cannot have the feeling of warm well-being in your body and at the same time experience psychological stress. Progressive relaxation of your muscles reduces pulse rate and blood pressure as well as decreasing perspiration and respiration rates. Deep muscle relaxation, when successfully mastered, can be used as an anti-anxiety pill.

Edmund Jacobson, a Chicago physician, published the book *Progressive Relaxation* in 1929. In this book he described his deep muscle relaxation technique, which he asserted required no imagination, willpower or suggestion. His technique is based on the premise that the body responds to anxiety-provoking thoughts and events with muscle tension. This physiological tension, in turn, increases the subjective experience of anxiety. Deep muscle relaxation reduces physiological tension and is incompatible with anxiety: The habit of responding with one blocks the habit of responding with the other.

Symptom Effectiveness

Excellent results have been found in the treatment of muscular tension, anxiety, insomnia, depression, fatigue, irritable bowel, muscle spasms, neck and back pain, high blood pressure, mild phobias and stuttering.

Time for Mastery

One to two weeks. Two 15 minute sessions per day.

Instructions

Most people do not realize which of their muscles are chronically tense. Progressive relaxation provides a way of identifying particular muscles and muscle groups and distinguishing between sensations of tension and deep relaxation. Four major muscle groups will be covered:

1. Hands, forearms and biceps.

2. Head, face, throat and shoulders, including concentration on forehead, cheeks, nose, eyes, jaws, lips, tongue and neck. Considerable attention is devoted to your head, because from the emotional point of view, the most important muscles in your body are situated in and around this region.

3. Chest, stomach and lower back.

4. Thighs, buttocks, calves and feet.

Progressive relaxation can be practiced lying down or in a chair with your head supported. Each muscle or muscle grouping is tensed from five to seven seconds and then relaxed for twenty to thirty seconds. This procedure is repeated at least once. If an area remains tense, you can practice up to five times. You may also find it useful to use the following relaxing expressions when untensing:

Let go of the tension.

Throw away the tension—I am feeling calm and rested.

Relax and smooth out the muscles.

Let the tension dissolve away.

Once the procedure is familiar enough to be remembered, keep your eyes closed and focus attention on just one muscle group at a time. The instructions for progressive relaxation are divided into two sections. The first part, which you may wish to tape and replay when practicing, will familiarize you with the muscles in your body which are most commonly tense. The second section shortens the procedure by simultaneously tensing and relaxing many muscles at one time so that deep muscle relaxation can be achieved in a very brief period.

Basic Procedure

Get in a comfortable position and relax. Now clench your right fist, tighter and tighter, studying the tension as you do so. Keep it clenched and notice the tension in your fist, hand and forearm. Now relax. Feel the looseness in your right hand, and notice the contrast with the tension. Repeat this procedure with your right fist again, always noticing as you relax that this is the opposite of tension—relax and feel the difference. Repeat the entire procedure with your left fist, then both fists at once.

Now bend your elbows and tense your biceps. Tense them as hard as you can and observe the feeling of tautness. Relax, straighten out your arms. Let the relaxation develop and feel that difference. Repeat this, and all succeeding procedures at least once.

Turning attention to your head, wrinkle your forehead as tight as you can. Now relax and smooth it out. Let yourself imagine your entire forehead and scalp becoming smooth and at rest. Now frown and notice the strain spreading throughout your forehead. Let go. Allow your brow to become smooth again. Close your eyes now, squint them tighter. Look for the tension. Relax your eyes. Let them remain closed gently and comfortably. Now clench your jaw, bite hard, notice the tension throughout your jaw. Relax your jaw. When the jaw is relaxed, your lips will be slightly parted. Let yourself really appreciate the contrast between tension and relaxation. Now press your tongue against the roof of your mouth. Feel the ache in the back of your mouth. Relax. Press your lips now, purse them into an "O." Relax your lips. Notice that your forehead, scalp, eyes, jaw, tongue and lips are all relaxed.

Press your head back as far as it can comfortably go and observe the tension in your neck. Roll it to the right and feel the changing locus of stress, roll it to the left. Straighten your head and bring it forward, press your chin against your chest. Feel the tension in your throat, the back of your neck. Relax, allowing your head to return to a comfortable position. Let the relaxation deepen. Now shrug your shoulders. Keep the tension as you hunch your head down between your shoulders. Relax your shoulders. Drop them back and feel the relaxation spreading through your neck, throat and shoulders, pure relaxation, deeper and deeper.

Give your entire body a chance to relax. Feel the comfort and the heaviness. Now breathe in and fill your lungs completely. Hold your breath. Notice the tension. Now exhale, let your chest become loose, let the air hiss out. Continue relaxing, letting your breath come freely and gently. Repeat this several times, noticing the tension draining from your body as you exhale. Next, tighten your stomach and hold. Note the tension, then relax. Now place your hand on your stomach. Breathe deeply into your stomach, pushing your hand up. Hold, and relax. Feel the contrast of relaxation as the air rushes out. Now arch your back, without straining. Keep the rest of your body as relaxed as possible. Focus on the tension in your lower back. Now relax, deeper and deeper.

Tighten your buttocks and thighs. Flex your thighs by pressing down your heels as hard as you can. Relax and feel the difference. Now curl your toes downward, making your calves tense. Study the tension. Relax. Now bend your toes toward your face, creating tension in your shins. Relax again.

Feel the heaviness throughout your lower body as the relaxation deepens. Relax your feet, ankles, calves, shins, knees, thighs and buttocks. Now let the relaxation spread to your stomach, lower back and chest. Let go more and more. Experience the relaxation deepening in your shoulders, arms and hands. Deeper and deeper. Notice the feeling of looseness and relaxation in your neck, jaws and all your facial muscles.

Shorthand Procedure

The following is a procedure for achieving deep muscle relaxation quickly. Whole muscle groups are simultaneously tensed and then relaxed. As before, repeat each procedure at least once, tensing each muscle group from five to seven seconds and then relaxing from 20 to 30 seconds. Remember to notice the contrast between the sensations of tension and relaxation.

1. Curl both fists, tightening biceps and forearms (Charles Atlas pose). Relax.

2. Wrinkle up forehead. At the same time, press your head as far back as possible, roll it clockwise in a complete circle, reverse. Now wrinkle up the muscles of your face like a walnut: frowning, eyes squinted, lips pursed, tongue pressing the roof of the mouth, and shoulders hunched. Relax.

3. Arch back as you take a deep breath into the chest. Hold. Relax. Take a deep breath, pressing out the stomach. Hold. Relax.

4. Pull feet and toes back toward face, tightening shins. Hold. Relax. Curl toes, simultaneously tightening calves, thighs and buttocks. Relax.

Special Considerations

1. If you make a tape of the basic procedure to facilitate your relaxation program, remember to space each procedure so that time is allowed to experience the tension and relaxation before going on to the next muscle or muscle group.

2. Most people have somewhat limited success when they begin deep muscle relaxation, but it is only a matter of practice. Whereas 20 minutes of work might initially bring only partial relaxation, it will eventually be possible to relax your whole body in a few moments.

3. Sometimes in the beginning, it may seem to you as though relaxation is complete. But although the muscle or muscle group may well be partially relaxed, a certain number of muscle fibers will still be contracted. It is the act of relaxing these additional fibers that will bring about the emotional effects you want. It is helpful to say to yourself during the relaxation phase, "Let go more and more."

4. Caution should be taken in tensing the neck and back. Excessive tightening can result in muscle or spinal damage. It is also commonly observed that over-tightening the toes or feet results in muscle cramping.

Further Reading

Jacobson, Edmund. *Progressive Relaxation.* Chicago: The University of Chicago Press, Midway Reprint, 1974.

Wolpe, Joseph. *The Practice of Behavior Therapy.* New York: Pergamon Press, 1969.

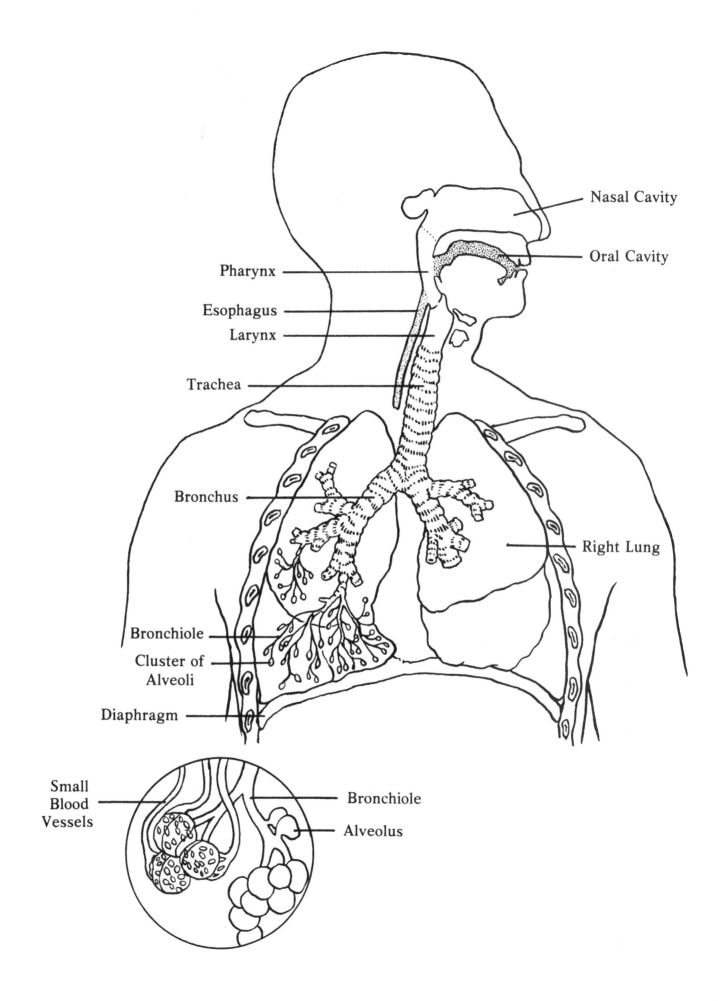

Nasal Cavity

Oral Cavity

Pharynx

Esophagus

Larynx

Trachea

Bronchus

Right Lung

Bronchiole

Cluster of
Alveoli

Diaphragm

Small
Blood
Vessels

Bronchiole

Alveolus

Adapted from *The Anatomy Coloring Book* by Wynn Kapit and Lawrence M. Elson, Harper & Row, New York, 1977.

4

Breathing

Breathing is essential for life. Proper breathing is an antidote to stress. Although we all breathe, few of us retain the habit of natural, full breathing experienced by an infant or by primitive man.

Let's examine what we all take for granted — a breath. When you inhale, air is drawn in through your nose and warmed by the mucous membrane of your nasal passages. The bristly hairs of your nostrils filter out impurities, which are expelled on the next exhalation.

The diaphragm is a sheet-like muscle that stretches across your chest, separating your chest from your abdomen. Although you can voluntarily expand and contract your diaphragm, it operates largely on an automatic basis. When the diaphragm relaxes, the lungs contract and air is forced out.

Your two lungs are made up of bronchi which transport oxygen to your veins and arteries. When the blood leaves your lungs through the arteries, it is bright red due to its high oxygen content (about 25 percent). It is pumped out by your heart through the arteries into the capillaries, reaching all parts of your body. As the life supporting oxygen is exchanged for the waste products in the cells, your blood dulls in color. It returns to the right side of your heart, and is pumped into the lungs where it is distributed by millions of hair-like blood vessels. When the oxygen contacts the waste-laden blood, a form of combustion occurs in which the blood cells take up oxygen and release carbon dioxide. After being purified and oxygenated, the blood is then returned to the left side of your heart and driven back out into the body.

When an insufficient amount of fresh air reaches your lungs, your blood is not properly purified or oxygenated. Waste products that should have been removed are kept in circulation, slowly poisoning your system. When your blood lacks enough oxygen, it is bluish and dark in color, and can be seen in poor complexion. Digestion is hampered. Your organs and tissues become undernourished and deteriorate. Poorly oxygenated blood contributes to anxiety states, depression and fatigue, and makes each stressful situation many times harder to cope with. Proper breathing habits are essential for good mental and physical health.

Westerners have only recently become aware of the importance of correct breathing habits. For centuries, breathing exercises have been an integral part of mental, physical and spiritual development in the orient and India. As the west hurries to catch up with the east in understanding and utilizing proper breath control, it has borrowed heavily from the teachings of Yoga. The underlying goal of all Yoga is to enable you, through discipline, to control the body and mind. The first three exercises in this chapter are simple American techniques reflecting an eastern heritage. Exercises four through eleven are Yoga exercises developed and refined in India over hundreds of years.

Symptom Effectiveness

Breathing exercises have been found to be effective in reducing anxiety, depression, irritability, muscular tension and fatigue. They are used in the treatment and prevention of breathholding, hyperventilation, shallow breathing, and cold hands and feet.

Time for Mastery

While a breathing exercise can be learned in a matter of minutes, and some immediate benefits experienced, the profound effects of the exercise may not be fully appreciated until months of persistent practice have passed. After you have tried the exercises presented in this chapter, develop a breathing program incorporating those exercises you find most beneficial, and follow your program with patience and persistence.

"Dead body" pose

Breathing Awareness

1. Lie down on a rug or blanket on the floor in a "dead body" pose—your legs straight, slightly apart, your toes pointed comfortably outwards, your arms at your sides, not touching your body, your palms up, and your eyes closed.

2. Bring your attention to your breathing, and place your hand on the spot that seems to rise and fall the most as you inhale and exhale. Note that if this spot is in your chest, you are not making good use of the lower part of your lungs. People who are nervous tend to breathe many short, shallow breaths in their upper chest.

3. Place both of your hands gently on your abdomen and follow your breathing. Notice how your abdomen rises with each inhalation and falls with each exhalation.

4. It is best if you breathe through your nose. If possible, clear your nasal passages before doing breathing exercises.

5. Is your chest moving in harmony with your abdomen, or is it rigid? Spend a minute or two letting your chest follow the movement of your abdomen.

6. Scan your body for tension, especially your throat, chest and abdomen.

Deep Breathing

1. Although this exercise can be practiced in a variety of poses, the following is recommended: lie down on a blanket or rug on the floor. Bend your knees and move your feet about eight inches apart, with your toes turned outward slightly. Make sure your spine is straight.

2. Scan your body for tension.

3. Place one hand on your abdomen and one hand on your chest.

4. Inhale slowly and deeply through your nose into your abdomen to push up your hand as much as feels comfortable. Your chest should move only a little and only with your abdomen.

5. When you feel at ease with step 4, smile slightly, inhale through your nose and exhale through your mouth, making a quiet, relaxing, whooshing sound like the wind as you blow gently out. Your mouth, tongue and jaw will be relaxed. Take long, slow, deep breaths which raise and lower your abdomen. Focus on the sound and feeling of breathing as you become more and more relaxed.

6. Continue deep breathing for about five or ten minutes at a time, once or twice a day, for a couple of weeks. Then if you like, extend this period to 20 minutes.

7. At the end of each deep breathing session, take a little time to once more scan your body for tension. Compare the tension you feel at the conclusion of the exercise with that which you experienced when you began.

8. When you become at ease with breathing into your abdomen, practice it whenever you feel like it during the day when you are sitting or standing. Concentrate on your abdomen moving up and down, the air moving in and out of your lungs, and the feeling of relaxation that deep breathing gives you.

9. When you have learned to relax yourself using deep breathing, practice it whenever you feel yourself getting tense.

The Relaxing Sigh

During the day you probably catch yourself sighing or yawning. This is generally a sign that you are not getting enough oxygen. Sighing and yawning are your body's way of remedying the situation. A sigh is often accompanied by a sense that things are not quite as they should be and a feeling of tension. A sigh releases a bit of tension and can be practiced at will as a means of relaxing.

1. Sit or stand up straight.

2. Sigh deeply, letting out a sound of deep relief as the air rushes out of your lungs.

3. Don't think about inhaling—just let the air come in naturally.

4. Repeat this procedure eight to twelve times whenever you feel the need for it, and experience the feeling of relaxation.

Complete Natural Breathing

Healthy infants and prehistoric men breathe in this complete, natural manner. Civilized man, with his penchant for tight clothing, a sedentary and stressful life style and poor posture, has tended to move away from this form of breathing. The following Yoga exercise, with practice, will become almost automatic.

1. Begin by sitting or standing up straight in good posture.

2. Breathe through your nose.

3. As you inhale, *first* fill the lower section of your lungs. Your diaphragm will push your abdomen outward to make room for the air. *Second,* fill the middle part of your lungs as your lower ribs and chest move forward slightly to accommodate the air. *Third,* fill the upper part of your lungs as you raise your chest slightly and draw in your abdomen a little to support your lungs. These three steps can be performed in one smooth, continuous inhalation, which with practice can be completed in a couple of seconds.

4. Hold your breath for a few seconds.

5. As you exhale slowly, pull your abdomen in slightly and lift it up slowly as the lungs empty. When you have completely exhaled, relax your abdomen and chest.

6. Now and then at the end of the inhalation phase, raise your shoulders and collarbone slightly so that the very top of your lungs are sure to be replenished with fresh air.

Purifying Breath

This exercise not only cleans your lungs, it also stimulates and tones up your entire breathing apparatus and refreshes your whole body. It may be practiced by itself or combined with other breathing exercises.

1. Begin by sitting or standing up straight in good posture.

2. Inhale a complete natural breath as described in the previous exercise.

3. Hold this breath for a few seconds.

4. Exhale a little of the air with considerable force through a small hole between your lips as though you were blowing through a straw. Stop exhaling for a moment and then blow out a bit more air. Repeat this procedure until all the air is exhaled in small, forceful puffs.

Tap Away Tension

This exercise will make you feel relaxed and alert.

1. Stand up straight with your hands at your sides.

2. As you slowly inhale, softly tap your chest with your fingertips. Continually move your hands around so that your entire chest is tapped. Women may choose not to tap their breasts.

3. When you have inhaled as much air as feels comfortable, hold your breath and pat your chest with your palms. Again, continue to move your hands around.

4. Exhale, using the purifying breath described above.

5. Practice a few more purifying breaths and then repeat the exercise beginning with step one as many times as it feels comfortable to you.

6. After you have repeated this exercise a few times tapping your chest, you may switch to tapping those areas of your back that you can reach with your hands.

The Bracer

Try this exercise when you feel low on energy, stiff and are having a hard time getting going. It will stimulate your breathing, circulation and nervous system.

1. Stand up straight with your hands at your sides.

2. Inhale and hold a complete natural breath as described above.

3. Raise your arms out in front of you, using just enough energy to keep them up and relaxed.

4. Gradually bring your hands to your shoulders. As you do, slowly contract your hands into fists so that when they reach your shoulders they are clenched as tight as you can make them.

5. Keep the fists tense as you push your arms out straight again very slowly.

6. Pull your arms back to your shoulders and straighten them out, fists tense, as fast as you can, several times.

7. Relax your hands to your sides and exhale forcefully through your mouth.

8. Practice a few purifying breaths as described above.

9. Repeat this exercise several times until you feel its stimulating effects.

The Windmill

When you have been bent over your work for several hours and are feeling tense, this exercise will relax you and make you more alert.

1. Stand up straight with your arms out in front of you.
2. Inhale and hold a complete natural breath.
3. Swing your arms backward in a circle several times and then reverse directions. For variety, try rotating them alternately like a windmill.
4. Exhale forcefully through your mouth.
5. Practice a couple of purifying breaths.
6. Repeat this exercise as often as you like.

Bending

Again, this exercise is a useful one to use when you feel stiff and tense. It has the added benefit of stretching your torso, making it more flexible for breathing.

1. Stand up straight with your hands on your hips.
2. Inhale and hold a complete natural breath.
3. Let the lower part of your body remain stiff. Bow forward as far as you can, slowly exhaling completely through your mouth.
4. Stand up straight again and inhale and hold another complete natural breath.
5. Bend backwards as you slowly exhale.
6. Stand up straight again and inhale and hold another complete natural breath.
7. Continue this exercise, bending first backwards and then to the left and right sides.
8. After each round of four bends, practice one purifying breath.
9. Do four full rounds.

Complete Natural Breathing and Imagination

This exercise combines the relaxing benefits of complete natural breathing with the curative value of positive auto-suggestions.

1. Lie down on a rug or blanket on the floor in a "dead body" pose.

2. Place your hands gently on your solar plexus (that point where your ribs start to separate above your abdomen) and practice complete natural breathing for a few minutes.

3. Imagine that, with each incoming breath of air, energy is rushing into your lungs and being immediately stored in your solar plexus. Imagine that as you exhale, this energy is flowing out to all parts of your body. Form a mental picture of this energizing process.

4. Continue on a daily basis for at least five to ten minutes a day.

Alternatives to step 3:

A. Keep one hand on your solar plexus and move the other hand to a point on your body that hurts. As you inhale, imagine energy coming in and being stored as in step 3. As you exhale, imagine the energy flowing to the spot that hurts, stimulating it. Inhale more energy, and when you exhale, imagine the energy driving out the pain. It is useful for you to have a clear picture of this process in your mind as you alternately stimulate the spot that hurts and then drive out the pain.

B. Keep one hand on your solar plexus and move the other hand to a point on your body that has been injured or is infected. Proceed as in alternative A, except as you exhale, imagine you are directing energy to the affected point and are stimulating it, driving out the infection and/or healing it. See this in your mind's eye.

Alternative Breathing

While this is a general relaxation exercise, people suffering from tension or sinus headaches find it particularly beneficial.

1. Sit in a comfortable position with good posture.
2. Rest the index and second finger of your right hand on your forehead.
3. Close your right nostril with your thumb.
4. Inhale slowly and soundlessly through your left nostril.
5. Close your left nostril with your ring finger and simultaneously open your right nostril by removing your thumb.

6. Exhale slowly and soundlessly and as thoroughly as possible through your right nostril.

7. Inhale through your right nostril.

8. Close your right nostril with your thumb and open your left nostril.

9. Exhale through your left nostril.

10. Inhale through your left nostril.

11. Begin by doing five cycles. Then raise the number of cycles slowly to ten or 25.

Alternative breathing

Further Reading

Ramacharaka, Yogi. *Science of Breath.* Chicago: Yogi Publication Society, 1905.

Saraswati, Swami Janakananda. *Yoga, Tantra and Meditation.* New York: Ballantine, 1976.

Spreads, Carol. *Breathing — The ABC's.* New York: Harper and Row, 1978.

5

Meditation

Meditation is the practice of uncritically attempting to focus your attention on one thing at a time. Exactly what that thing is is relatively unimportant and varies from one tradition to the next. Often the meditator repeats, either aloud or silently, a syllable, word, or group of words. This is known as mantra meditation. Gazing at a fixed object such as a flame or flower can also anchor the attention. Many meditators find that a convenient and relaxing point of focus is the rising and falling of their own breath. But you can use anything as an object of meditation . . . Aunt Mary's maiden name, the calendar on your desk, or even the tip of your nose.

It is important to understand that the heart of meditation lies not simply in focusing on one object to the exclusion of all other thought, but rather in the *attempt* to achieve this type of focus. The nature of the mind is such that it does not want to stay concentrated. Myriads of thoughts will appear and seemingly interfere with the meditation. A typical meditation might go something like this (the meditator in this case has chosen the task of counting to three repeatedly):

> One . . . two . . . This isn't so hard . . . one . . . two . . . three . . . one . . . I'm not having many thoughts at all . . . Oh, oh, I just had a thought . . . That was another one . . . two . . . My nose itches . . . one . . . I wonder if it's okay to scratch it . . . Darn, there was another thought. I've got to try harder . . . one . . . two . . . three . . . one . . . two . . . I was judging myself pretty harshly. I'm not supposed to do that . . . one . . . two . . . three . . . one . . . I'm hungry . . . Wonder what I'll cook tonight . . . one . . . two . . . three . . . I'm having way too many thoughts . . . I'll never get this right . . . one . . . two . . . Now don't judge . . . one . . .two . . . three . . . one . . .

Each time this meditator realizes that his mind has drifted to other thoughts, he chooses instead to dwell on the original object of his attention. By repeating this one moment of awareness, a moment which consists of noticing the thought and then refocusing the attention, over time a number of surprising realizations will become apparent:

- It is impossible to worry, fear, or hate when your mind is thinking about something other than the object of these emotions.

- It isn't necessary to think about everything that pops into your head. You have the ability to choose which thoughts you will think about.

- The seemingly diverse contents of your mind can really fit into a few simple categories, such as: grudging thoughts, fearful thoughts, angry thoughts, wanting thoughts, planning thoughts, memories, and so on.

- You act in certain ways because you have certain thoughts which, over your lifetime, have become habitual. Habitual patterns of thought and perception will begin to lose their influence over your life once you become aware of them.

- Emotion, aside from the thoughts and pictures in your mind, consists entirely of physical sensations in your body.

- Even the strongest emotion will become manageable if you concentrate on the sensations in your body, and not the content of the thought that produced the emotion.

- Thought and emotion are not permanent. They pass into and out of your body and mind. They need not leave a trace.

- When you are awake to what is happening *right now,* the extreme highs and extreme lows of your emotional response to life will disappear. You will live life with equanimity.

Members of many Eastern religions have long realized the benefits of meditation, but most Westerners have approached the practice with a skeptical eye. Weren't the only people who practice meditation members of non-Christian religions? That in itself was reason enough for many to view it with suspicion. And anyone who touted meditation as a sure way to achieve mental and physical well being was seen as a fanatic trying to make a quick buck from a totally untested method.

In 1968, Dr. Herbert Benson and his colleagues at Harvard Medical School decided to put meditation to the test. Volunteer practitioners of Transcendental Meditation were tested to see if meditation really could counter the physiological effects of stress. Benson scientifically proved that: (1) Heart beat and breathing rates slow down. (2) Oxygen consumption falls by 20 percent. (3) Blood lactate levels drop. This level rises with stress and fatigue. (4) Skin resistance to electrical current, a sign of relaxation, increases fourfold. (5) EEG ratings of brain wave patterns indicate increased alpha activity, another sign of relaxation.

Benson went on to prove that any meditational practice could duplicate these physiological changes as long as four factors were present: (1) a relatively quiet environment, (2) a mental device that provides a constant stimulus, (3) a comfortable position, and (4) a passive attitude (this aspect will be discussed in depth later).

Symptom Effectiveness

Meditation has been used successfully in the treatment and prevention of high blood pressure, heart disease, strokes, migraine headaches, and autoimmune diseases such as diabetes and arthritis. It has proved helpful in curtailing obsessive thinking, anxiety, depression, and hostility.

Time for Mastery

You can learn to meditate within a few minutes. Immediately your body will use less oxygen (a sign of deep relaxation) while you are meditating. However, as with most things, the benefits of meditation increase with practice. Levels of relaxation deepen. Attention becomes more steady. You become more adept at living in the present moment. Therefore, it is important to meditate regularly.

Instructions

Establishing Your Posture

A. From the following, select a position that is comfortable for you:
  - In a chair with your knees comfortably apart and your hands resting in your lap.
  - Tailor-fashion (cross-legged) on the floor. This position is most comfortable and stable when a cushion is placed under your buttocks so that both knees touch the floor.
  - Japanese fashion on your knees with your big toes touching and your heels pointed outward so that your buttocks rest on the soles of your feet. Again, if you place a cushion between your feet on which your buttocks can rest, you will be able to hold the position for a much longer period of time.
  - The yoga full lotus position. This position requires so much physical conditioning that it is not recommended for beginners.

B. Sit with your back straight (but not ramrod rigid) and let the weight of your head fall directly down upon your spinal column. This can be accomplished by pulling your chin in slightly. Allow the small of your back to arch.

C. Rock briefly from side to side, then from front to back and establish the point at which your upper torso feels balanced on your hips.

D. Close your mouth and breathe through your nose. Place your tongue on the roof of your mouth.

Establishing Your Posture

Yoga lotus position

Japanese-fashion

Tailor-fashion

Centering Yourself

A. Grounding

Close your eyes and focus on the place where your body touches the cushion or chair. What are the sensations there? Next notice the places where your body touches itself. Are your hands crossed? Your legs? Pay attention to the sensation at these places of contact. Finally focus on the way your body takes up space. Does it take up a lot of space? A small amount? Can you feel the boundary between your body and space? Notice the feelings there.

B. Breathing

With your eyes closed, take several deep breaths and notice the quality of your breathing. Is it fast or slow? Deep or shallow? Notice where your breath rests in your body. Is it up high in your chest? In the midsection around your stomach? Down low in your belly? Try moving your breath from one area to the other. Breathe into your upper chest, then into your stomach, then drop your breath into your lower belly. Feel your abdomen expand and contract as the air goes in and out. Notice how the upper chest and stomach areas seem almost still. This "dropped breath" is the most relaxing stance from which to meditate. However, if you have difficulty taking deep belly breaths, pay this no mind. Your breath will drop of its own accord as you become more practiced in meditation.

Attitude

Maintaining a passive attitude during meditation is perhaps the most important element in eliciting relaxation. It is important to realize that, especially as a beginner, you will have many thoughts and relatively few moments of clear concentration. This is natural and to be expected. Realize that your thoughts are not really interruptions, but are an integral part of meditation. Without thoughts, you would not be able to develop the ability to let them go.

A passive attitude includes a lack of concern about whether you are doing things correctly, whether you are accomplishing any goals, or whether this meditation is right for you. Sit with the intention of "I'm going to put in my time here, just sitting, and whatever happens is exactly what should happen."

A Word About Time

In general, any amount of time spent in meditation is more relaxing than not meditating at all. When you first begin to practice, maintain the meditation for only as long as is comfortable, even if this is only for five minutes a day. If you feel that you are forcing yourself to sit, you may develop an aversion to practicing meditation at all. As you progress in your practice and meditation becomes easier, you will find yourself wanting to extend your time. In terms of relaxation, twenty to thirty minutes once or twice a day is sufficient.

Exercises

The following exercises are divided into five groups.

Group 1 explains the mechanics of three basic meditations. Try each one a few times, then settle on the one you like best. Practice it regularly, at least once a day.

Group 2 consists of meditational exercises which will help you to develop the skill of relaxing muscle groups at will.

Group 3 introduces minor irritants into the basic sitting practice you selected from Group 1. In real life you may often find yourself in the presence of minor pain, annoyances, or disappointments which cause you to tense up. By practicing feeling relaxed around small irritations while you meditate, you will become more adept at handling life's larger irritations when they occur.

Group 4 contains exercises that can be practiced inconspicuously. You may often be in situations where you feel tense but don't have the opportunity to sit in a quiet place and relax. These exercises will help you to relax while blending in with your everyday world.

Group 5. Often it is difficult to relax because your mind wants to hold on to an idea or emotion that you experienced at an earlier time. This final exercise teaches you how to let go of obsessive thoughts and feelings.

Group 1. Three Basic Meditations

1. *Mantra Meditation*

This is the most common form of meditation throughout the world. Before you begin, select a word or syllable that you like. It may be a word which has meaning for you. Or it may be two nonsense syllables, the sound of which you find pleasant. Benson recommended using the word "one." Many meditators prefer the universal mantra, "OM."

A. Find your posture and center yourself. Take several deep breaths.

B. Chant your mantra silently to yourself. Say the word or syllables over and over within your mind. When your thought strays, note that, then bring your attention back to your mantra. If you notice any sensations in your body, note the feeling, then return to the repetition of your own special word. You needn't force it. Let your mantra find its own rhythm as you repeat it over and over again.

C. If you have the opportunity, you may want to try chanting your mantra aloud. Let the sound of your own voice fill you as you relax. Notice whether the sensations in your body are different from those you felt when you chanted silently. Which is more relaxing?

D. Remember, meditation is to be practiced with awareness. You may find that the repetition of a mantra, especially when repeated silently, can easily become mechanical. When this happens, you may have the sense that an inner voice is repeating your mantra while you are actually lost in thought or rapidly approaching sleep. Try to stay aware of each repetition of each syllable.

2. Breath Counting Meditation

This is perhaps the most relaxing form of meditation. Following the gentle ins and outs of the breath creates a sense of peace and restfulness.

A. Find your posture and center yourself. Take several deep breaths. Either close your eyes or fix them on a spot on the floor about four feet in front of you. Your eyes may or may not be focused.

B. Take deep but not forced belly breaths. As you do, focus your attention on each part of the breath: the inhale, the turn (the point at which you stop inhaling and start exhaling), the exhale, the pause (between the exhale and inhale), the turn (the point at which you start to inhale), the inhale, and so on. Pay careful attention to the pause. What are the sensations in your body as you pause between breaths?

C. As you exhale, say "one." Continue counting each exhale by saying "two . . . three . . . four." Then begin again with "one." If you lose count, simply start over with "one."

D. When you discover that your mind has slipped into thought, note this, then gently return to the counting of your breath.

E. If a particular sensation in your body catches your attention, focus on the sensation until it recedes. Then return your attention to the inhale and the exhale and the counting of your breath.

F. If you wish, try the following variation. Begin by counting your breath for several minutes. Then stop the actual counting and put your attention on the sensations of breathing. Focus on your abdomen as it expands and contracts. Can you sense how the size of the empty space in your abdomen grows and shrinks as your breath goes in and out of your belly? At first, you may have more thoughts when you practice this way than you had when you were counting breaths. The counting kept your mind returning in a small circle of numbers which left less room for rising thoughts. Do not be disturbed by this. Simply note each thought and then return your awareness to the sensations of your breath. Every now and then, you may come across a thought that you find enticing and want to contemplate. Tell yourself you will consider this thought when the meditation period is over and let it go. Sensations other than breathing may call your attention from time to time:

a strain in your shoulder, or the pins and needles of your legs falling asleep. When this happens, let your attention focus on these new sensations until they fade into the background. Then go back to your breath. The sounds of the outside world will cross and recross the boundaries of your awareness. Note their passing and return to your breath.

3. *Gazing*

This form of meditation involves fixing your gaze on an object without thinking about it in words. Select a small object that you like. A stone, a candle, a piece of wood, or anything else that you feel is appropriate.

A. Find your posture, center yourself and take several deep breaths.

B. Set your object on a surface which is at eye level and about a foot or so away from you. Look at it carefully. Gaze rather than stare. Keep your eyes soft and relaxed, without frowning. Notice the object's color, texture, size and shape. Trace its edges with your eyes. Cover every inch that is visible to you, and see if you can have the feeling of experiencing its qualities. Allow yourself to become totally involved in the exploration, as though you had never seen this object before.

C. As thoughts or words you associate with the object pop up, simply note them and let them go. Return your attention to your object.

D. If sensations in your body attract your attention, allow yourself to stay with the sensations until they fade while continuing to gaze at your object.

Special Considerations

1. It is not necessary to feel as though you are relaxing while you meditate in order for you to actually become relaxed. You may feel as though you are thinking thousands of thoughts and are very restless. However, when you open your eyes at the end of your meditation, you will realize you feel much more relaxed than you did before meditating.

2. As your mind quiets with meditation, old or hidden pain can arise from your subconscious. If you find that when you meditate you suddenly feel angry, depressed, or frightened, try to gently allow yourself to experience the feeling while resisting the temptation to make sense out of your feelings. If you feel the need, talk to a friend, counselor, or meditation teacher.

3. You may hear or read about ideal conditions for meditation: that you should meditate only in a quiet place. Or meditate only two hours after you've eaten. Or meditate only in a position that you can hold comfortably for twenty minutes, and so on. Yes, these are ideal conditions, but life is seldom ideal. If the place isn't absolutely quiet or the only time you have to meditate is

right after lunch, don't let these small obstacles keep you from meditating. If you find yourself being particularly bothered by noises or the rumblings of a full stomach, simply incorporate the annoying sensation in with the object of your meditation.

4. If you adopt a daily sitting practice, you may find that there are stretches of time during which you will not want to meditate. Do not expect that your desire to meditate will grow constantly with your practice. If you feel discouraged, be gentle with yourself and try to work creatively on ways to make your practice more comfortable. Know that these periods of discouragement will go away by themselves in time. For helping to maintain a schedule, the value of finding a group with which you can meditate at least once a week cannot be overstated.

Group 2. Releasing Muscular Tension

1. *The Moving Band Meditation*

A. Find your posture, center yourself and take several deep breaths.

B. Imagine that a three-inch-wide band encircles the top of your head. Focus your attention on that part of your head which is surrounded by the imaginary band. Notice the sensations. Is there any tension in your forehead? If so, try to relax it. Are there any other sensations in this area? Focus on them for a moment.

C. Lower the imaginary band three inches—the width of the band. Again focus your attention on the area encompassed by the band. Really try to feel around in there. What does the back of your eyeball feel like? Or the right wall of your nose? How are the muscles of your upper lip set? Any tension? Try to completely relax this area of your head. Breathe deeply and whisper to yourself, "Let it go, let it all go."

D. Continue to move the band down your body. Focus intently on any sensations. Wherever you notice tension, try to release it. As you do, take several deep belly breaths and relax. See if you can be aware of how the muscles feel as they relax.

E. When the band gets down to your torso, imagine that the band goes around one arm, then across your upper body, around the other arm, then across your back. Scan a section of each arm and your torso at the same time as though they were one part. Notice the sensations where the arms are separate from the body. What do these boundaries feel like? Can you make the sensation of the boundaries less distinct so that your arms feel like they are merging with your torso? Is there any tension? In the shoulders? The back? If so, relax these areas.

F. Move the band down your torso and arms to your legs, noting tension and releasing it. Focus on the sensation where your legs touch each other (if they do), and where they touch the floor. Again, feel the sensations at the points of contact, then try to experience the sensation of your legs merging together.

G. This exercise can be practiced in two different ways:

1. Move the band slowly down your body, carefully experiencing each sensation, noting all the points of tension and letting them go.

2. Quickly lower the band down your body. Move it as soon as your attention has given the encompassed area a brief scan. If practiced this way, repeat the entire exercise several times in a row.

Try both ways and see which is more relaxing.

2. *The Inner Exploration*

A. Find your posture and center yourself. Take two or three deep breaths.

B. Pick a part of your body on which to focus your attention. Explore it thoroughly with your awareness. For example, if you were concentrating on your jaw bone, you would want to have an idea about what it looks like. How is it attached to your head? Where are the muscles that move it? Can you tense and relax these muscles? What are the sensations when the jaw moves? When is it still? How are the teeth attached to it? What do your teeth feel like? The left front tooth? The last molar on the right? In what position is your jaw most relaxed?

C. It is helpful to explore any part of your body with the focal point of your mind, but especially those that fit into the following categories:

1. Parts of your body that are prone to hold tension. Some of these are the brow, jaw, neck, shoulders, and lower back.

2. Internal areas that tend to hold tension. Pay special attention to your stomach, chest, lower abdomen, and heart.

3. Areas of your body that you almost never think about in your daily life, such as your middle toe, your elbow, or the back of your knee.

Group 3. Softening

People usually respond to pain, irritation, or any discomfort by trying to build a solid wall of tightness around it, attempting to block off the feeling. However, the more you resist pain, the more it hurts. And the more it hurts, the more you will try to resist it. This vicious circle produces one big knot of pain and resistance that is extremely difficult to untie.

An alternative way to deal with pain is to learn to soften around it. This means you first acknowledge pain's presence, and then simply allow yourself to experience, physically and mentally, whatever it is that hurts. Be your own good nurse, hold your own hand, tell yourself it's all right, and then sit with yourself compassionately as you experience sensations of discomfort.

When you soften around an irritation, you consciously relax your tense, clenched muscles around the spot that hurts. You focus on the hurting itself, without all the tightness you tend to add to it.

Softening also means that you notice but disregard your thoughts about how awful the discomfort is, how you have to move, how you have to scratch, how you can't stand it, and so on.

A metaphor may help you understand softening. It's like working the hard lumps out of a mound of clay so that you can feel a tiny pearl in the center. It's like removing screens placed around a candle flame so that you can see it clearly. It's like thawing out the frozen core of a large piece of meat so that you can remove the bone. It's like cleaning layers of grime off of the outside of a window so that you can see what's inside more clearly.

The following exercises introduce minor irritations into your basic meditation. By practicing with small irritations in a safe setting, you can begin to understand the process of softening.

1. *Don't Move*

A. Find your posture and center yourself. Take several deep breaths.

B. Make an agreement with yourself that for a preset period of time you will not move. Then begin your basic meditation.

C. As time passes, you may find yourself moving your head or shifting in your seat without realizing it. This is fine. Note the movement and return to your meditation. After a while you will be able to notice your intention to move a part of your body before you actually move it.

D. Once you are able to identify your intention to move, try to focus on what exactly your desire is. Do you want to squirm around in your chair? Stretch your back muscles? Maybe you have an itch, or an ant is crawling across your foot. Try to precisely identify the uncomfortable sensation. Remember now, don't move.

E. As you focus on the discomfort, try to soften around it. If muscle groups are tightening, try to relax them. Check these muscle groups often. They will not want to stay relaxed. Where is your breath? Is it high in your chest? If so, try to drop it into your belly. Focus on the sensation of discomfort. What is the feeling here? Stay with it for a while.

F. When time is up, move your body slowly to the position in which you've been wanting to sit. Focus on the sensations. Is the relief immediate? Is the relief gradual? In what way does your body feel better? Is there any tension? If so, release it.

2. *The Lifted Arm*

A. Find your posture and center yourself. Take several deep breaths.

B. Place your left hand on your lap. Bend your right arm at your elbow and lift the arm so that the tips of your fingers are about even with the top of your head. In other words, raise your hand as though you want to answer a question.

C. Begin your basic meditation. As the right arm begins to tire, focus on the sensation of tiredness. Which muscles are actually holding the arm up? Can you find a way to relax them somewhat without letting the arm fall? Scan your body and see if other groups are tightening. Are your legs tensing because your arm hurts? If so, can you relax them? Focus on your heart, stomach and lungs. Are you beginning to feel a little anxious? If so, can you find a way to calm yourself? Take several deep breaths and say to yourself gently, "Relax," or "Let it go."

D. When you've finished meditating, lower your right arm very slowly until it rests in your lap. As you lower it, focus on the sensations. Which muscles are strained and which are not? Can you find the point at which the muscles that held up the arm relax? How does the discomfort change? Does it go away as soon as the arm moves? Does it go away gradually? Is there any discomfort as your hand rests in your lap? Can you still feel the muscles you were so aware of when your arm was raised? Scan your body for tension, take several deep breaths, and relax.

3. *Warming Up and Cooling Down*

This exercise involves working with temperatures that are slightly warmer or slightly cooler than those with which you are comfortable. Find an area where you can meditate that's a little warmer or cooler than you would normally like it. This could be in your living room before you turn on the heat in the morning. Or perhaps in front of (but not too close to) a fireplace or heater. Or this could be a matter of putting on or taking off an extra sweater. The point is to be *slightly* warmer or cooler than usual.

A. Find your posture and center yourself. Take several deep breaths. Practice your basic meditation.

B. As the warmth or coolness around you becomes irritating, focus on your body's reaction to it. Are your muscles tensing? Which ones? Is perspiration about to form? If so, what does this feel like? Or is your body beginning to shiver? If so, how does it do this? What tightens? Does it stay tight? Does your whole body shiver or only certain parts? Can you find a way to soften your body's reaction to the temperature? Can you concentrate on your object of meditation and not notice your reactions to the temperature?

C. When you have finished meditating, find an area that's comfortably heated and spend a few minutes quietly noticing how your body adjusts from discomfort to comfort.

Any irritating sound or sensation can be used as a focal point for meditation. Focusing on your body's minor aches, or the sound of a lawn mower, or a dog barking, can teach you how your body responds to life's irritations. Once you realize this, you can begin to learn how to soften around them.

Group 4. Being Present in the Present

Most stress comes from thinking about the past or worrying about the future. When you live in the present moment, when all of your attention is focused on what you are doing *right now,* there is no room for anything else to enter—including fears, desires, or anything that could be stressful.

In the meditative state all of your attention is focused on the present moment: the inhale, the exhale, the mantra, the object of meditation. When thoughts of past or future, desires or aversions, or anything else arise, you note this and then turn your awareness gently back to the present. It is this concentration on the *now* which allows your body and mind to enter a state of relaxation.

But you needn't go off by yourself and sit in silence in order to concentrate. In fact, the odds are that you have moments every day which demand and get your complete attention. What about those times you try to make a left-hand turn across the path of heavy oncoming traffic? Or when your four-year-old runs home with tears in his eyes and a cut on his elbow? Where is your attention when you are watching the best movie you ever saw in your life?

The following exercises will show you how to focus your attention on the present even in the midst of a busy world. They can be practiced anywhere and can be very helpful in calming your body as it responds to stress throughout the day.

1. *Eating Meditation*

You eat every day, but how often do you really pay attention to what you are eating while you are eating it? Do you usually eat with other people? In front of TV? While reading a book? Can you usually finish a three-course meal in ten minutes or less?

This is a conscious eating meditation. Try it some place where it is unlikely anyone will want to come over and eat with you. For the sake of this exercise, the food in question *is* a cheese sandwich.

A. Sit down in front of your food and take several deep breaths. Note the color, shape and texture. Does it seem appealing to you? Can you barely restrain yourself from gobbling it up? Whatever your feeling is, notice it.

B. Be aware of your intention to begin eating. Move your hand slowly toward the sandwich. As you do this, make a quiet mental note of the action. You may say to yourself, "Reaching . . . reaching . . . reaching." By labeling your actions you are more likely to keep in mind your purpose—to stay aware. As you pick up the sandwich, notice that you are "lifting . . . lifting . . . lifting."

C. Watch your hand move the sandwich closer to your mouth. When it nears your mouth, take a moment to smell the food. What smells do you recognize? Can you smell the mayonnaise? How is your body reacting to the smell? Is your mouth watering? Notice the sensation of your body desiring food.

D. As you take your first bite, feel your teeth penetrate the bread. When the bite is complete, how is the food positioned in your mouth? How does your tongue position the food so that it's in between your teeth? Begin chewing slowly. What are the sensations in your teeth? Your tongue? How does your tongue move when you chew? What tastes are you experiencing? The tomato? The cheese? What part of your tongue experiences the taste? And where is your arm? Did you put it back on the table? If so, did you notice the motion?

E. When you swallow, try to be aware of how the muscles in your esophagus contract and relax as they push the food to your stomach. Where is the food when you have finished swallowing? Can you feel the sensations in your stomach? Where is your stomach? What size is it? Is it empty, full, or somewhere in between?

F. As you continue to eat your sandwich, try to stay aware of as many sensations as you can. Silently label each movement if this helps. If you eat with the hand you don't normally use, the awkwardness may serve as a reminder to pay attention. As with your basic meditation, when thoughts arise, notice them. Then return your attention to your food.

2. Walking Meditation

Most people cover miles in the course of their daily routines. This makes walking a good activity on which to practice one-pointed concentration. The following exercise incorporates walking, breathing, and counting as a focal point.

A. Stand up and relax your abdominal muscles. Take several deep belly breaths. Feel your abdomen expand and contract with each breath. As you practice this exercise, try to continue breathing from this dropped stance. Mentally repeat the word "in" with each inhalation and "out" with each exhalation.

B. Without controlling your breathing too much, try to arrange it so that one of your feet touches the ground at the beginning of each *in* breath and each *out* breath. Now, see how many steps it seems natural to take during each inhalation and each exhalation.

C. Count your steps in time with your breathing as you walk. If you are taking three steps during each inhalation and exhalation, mentally say to yourself, "In . . . two . . . three. Out . . . two . . . three. In . . . two . . . three . . . " and so on. Your *in* breaths may be longer or shorter than your *out* breaths and therefore may accommodate either more or fewer steps. Or your step count may vary from breath to breath. Just pay attention and readjust your walking to the ins and outs of your breathing as is needed.

D. As with all meditations, when thoughts or images interrupt your counting, make a mental note of this and then return to your walking and counting and breathing.

E. A different way of practicing this meditation is, instead of counting steps, to pay attention to the sensations of walking. Concentrate on your feet and lower legs. Notice which muscles contract and which relax as you lift your legs up and down. Which part of your foot touches the ground first? Pay attention to how your weight shifts from one foot to the other. What are the feelings in your knees as they bend and straighten? And, while you're at it, pay attention to the ground. What is its texture? Is it hard or soft? Notice any cracks or stones. How does the sensation of walking on grass differ from that of walking on a sidewalk? Catch the thoughts, let them go, and notice everything.

3. *Gazing*

Basic instructions were given earlier for using a small object such as a stone or candle as a focal point for meditation. This same exercise can be practiced anywhere using a variety of objects, both large and small. You can gaze during a meeting, on a bus, or in a waiting room. It is a wonderfully inconspicuous practice.

A. Find an object within your line of vision on which you want to fix your eyes. Take several belly breaths as you glue your eyes to the object. Let it capture your interest, as though it were the only object around you. (For more detailed instructions, see Meditation 3 in the Basic Meditation section.)

   B. Try not to judge what you are seeing or have any thoughts about it at all. See if you can have the experience of "just seeing." When thoughts arise, note them, then return your focus to the object.

   C. Try practicing this exercise with different types of objects. Here are a few suggestions:

- Concrete objects — objects with a definite size and shape that are usually stationary.

- Natural objects — such as clouds, sand, a pile of dry leaves, the ocean, and so on.

- Vastness — any large, uniform surface such as a wall or a finely patterned rug.

- Moving objects — a crowd of people, cars on a busy street, and so on. With objects of this nature, don't follow individual shapes with your eyes. Instead, fix your eyes on a point in space and let the movement pass in front of you.

Any simple activity can become a meditation when you try to continuously focus your attention on it. A good mindfulness exercise is to choose an activity you do every day, preferably a short one. Concentrate on every action and every sensation involved in the activity. Use the type of mental notation discussed in the Eating Meditation if that helps. You could practice concentrating when you shave, brush your teeth, wash dishes, fold clothes, or pull up weeds. As thoughts occur, note them, and then go back to the task with renewed concentration. It is often helpful to switch to your unaccustomed hand (you might not want to do this while shaving). The resulting awkwardness will serve as a constant reminder that you want to concentrate on what you are doing.

Group 5. Letting Go of Thoughts

This highly structured exercise is found in many cultures in one form or another. In it, you passively observe the flow of your thoughts, feelings, and perceptions, one after another, without being concerned with their meaning or their relationship to one another. This will allow you to literally see what's on your mind and then let it go.

   A. Find your posture and center yourself. Take several deep breaths.

B. Close your eyes and imagine yourself sitting at the bottom of a deep pool of water. When you have a thought, feeling, or perception, see it as a bubble and let it rise away from you and disappear. When it's gone, wait for the next one to appear and repeat the process. Don't think about the contents of the bubble. Just observe it. Sometimes the same bubble may come up many times, or several bubbles will seem related to each other, or the bubbles may be empty. That's okay. Don't allow yourself to be concerned with these thoughts. Just watch them pass in front of your mind's eye.

C. If you feel uncomfortable imagining being under water, imagine that you are sitting on the bank of a river, watching a leaf drift slowly downstream. Observe one thought, feeling, or perception as the leaf, and then let it drift out of sight. Return to gazing at the river, waiting for the next leaf to float by with a new thought. Or, if you prefer, you can imagine your thoughts rising in puffs of smoke from a campfire.

Further Reading

Friedman, Lenore. *Meetings With Remarkable Women*. Boston: Shambala Publications, 1987.

Goldstein, Joseph. *The Experience of Insight*. Boston: Shambala Publications. 1976.

Goldstein, Joseph, and Kornfield, Jack. *Seeking the Heart of Wisdom*. Boston: Shambala Publications, 1987.

Harp, David. *The Three Minute Meditator*. San Francisco: Mind's i press, 1987. (This book is particularly recommended as an excellent introduction to meditation practice.)

Hewitt, James. *The Complete Yoga Book*. New York: Shocken Books, 1978.

LeShan, Lawrence. *How To Meditate*. New York: Bantam Books, 1974.

Locke, Steve and Colligan, Douglas. *The Healer Within*. New York: E. P. Dutton, 1986.

Naranjo, Claudio and Ornstein, Robert. *The Psychology of Meditation*. New York: The Viking Press, 1971.

Needleman, Jacob. *The New Religions*. New York: Doubleday, 1970.

Saraswati, Swami Janakananda. *Yoga, Tantra, and Meditation*. New York: Ballantine, 1975.

Suzuki, Shunryll. *Zen Mind, Beginner's Mind*. New York: Weatherhill, 1970.

6

Visualization

You can significantly reduce stress with something enormously powerful: your imagination. The practice of positive thinking in the treatment of physical symptoms was popularized by Emil Coué, a French pharmacist, around the turn of this century. He believed that the power of the imagination far exceeds that of the will. It is hard to will yourself into a relaxed state, but you can imagine relaxation spreading through your body, and you can visualize yourself in a safe and beautiful retreat.

Coué asserted that all of your thoughts become reality—you are what you think you are. For example, if you think sad thoughts, you feel unhappy. If you think anxious thoughts, you become tense. In order to overcome the feeling of unhappiness or tension, you can refocus your mind on positive, healing images. When you predict that you are going to be lonely and miserable, it is likely your prediction will come true, because your negative thoughts will be reflected in asocial behavior. A woman who predicts that she will get a stomach ache when she is yelled at by her boss is likely to have her thoughts take a somatic form. Coué found that organic diseases such as fibrous tumors, tuberculosis, hemorrhages, and constipation are often worsened when you focus on them. He recommended to his patients that they repeat 20 times to themselves on waking, mechanically moving their lips, the now-famous phrase, "Every day in every way I am getting better and better."

Coué also encouraged his patients to get into a comfortable, relaxed position upon retiring, close their eyes and practice general relaxation of all their muscles. As they started to doze off in the "stage of semi-consciousness," he suggested that they introduce into their minds any desired idea, for example, "I am going to be relaxed tomorrow." This is a way of bridging your conscious and unconscious minds and allowing your unconscious to make a wish come true.

Carl Jung, in his work in the early part of this century, used a technique for healing which he referred to as "active imagination." He instructed his patients to meditate without having any goal or program in mind. Images would come to consciousness which the patient was to observe and experience without interference. Later, if he or she wanted, the patient could actually communicate with the images by asking them questions or talking to them. Jung used active imagination to help the individual appreciate his or her own rich inner life and learn to draw on its healing power in times of stress. Jungian and Gestalt therapists have since devised several stress-reduction techniques using the intuitive, imaginative part of the mind.

Visualization is practiced and studied in cancer and pain centers throughout the country. Stephanie Matthews and O. Carl Simonton, who pioneered the use of visualization with cancer patients, wrote *Getting Well Again* in 1980. Two other visualization scientists, therapists, and writers are Jeanne Achterberg, who wrote *Imagery in Healing* in 1985, and Connecticut surgeon and Yale professor Bernie S. Siegel, who wrote *Love, Medicine, and Miracles* in 1986.

Shakti Gawain, author of *Creative Visualization* and *Living in the Light,* states that visualization is a form of energy creating life and life's happenings. Everything is energy and our mind creates our world, much as a movie projector projects a world upon a blank screen.

Symptom Effectiveness

Visualization is effective in treating many stress-related and physical illnesses, including headaches, muscle spasms, chronic pain, and general or situation-specific anxiety.

Time for Mastery

Symptom relief can be immediate or take several weeks of practice.

Instructions

Kinds of Visualization

Everybody visualizes. Daydreams, memories, and inner talk are all types of visualization. You can harness your visualizations and consciously employ them for bettering yourself and your life. Visualizations or mental sense impressions that you create consciously can train your body to relax and ignore stress.

There are three types of visualization for change:

Receptive Visualization. Here you relax, empty your mind, sketch a vague scene, ask a question and wait for a response. You might imagine you are on the beach, the breeze is caressing your skin. You can hear and smell the sea. You can ask, "Why can't I relax?" The response might surface into your consciousness, "Because you can't say no to people," or "Because you can't detach yourself from your husband's depression."

Programmed Visualization. Create an image, replete with sight, taste, sound, and smell. Imagine a goal that you want to attain or a healing that you want to accelerate. Harriet used programmed visualization when she started to run. For her first race, she not only practiced, but after one run on the course, she daily would visualize her race on that course. She would feel the pressure to run up a hill, the exhaustion after several miles, the sprint to the finish line. When she ran that race she set a state record for 40- to 49-year-old women.

Guided Visualization. Again visualize your scene in detail, but omit crucial elements. Then wait for your subconscious, or your inner guide, to supply the missing pieces in your puzzle. Jane imagines visiting a special place where she likes to relax. She constructs the smells, tastes, sounds, touch, sights associated with this place, a forest clearing that she used to visit with the Girl Scouts. She sees herself roasting marshmallows over a campfire at twilight. (There are no mosquitoes.) She imagines her Girl Scout leader, someone whom Jane loves, and asks her teacher how she can relax. Sometimes her leader reminds her of some songs Jane loves and tells Jane to sing them whenever she feels tense. Sometimes her leader reminds Jane of some old jokes and old times that made Jane laugh, and tells Jane that she needs to laugh more. Often the leader gives Jane a hug, to remind her that she is loved and that she needs to search for affirmations of that love.

Rules for Effective Visualization

1. Loosen your clothing, lie down in a quiet place, and close your eyes softly.

2. Scan your body, seeking tension in specific muscles. Relax those muscles as much as you can.

3. Form mental sense impressions. Involve all your senses: sight, hearing, smell, touch, and taste. For instance, imagine the sights of a green forest with the trees, blue sky, white clouds, and pine needles underfoot. Then add the sounds: wind in the trees, water running, birdcalls, and so on. Include the feel of the ground under your shoes, the smell of pine, and the taste of chewing a grass stem or mountain spring water.

4. Use affirmations. Repeat short, positive statements that affirm your ability to relax now. Use the present tense and avoid negatives such as "I am *not* tense" in favor of positive versions such as "I am letting go of tension." Here are some other examples of affirmations:

   Tension flows from my body.
   I can relax at will.
   I am in harmony with life.
   Peace is within me.

5. Visualize three times a day. Visualization practice is easiest in the morning and night while lying in bed. After some practice, you will be able to visualize while waiting in the doctor's office, at the service station, before going into a parent-teacher conference, or during an IRS audit.

Basic Tension and Relaxation Exercises

1. *Eye Relaxation (Palming)*

Put your palms directly over your closed eyes. Block out all light without putting too much pressure on your eyelids. Try to see the color black. You may see other colors or images, but focus on the color black. Use a mental image to remember the color black (black fur, black object in the room).

Continue this way for two to three minutes, thinking and focusing on black. Slowly open your eyes, gradually getting accustomed to the light. Experience the sense of relaxation in the muscles that control the opening and closing of your eyes.

Color imagery and eye relaxation can be done when you need a technique and don't have very much time. They are designed to be fun and provide you with some alternatives to keep "relaxing" interesting. Try to slip one of these into your regular activities every now and then.

2. *Metaphorical Images*

Lie down, close your eyes, and relax. Visualize an image for tension and then supplant it with an image for relaxation. The best images are those you make up yourself. But to get you started, images for tension might include:

The color red
The screech of chalk on a blackboard
The tension of a cable
The scream of a siren in the night
The glare of a searchlight
The smell of ammonia
The confinement of a dark tunnel
The pounding of a jackhammer

These tension images during visualization can soften, expand, fade, creating relaxation and harmony.

The color red can fade to pale blue.
The chalk can crumble into powder.
The cable can slacken.
The siren might soften to a whisper of a flute.
The searchlight might fade into a soft rosy glow.
The dark tunnel might open into a light, airy beach.
The jackhammer might become the hands of a masseuse kneading your muscles.

As you scan your body, apply a tension image to a tense muscle. Allow it to develop into your relaxation image. For example, if your neck is tense, you may visualize a tightened vise. Imagine the vise opening as you say an affirmation such as "Relax," or "I can relax at will."

End by reciting your affirmation. Speak to the specific tenseness as you apply your relaxation image. Watch the tension disappear.

3. *Creating Your Special Place*

In creating your own special place you will be making a retreat for relaxation and guidance. This place may be indoors or out. In structuring your place, follow a few guidelines:

- Allow a private entry into your place.
- Make it peaceful, comfortable and safe.
- Fill your place with sensuous detail. Create a midground, a foreground, and a background.
- Allow room for an inner guide or other person to comfortably be with you.

A special place might be at the end of a path that leads to a pond. Grass is under your feet, the pond is about 30 yards away and mountains are in the distance. You can feel the coolness of the air in this shady spot. The mockingbird is singing everyone's song. The sun is bright on the pond. The honeysuckle's pungent odor attracts the bee buzzing over the flower with its sweet nectar.

Or your special place might be a sparkling clean kitchen, with cinnamon buns baking in the oven. Through the kitchen window you can see fields of yellow wheat. A window chime flutters in the breeze. At the table is a cup of tea for your guest.

Try taping this exercise and playing it, or have a friend read it to you slowly.

To go to your safe place, lie down, be totally comfortable. Close your eyes . . . Walk slowly to a quiet place in your mind . . . Your place can be inside or outside . . . It needs to be peaceful and safe . . . Picture yourself unloading your anxieties, your worries . . . Notice the view in the distance . . . What do you smell? . . . What do you hear? . . . Notice what is before you . . . Reach out and touch it . . . How does it feel? . . . Smell it . . . Hear it . . . Make the temperature comfortable . . . Be safe here . . . Look around for a special spot, a private spot . . . Find the path to this place . . . Feel the ground with your feet . . . Look above you . . . What do you see? . . . Hear? . . . Smell? . . . Walk down this path until you can enter your own quiet, comfortable, safe place.

You have arrived at your special place . . . What is under your feet? . . . How does it feel? . . . Take several steps . . . What do you see above you? . . . What do you hear? . . . Do you hear something else? . . . Reach and touch something . . . What is its texture? . . . Are there pens, paper, paints nearby, or is there sand to draw in, clay to work? . . . Go to them, handle them, smell them. These are your special tools, or tools for your inner guide to reveal ideas or feelings to you . . . Look as far as you can see . . . What do you see? . . . What do you hear? . . . What aromas do you notice?

Now you need to find a place for your inner guide and a path from which your guide can enter.

Sit or lie in your special place . . . Notice its smells, sounds, sights . . . This is your place and nothing can harm you here . . . If danger is here, expel it . . . Spend three to five minutes realizing you are relaxed, safe and comfortable.

Memorize this place's smells, tastes, sights, sounds . . . You can come back and relax here whenever you want . . . Leave by the same path or entrance . . . Notice the ground, touch things near you . . . Look far away and appreciate the view . . . Remind yourself this special place you created can be entered whenever you wish. Say an affirmation such as, "I can relax here," or "This is my special place. I can come here whenever I wish."

Now open your eyes and spend a few seconds appreciating your relaxation.

4. Finding Your Inner Guide

Your Inner Guide is an imaginary person or animal that clarifies and instructs. This being is your link to your inner wisdom and subconscious. Your Inner Guide can tell you how to relax and can clarify what is causing your stress. With practice, you can meet your Inner Guide in your special place whenever you want.

Perhaps you already have an Inner Guide, a deceased parent or other spiritual presence. If so, invite this person into your special place and ask him or her to show you how to relax.

Try this exercise using your tape recorder or a friend.

Relax and follow the path to your special place, as you have been doing. Invite an Inner Guide to your place. Wait. Watch your guide's path. Notice a speck in the distance. Wait. Watch your guide's approach. Listen to its footfalls. Can you smell its fragrance? As your guide gains shape and clarity, if you feel unsafe, send it away. Wait for other guides until you find one you like, even though its appearance may surprise you or seem odd.

When your guide is comfortable, ask it questions. Wait for its answers. An answer may be a laugh, a saying, a feeling, a dream, a frown, a purr. Ask your guide, "How can I relax? What is causing my tension?" When your Guide answers, you will probably be surprised at the simplicity, yet clarity of its answers.

Before your guide leaves you, or immediately after, say your affirmation to yourself. Affirm your ability to relax with a simple, "I can relax here," or "I can relax at will."

Do this exercise several times a day for at least seven days. By the seventh day, you will probably have found a guide and some answers.

A student who has lost his mother and his house and has a father unable to care for him, uses his mother as his Inner Guide. He goes to her to relax, to seek guidance when pressure from life and his peers is overwhelming. She doesn't say much, but her presence and her look of approval or disapproval is often enough.

One person's guide creates relaxation because of the emptying of the mind that occurs in her presence. Rarely are words spoken, but her actions in small stories guide her.

Each person's inner guide is different and instructs them in a unique manner.

5. Listening to Music

Listening to music is one of the most common forms of relaxation. Each person gives his own meaning to music. It is important, therefore, that you select music that you find peaceful and soothing when you want to listen to music for the purpose of relaxation. If possible, make a half-hour tape of uninterrupted relaxing music that you can play daily or whenever you decide to use music to relax. Repetition of the same music that helped you to relax in the past carries with it a positive association that is likely to be beneficial in the future.

To get the most out of your music session, find a half-hour of uninterrupted time alone. Put on the music you have chosen, settle back in a comfortable position, and close your eyes. Mentally scan your body, noting areas of tension, pain, and relaxation. Be aware of your mood as you focus your attention on the music. Each time an unrelated thought enters your head, note it and then discard it, remembering your goal of focusing on the music and relaxing. Say an affirmation such as "Relax," or "Music relaxes me." When the music ends, allow your mind to again scan your body and become aware of how it feels. Does your body feel different from how it felt before you started? Is there any difference in your mood?

Special Considerations

A. If you have trouble getting impressions from all senses, work on your strongest sense first. The rest will improve in time.

B. Practice often—three times a day. And be patient, it takes time.

C. If recording your own tapes doesn't work, you might want to buy a prerecorded tape. See the list of tapes offered by New Harbinger at the end of the book.

D. Laughter
Laughter reduces emotional and physical tension by producing an internal message. Laughing stimulates your circulatory, respiratory, vascular, and nervous systems. When the internal spasms subside, the release of pressure reduces muscle tension and creates a feeling of well-being.

In his book, *Anatomy of an Illness,* Norman Cousins describes how he used laughter to overcome a rare and painful illness. His laughter therapy included watching old Marx Brothers movies and Candid Camera shows. He says that laughter has astounding rejuvenating effects on mind and body and "serves as a bulletproof vest that protects you against the ravages of negative thinking."

It is difficult to remain anxious, angry or depressed when you are laughing. Laughter gets your attention off yourself and your situation. It gives you the distance necessary to gain a perspective on a situation you are probably taking too seriously. Besides serving these useful functions, laughter is just plain fun to do. Give yourself more opportunities to laugh as a break from your stressful life.

Here's a humor exercise.

Close your eyes . . . experience yourself becoming more and more relaxed as the tension gradually leaves your body . . . once you are relaxed, begin imagining yourself using humor in a difficult situation . . . it might be telling your boss you made a mistake . . . or presenting a paper you have written. Choose something that is happening in your life right now and create a humorous alternative to your usual stress response.

E. Creativity

Accessing or learning to "turn on" the imaginative, creative aspect of the brain can be a powerful stress management tool and a relief from anxiety, worrying, and negative thinking. Scientific research done since the 1950's supports the value and validity of creative thought and has demonstrated that there are two distinct hemispheres in the human brain that mediate and process different kinds of tasks and problems.

The left brain or hemisphere, named the major or dominant brain by scientists, controls verbal and numerical information processed sequentially in a linear fashion. The left brain is the active, verbal, logical, rational, and analytic part of our brain. In contrast, the right brain or hemisphere manages the intuitive, experimental, nonverbal part of our brain and deals in images and holistic patterns and structures. It deals in dreams, metaphors, analogies, and new combinations of ideas. The key concept is that there are two ways of perceiving the world, and the right brain mode is more conducive to the relaxation response.

In her book, *Drawing on the Right Side of the Brain,* Betty Edwards, an art teacher and researcher on the relationship of drawing and brain-hemisphere process, states that anyone can draw. Ms. Edwards writes, "It is not a matter of 'talent,' but a process of developing and turning on the perceptual skills available in the right hemisphere." In her work with beginning art students, Ms. Edwards uses upside down or inverted drawing to force a cognitive shift from the dominant left brain to the subdominant right brain. This shift takes the student out of the labeling, rational, abstract mode, and puts them in the nonverbal, visual, concrete, intuitive mode which allows them to learn the artist's way of perceiving and attending to visual information that the left brain cannot or will not process. After experiencing this shift, the students reported less time urgency, less attachment to meaning, and a heightened sense of alertness, while feeling relaxed, calm, confident, and exhilarated. This pleasurable experience is derived from resting the left hemisphere, stopping its chatter, and keeping it quiet for a change. Visualization and guided imagery are methods of accessing the right brain and using its relaxing power.

Here is an exercise taken in part from *Drawing on the Right Side of the Brain* by Betty Edwards.

Find a quiet place to draw where no one will disturb you . . . play music if you like . . . From an art book choose a drawing that interests you . . . Turn the drawing you are going to copy upside down . . . Do not turn the drawing rightside up until you have finished . . . Finish the drawing in one sitting . . . Allow 30 to 40 minutes to complete the drawing . . . You might want to set a timer so you can forget about keeping time.

Look at the upside-down drawing for a minute . . . Regard the angles and shapes and lines . . . You can see the lines all fit together . . . Where one line ends another starts . . . When you begin to draw start at the top and copy each line . . . moving from line to adjacent line, putting it all together just like a jigsaw puzzle . . . Stay away from naming parts.

Begin to draw . . . work your way through the drawing by moving from line to line, part to adjacent part . . . Take your time . . . Don't make the exercise too complicated . . . Allow your movements to be slow and easy.

After you have finished, notice your state of mind . . . Do you feel calm and relaxed? . . . Did you lose track of time and meaning? . . . Did you turn off the chatter? . . . Were you able to get away from labeling and focus on the whole rather than the parts of the drawing? . . . Turn your drawing rightside up . . . You will probably be quite surprised by how well your drawing came out . . . Give yourself a pat on the back.

Further Reading

Fanning, Patrick. *Visualization for Change*. Oakland, California: New Harbinger Publications, 1988.

Gawain, Shakti. *Creative Visualization*. Mill Valley, California: Whatever Publishing, 1978.

Ornstein, Robert. *The Psychology of Consciousness*. San Francisco: W. H. Freeman & Company, 1972.

Oyle, Irving. *The Healing Mind*. New York: Pocket Books, 1976.

Samuels, Mike, and Samuels, Nancy. *Seeing With the Mind's Eye*. New York: Random House, 1975.

Shealy, C. Norman. *90 Days to Self-Health*. New York: Dial Press, 1977.

Siegel, Bernie S. *Love, Medicine, and Miracles*. New York: Harper & Row, 1986.

Simonton, O. C., Matthews-Simonton, S., and Creighton, J. L. *Getting Well Again*. New York: Bantam Books, 1980.

7

Self Hypnosis

Self hypnosis is a powerful weapon to counteract stress and stress-related illness. It is one of the fastest, easiest methods of inducing relaxation.

In some ways, hypnosis is very similar to sleep: There is a narrowing of consciousness, accompanied by inertia and passivity. But unlike sleep, there is never a complete loss of awareness.

Every hypnotic trance includes the following elements:

1. Economy of action and relaxation. A reduction of muscular activity and energy output.

2. Limb catalepsy: a sort of rigidity in the muscles of the limbs, with the tendency for them to stay in any position in which they are placed. This is sometimes described as the lead pipe effect.

3. Taking words at their literal meaning. If you asked a hypnotized person, "Would you tell me your birthday?" he would simply reply, "yes."

4. Narrowing of attention.

5. Increased suggestibility. For example, the ability to produce the sensation of lightness or heaviness in the limbs.

Optional benefits from hypnosis include:

1. The ability to produce anesthesia in any part of the body.

2. The ability to make post-hypnotic suggestions to improve sleep, coping, control painful symptoms, etc.

3. Control of some organic functions such as bleeding, heart rate, etc.

4. Partial age regression: the experience of going back to relive something in the distant past, just as it occurred, with all five senses operating to bring the sound, smell, sight, etc. alive. This memory is frequently one that would not be available to the conscious mind. It has been forgotten, or submerged, because it is painful.

5. Abnormal abilities of concentration: the capacity to learn and remember in enormous detail.

6. Time distortion: the capacity to compress a great deal of thinking and recall into a very short amount of real time.

Dr. David Cheek, who with Leslie LeCron wrote *Clinical Hypnotherapy,* has argued that hypnosis is a defense mechanism natural to all animals. When injured and in shock, we enter a hypnotic trance which cools skin temperature, minimizes bleeding and decreases movement and breathing. With self hypnosis you can enter such a trance and enjoy its therapeutic properties without trauma or injury. You can gain increased control of your emotions and improve concentration on tasks. Relaxation and calm can exist side-by-side with clearheaded focus and intense mental activity.

You are no stranger to hypnosis. Dr. Griffith Williams described spontaneous states of hypnosis in his article in *Experimental Hypnosis* (edited by LeCron). Frequently, when losing ourselves in concentration, we enter hypnosis without any formal induction. Daydreaming is an hypnotic state. Long distance driving is highly conducive to hypnosis, and commonly results in amnesia for various parts of the trip. You may have entered hypnosis many times while attempting to remember sequential things, watching TV, or feeling a strong emotion such as fear.

The term "hypnotism" was coined by James Braid in 1843, but his description of the hypnotic experience was identical to what Franz Mesmer and his disciples had earlier called "animal magnetism." Prior to the introduction of ether in 1846, *Mesmerism* was beginning to show great promise for painless surgery. Interest was lost, however, as reliable anesthetics were developed. Not until Hyppolite Bernheim's book, *Suggestive Therapeutics,* appeared in 1895 was hypnosis again recognized as a treatment by the medical profession. Together with a little-known country doctor named Lieubeault, he started a clinic in Nancy, France that treated more than 30,000 patients in 20 years. They used hypnosis with such success that doctors came from all over Europe to learn the technique. Jean Charcot and his pupil Sigmund Freud were also experimenting with hypnosis during this period, putting it to use in the treatment of neuroses.

You can learn self hypnosis quickly and safely. There are no reported cases, even for the most inexperienced practitioners, of harm resulting from self hypnosis.

Symptom Effectiveness

Self hypnosis has been clinically effective with symptoms of insomnia, minor chronic pain, headache, nervous tics and tremors, chronic muscular tension and minor anxiety. It is a well established treatment for chronic fatigue.

Time for Mastery

Significant relaxation effects can be achieved within two days.

Instructions

You can use hypnosis to relax, to make positive suggestions for changes in your life, and to uncover forgotten events that continue to influence you. The first step in self hypnosis is learning the power of suggestion. Make a pendulum by tying about ten inches of thread to a small, light object such as a paper clip, steel washer or finger ring. Some pendant necklaces, particularly ones with a single ball, can easily be adapted into pendulums. Hold the thread or chain between the thumb and forefinger of your dominant hand. Make sure your elbow is resting on a table, chair arm, etc. Let the weight dangle above the point where lines AB and CD cross on the diagram on the next page.

Run your eye from C to D, and back again. You will notice the pendulum starting to pick up the same movement. Now change direction and run your eye along the line from A to B. Eventually, the pendulum should also pick up the AB direction. Now allow your eyes to move around the circle clockwise until you notice the pendulum is beginning a similar clockwise motion. Repeat this movement with a counterclockwise eye movement. These are the four basic pendulum motions. In each case, the pendulum has been pushed by subtle muscle contractions which you did not consciously control. Your subconscious is at work, responding to suggestion.

Some people find at first that the pendulum doesn't move in a consistent direction. This is because the muscles of your hand and arm haven't learned yet how to manipulate the pendulum. Practice making it move along the two axis lines, and in circles without noticeably moving your hand. When you are able to produce easily the four basic pendulum motions, try again to influence it only with your eyes.

The pendulum is a tool for asking direct questions of your subconscious mind. Hold the pendulum motionless and ask which direction means "yes." Repeat to yourself: yes . . . yes . . . yes, until the pendulum begins a definite movement. LeCron has suggested that you word it in this way: "My subconscious is to select one of these four motions of the pendulum to mean 'yes' in answer to questions." Don't try to anticipate what the movement will be. Next, concentrate on the "no" movement, the "I don't know" movement and the "I don't want to answer" movements. There should be one distinct pendulum motion for each of these four answers. As an example, "yes" might be expressed by a pendulum movement along the CD line, "no" along the AB line, "I don't know" a counterclockwise circle, and "I don't want to answer" a clockwise circle.

Always try to hold the pendulum still during each of these procedures. Inevitably it will start to move on its own. If you have difficulty getting clear responses from the pendulum, have a friend ask the questions.

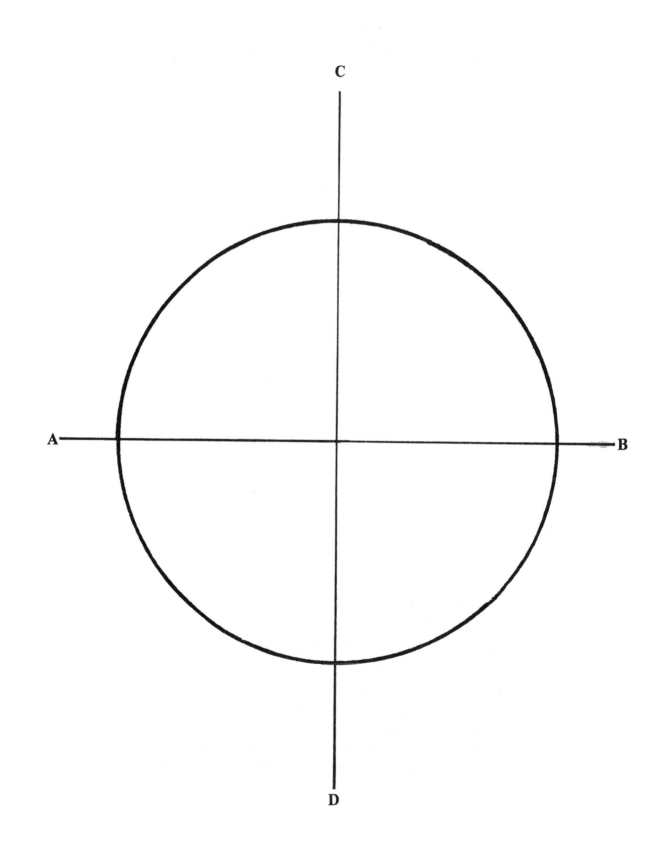

Practice with the pendulum can awaken you to the power of your subconscious. Your subconscious can control your muscle movements, and in fact does take over most automatic responses such as shifting gears in a car, shuffling cards, dialing well known numbers, etc. If you still aren't convinced, try these two exercises:

1. **Postural sway.** Stand up with your eyes closed and imagine holding a suitcase in your right hand. Imagine bigger and bigger suitcases weighing down your right side, pulling you over. After two or three minutes, open your eyes and notice any changes in your posture. Again close your eyes and imagine that the north wind is blowing you, pushing you back on your heels. Feel the gusts. Notice if your weight is shifting in response to your imagination.

2. **Postural suggestion.** Stretch both arms in front of you at shoulder level. With eyes closed, imagine a weight being tied onto your right arm as it strains to stay up. Imagine a second weight, a third. Feel the strain in that arm as it gets heavier and heavier. Open your eyes and notice where your arms are relative to each other.

Questioning Your Inner Mind

Using the pendulum, you are now in a position to ask questions of your subconscious mind. Your subconscious is usually dependable and remembers everything from your past. Here are some guidelines to follow:

Always ask permission of your inner mind before uncovering any particular memory. Ask questions such as "When it's all right for me to know about my fear of being embarrassed, the pendulum will make a 'yes' motion." Your subconscious tends to be responsive to questions that suggest alternatives, and will often resist questions that demand an answer.

Ask questions that have yes or no answers.

Ask if there is an experience that set the stage for your symptom or problem. Keep asking for earlier and earlier experiences. Nail down the time and setting for each experience.

Don't ask your subconscious to soothsay or predict the future. You can, however, ask if your inner mind knows that you can get over the problem.

If you recall a traumatic experience from the past, don't try to relive it. Look back on it from the present time. Ask the pendulum if there is something you can learn from this memory that would be of value to you. Suggest that the pendulum will make a "yes" motion when you are ready to know what you have learned. Examine the first thought that pops into your mind as the pendulum says "yes."

Don't try to turn off a symptom. Instead, suggest, "When I know I can feel good about myself, even when I am sometimes foolish or make mistakes, the pendulum will make a 'yes' motion."

The following illustration of questioning techniques involves a legislative assistant who was very uncomfortable in meetings.

Question	*Pendulum*
Is it all right for me to find out why I am anxious at meetings?	Yes
Is there anything that happened to me in the past that set the stage for my anxiety in meetings?	Yes
Is it something that happened before I was 20?	Yes
Before I was 10?	No
When I was 11, 12, 13?	No, no, no
When I was 14?	Yes
Was it at home?	No
Was it at school?	No
Was it with a group of friends?	Yes
Was it indoors?	Yes
Was it daytime?	No

[*Suddenly he recalled a scout meeting where he had been unexpectedly called on to make an oral report. He had stood up and his mind went completely blank. At the first nervous titters, he had fled the room.*]

Now that I know why I'm nervous at meetings, can I be more confident?	Don't know
When I know what I need to learn from this memory, today in 19__, the pendulum will say "yes."	Yes

[*When the pendulum started moving, he was thinking that his skills and abilities had been a lot less developed at 14 than they were at 40*]

Is it possible for me not to feel that helplessness and pain now?	Yes
When I know that I can go to the next meeting with a sense of confidence and freedom from that long-ago scare, the pendulum will say "yes."	Yes

Many symptoms and problems can be traced back to a traumatic event that was the precipitant. You can bring these up to be examined in the light of day. You can cope with the experience as an adult, rather than as the child you were. What was frightening then, and launched you into a habit of fear, you don't need to be afraid of with the skills and knowledge you have now.

The Self Induction

Sit in a comfortable position with legs uncrossed. The first thing you need is something to encourage eye fixation. A candle works well, or you can use a picture, a crack on the ceiling, a fire in the fireplace, etc. As you watch, suggest to yourself that your eyes are getting heavier, or are beginning to sting, or are starting to blink and flutter—whichever works best for you. Take several deep breaths, letting go of the air with a sigh. Silently suggest: "As I look at the candle, my eyelids are feeling heavier and heavier. They feel like little weights are dragging them down. They are almost heavy enough to close. Heavier and heavier. In a little while I will be so relaxed and sleepy that they will close."

Preselect a key word or phrase to say at the moment your eyes close. LeCron suggests a phrase such as "relax now." You could also use your favorite color, or a place that is very beautiful and has special meaning to you. Repeat this slowly as your eyes close. With enough practice, this word alone will be sufficient to induce hypnosis.

With your eyes closed, begin the relaxation of all your muscles. Start with your forearms and biceps. Tighten them first, then allow them to go completely slack. Tighten and relax your face, your neck and shoulders. Relax your chest as you breathe deeply into your abdomen. Tighten and relax simultaneously your stomach and lower back. Tighten and relax your buttocks, thighs and calves. Wriggle your toes. Notice that as your muscles become relaxed, they take on a wooden or heavy feeling.

Suggest to yourself that you are going deeper and deeper. Imagine riding an escalator down to the next floor of a department store. Notice everything about the escalator as you descend, and count back slowly from ten to zero. At zero imagine yourself stepping off at the bottom. Go down two more floors, counting backwards from ten to zero each time. Eventually you will only need to descend one level to achieve hypnosis.

When you wish to come back to full alertness, you can waken yourself by thinking, "Now I am going to wake up," pausing and counting slowly to three. Almost without exception, you will waken refreshed and relaxed, fatigue drained away.

Here are the key rules for successful self induction:

1. Allow at least 20 minutes to enter and deepen the hypnotic state.

2. Don't worry about success or how you are doing. Hypnosis will get easier with practice.

3. Always allow time to relax your muscles and take deep breaths.

4. Use compelling instructions ("I am feeling more and more heaviness in my arms.").

5. Use adjectives such as "drowsy, peaceful, comfortable" during self induction.

5. Repeat everything until the suggestion begins to take hold.

7. Use creative imagery. To induce heaviness, imagine weights hanging off your arms or eyelashes. For lightness, imagine helium-filled balloons pulling up your arm, etc.

8. Time your key word to exactly coincide with your eyes closing.

Your Own Induction Talk

Record the following on tape, and play it back for your initial inductions. Later you can change and adapt it to fit your personal style and needs.

"Make yourself comfortable and listen to my voice. Relax. Look at the candle in front of you, and as you watch it there will be heaviness in your eyelids, almost as if they were made of lead, or little weights had been tied on the lashes. Soon it will be too much work to hold them up. As your eyes close, say to yourself [*Insert here your key word or phrase*]. Now take some deep breaths, and let yourself slip into drowsiness. Tighten and relax your arms. Tighten and relax the muscles of your face where so much tension is often felt. Tighten and relax your neck and shoulders. Breathe deeply into your abdomen. Tighten and relax your stomach and lower back. At the same time, tighten and relax your buttocks, thighs and calves. Let the relaxation spread over your entire body, deeper and deeper, more and more peaceful and comfortable. Let a heaviness and relaxation come into your body as you picture the top of an escalator. Soon you will grab the rail and step on. The steps are moving down in front of you. As you step on, count slowly backward from ten to zero. Count with me: ten, nine, eight . . . going deeper and deeper . . . seven, six, five . . . deeper with each breath . . . four, three, two, one, zero . . . breathing slowly and deeply. [*Repeat the descent on the escalator for two more floors.*]

"In a while, you will notice that your right arm [*left if you are left handed*] is losing the feeling of heaviness. It is getting lighter and lighter, as if one after another, balloons were being tied to your arm. Lighter and lighter, and soon it will begin to lift. Imperceptibly at first, but soon the hand will start to float, and the arm will float, pulled by the balloons. Or imagine a powerful magnet pulling your arm higher. It is so light now, it is drifting in the air current of the room. Drifting higher and closer to your face. Soon the fingers will touch your face. If it doesn't lift up on its own, give your arm a little help. Lift it a few inches until it can catch the air currents and begin drifting. The higher it floats, the deeper you will go. When your hand touches your face, you will know that you are in hypnosis.

"Now let yourself slip a little deeper as you imagine the candle flame flickering and weaving. Suggest to yourself that in a moment, when you wake up, you will feel alert, refreshed and good about what you have done. When you are ready to awaken, say to yourself, 'Now I am going to wake up' and count to three."

When you record the induction, let your voice have a normal pitch, but do not vary the tempo. Speak one word after another with an even beat. Make long pauses between each sentence. By the tenth time you have practiced this induction, you will probably have achieved as deep an hypnotic state as you will need.

Deepening Hypnosis

Arm levitation. This has been previously described in the induction script. As you think, "My right arm is getting lighter and lighter" and the arm slowly drifts up, you are deepening the hypnotic trance. Suggest to yourself that as your hand touches your face, you will know that you are at a medium level of hypnosis.

Glued eyelids. Suggest that your eyelids are glued (sewn, padlocked, etc.) shut. Imagine the glue being spread on them, or see the tiny padlocks being snapped on. When the image is very clear, suggest that on the count of three, you will be unable to open your lids. LeCron uses the paradoxical suggestion, "The harder

I try to open them, the tighter the lids will stick together." Write a little script for your count of three: "One, the glue is being brushed on by little elves . . . two, my eyes are closed tight, it would take pliers to open them . . . three, they are locked now, I cannot open them." When you are sure that it would be very difficult to open your eyes, and thinking about opening them brings no results, you will know that you have achieved a medium level of hypnosis.

Hand clasp. Clasp your hand in front of you as if you were praying, and push them tightly together. As you hold them tightly, use the same suggestions as with your eyes. You should experience great difficulty in pulling them apart.

Anesthesia. Suggest to yourself there is a little numbness in your arm, just as if you had slept on it. Imagine your skin feeling thick and insensitive. There might even be a little tingling sensation. Lightly touch the skin of that arm and feel a slight numbness. Remember to suggest that the feeling will come back to your arm after waking up.

Anesthesia can also be used to reinforce other suggestions made during hypnosis. Say to yourself, "My arm will remain numb for one minute after I wake. When I feel the numbness, I will know that my subconscious is accepting all the suggestions I have made." Lightly touch your arm when you waken to verify the temporary anesthesia.

Abbreviated Inductions

These are shorthand techniques that can produce hypnosis in 30 seconds to two minutes:

Pendulum drop. Hold the pendulum in your dominant hand. Ask your subconscious for permission to go into hypnosis for two minutes. If the pendulum says yes, close your eyes and picture the candle flame. Take several deep breaths, and allow yourself to slip deeper and deeper. Suggest to yourself that when you have entered hypnosis, your hand will relax, dropping the pendulum. Count back slowly from ten.

Pencil drop. Same as above, except that you are holding a pencil poised above a table. Pinch the point between your thumb and index finger.

Yes repetition. Think the thought "yes" over and over, as you focus on the imagined candle flame. Go down the escalator while you continue to think "yes."

Coin flip. Place a penny in your palm. Suggest to yourself that the hand will begin to turn over gradually. Just allow your hand to turn slowly, until the coin drops out. As the coin drops, permit your eyes to close, and enter hypnosis.

Eye fixation. Fix your eyes slightly above your normal line of vision. Let your periphery vision narrow, and your eyes lose focus. Allow your eyes to close, accompanied by a feeling of drowsiness. To increase the drowsiness, roll your eyes up to the top of your head two or three times.

Key word or phrase. Breathe deeply and slowly, and repeat your key word or phrase from your induction talk. As you say it, close your eyes and enter hypnosis.

The abbreviated methods are useful after you have become relatively proficient at self hypnosis. Always remember to suggest that you will awaken refreshed and feeling good. Other suggestions to deal with such problems as insomnia, fatigue, finding lost articles, etc. should be written out in advance before going into hypnosis. After writing them down, summarize them in a key phrase that you can remember during the hypnotic state.

Five Finger Exercise

The following exercise has been used very effectively for relaxation. Memorize the following steps, and then enter hypnosis.

1. Touch your thumb to your index finger. As you do so, go back to a time when your body felt healthy fatigue, when you had just engaged in an exhilarating physical activity. You might imagine that you had just played tennis, jogged, etc.

2. Touch your thumb to your middle finger. As you do so, go back to a time when you had a loving experience. It may be sexual, it may be a warm embrace, or an intimate conversation.

3. Touch your thumb to your ring finger. As you do so, go back to the nicest compliment you have ever received. Try to really accept it now. By accepting it, you are showing your high regard for the person who said it. You are really paying him or her a compliment.

4. Touch your thumb to your little finger. As you do so, go back to the most beautiful place you have ever been. Dwell there for awhile.

The five finger exercise takes less than ten minutes, but it pays off with increased vitality, inner peace and self esteem. It can be done at any time you feel tension.

Rules for Hypnotic Suggestions

- Autosuggestions should be direct.

- Autosuggestions should be positive. Avoid wording suggestions with negatives such as "I won't feel tired tonight."

- Permissive suggestions meet less resistance. "I *can* feel relaxed and refreshed tonight" instead of "I *will* feel relaxed and refreshed." It should be noted, however, that some people respond better to commands. You should experiment with yourself.

- Make suggestions for the immediate future, not the present: "Soon the drowsiness is going to come."

- Repeat all suggestions at least three times.

- Attach a visual image to your suggestions. If you are exhausted, imagine yourself walking along with springs on your feet, bouncing, looking athletic and happy.

- Attach an emotion to your suggestions. For example, if you are attempting to give up cigarettes, imagine how bad the first one tasted, think of the unpleasant burning in your lungs, etc. If you are attempting to improve confidence on a first date, imagine the feeling of closeness and belonging you are looking for.

- Never use the word "try" in any suggestion. It implies doubt and the possibility of failure.

- When working toward the control of unpleasant emotions or painful physical symptoms, initially suggest that the emotion or symptom grow more intense. You might say, "My anger is getting bigger, I can feel the blood pushing at my veins, I'm getting hot, my muscles are tensing." Bring it up to a peak. If you can make it worse, you can make it better. Now suggest that it is diminishing: "My anger is subsiding, my heart is slowing, beating normally, my flush is receding, my muscles are unknotting and beginning to relax." When an emotion or symptom reaches its peak, it can only get better. Suggestion can rush that process of recovery. When you can turn your emotions and symptoms on and off during hypnosis, you will have gained enormous control over your life.

- Write your suggestions out in advance, and then distill them to a catchword or phrase that you can easily remember when you are in the hypnotic state.

Practice Writing Hypnotic Suggestions

Once hypnotized and relaxed, your subconscious mind is ready to believe what you tell it. Many of the symptoms that bother you, as well as the habitual tension responses to stress, were learned through suggestion. They can be unlearned through suggestion. If you watched your father blow his stack every time he was forced to wait, and if on the first occasion when you delayed him he became angry at you, you may have learned by suggestion to be exactly the same way. You can use hypnosis to learn new methods of coping with delay. Suggestions such as "Waiting is a chance to relax" and "I can let go of rushing" may undo the old habit.

In order to get the flavor of how suggestions can be written, write the hypnotic suggestions that you would use for the following problems:

1. Fear of coming into the dark house at night.

2. Deadlines, but too anxious to work or study.

3. Insomnia.

4. Chronic fatigue.

5. Obsessive and fearful thoughts about death.

6. Fear of illness.

7. Minor chronic head or back pain.

8. Feelings of inferiority.

9. Anxiety about upcoming evaluation or test.

10. Chronic anger, chronic guilt.

11. Worry about interpersonal rejection.

12. Chronic tension in a particular part of the body.

Now that you have written your own, examine these suggestions for each of the above problems:

1. I can come in tonight feeling relaxed and glad to be home.

2. I can work steadily and calmly. My concentration is improving as I become more relaxed.

3. I will gradually become more and more drowsy. In just a few minutes I will be able to fall asleep, and sleep peacefully all night.

4. I can waken refreshed and rested. I can enjoy the evening ahead.

5. I am full of life now. I will enjoy today. Very soon I can let go of these thoughts (visualize a blackboard and see the date written there).

6. My body is feeling more and more healthy, strong, etc. Each time I relax, my body becomes stronger.

7. Soon my head will be cool and relaxed. Gradually I will feel the muscles in my back loosen. In an hour, they will be completely relaxed. Whenever these symptoms come back, I will simply turn my ring a quarter turn to the right and the pain will relax away.

8. The next time I see _____, I can feel secure in myself. I can feel relaxed and at ease because I am perfectly all right.

9. Whenever I feel nervous, I can say to myself . . . [*Insert your key word or phrase*] . . . and relax.

10. I can turn off anger and guilt because I am the one who turns it on. I will relax my body and breathe deeply.

11. Whenever I lace my fingers together, I will feel confidence flowing throughout my entire body.

12. Every hour I will think about my _____ and let it relax.

Hypnosis, just by itself, is highly relaxing. You don't have to make specific suggestions to reap its stress reducing benefits. Suggestions tailored to your particular needs will simply increase its effectiveness.

You should use hypnosis while you are right in the middle of a painful emotion or symptom. Rehearse the symptom, make it worse, then make suggestions that will begin to quiet it. As you learn to turn it on and off, you are taking away its power over you. Under hypnosis, you can ask your subconscious mind to recall the first moment the symptom was experienced by you. Ask: "What set the stage for the development of this symptom?" If no memories come up, use the pendulum to narrow the incident down in time. Getting in touch with the origin of a habit is a good way to start breaking it.

Further Reading

Cheek, D. B. and LeCron, Leslie. *Clinical Hypnotherapy.* New York: Grune and Stratton, 1968.

Haley, Jay. "Advanced Techniques of Hypnosis and Therapy." *Selected Papers of Milton Erickson.* New York: Grune and Stratton, 1967.

Haley, Jay. "Uncommon Therapy." *The Psychiatric Techniques of Milton Erickson.* New York: Norton, 1973.

LeCron, Leslie (ed.). *Experimental Hypnosis.* New York: MacMillan, 1952.

LeCron, Leslie (ed.). *Techniques of Hypnotherapy.* New York: Julian Press, 1961.

LeCron, Leslie. *Self-Hypnosis.* New York: New American Library, 1970.

Morris, Freda. *Self-Hypnosis in Two Days.* Berkeley: Intergalactic, 1974.

8

Autogenics

Autogenic Training (AT) is a systematic program that will teach your body and mind to respond quickly and effectively to your verbal commands to relax and return to a balanced, normal state. It is one of the most effective and comprehensive reducers of chronic stress.

In stress reduction and holistic health centers across the country AT is being increasingly used with Biofeedback. Other health professionals use it as the treatment of choice to teach self-regulation of the autonomic nervous system.

When you do not have time to recuperate from emotionally and physically stressful events, your body chemistry becomes imbalanced and your mood is disturbed. In extreme cases, you may develop high blood pressure, hardening of the arteries, peptic ulcers, migraines or rheumatoid arthritis. Feelings of anxiety and depression often accompany these psychosomatic diseases. In less extreme cases, you may experience the imbalance in the form of muscle tension, neck and backache, indigestion or cold hands and feet. The goal of AT is to normalize your physical, mental and emotional processes which get out of balance due to stress.

AT has its origins in the research in hypnosis conducted by the famous brain physiologist Oskar Vogt. He worked at the Berlin Institute during the last decade of the 19th century. Vogt taught some of his experienced hypnotic subjects to put themselves in a trance that had the effect of reducing fatigue, tension and painful symptoms such as headaches. It appeared to help the subjects deal more effectively with their everyday lives. The subjects usually reported that when their fatigue and tension lifted, they felt warm and heavy.

Johannes H. Schultz, a Berlin psychiatrist, became interested in Vogt's work. He found that you can create a state very much like an hypnotic trance just by thinking of heaviness and warmth in your extremities. Essentially, all you have to do is relax, undisturbed, in a comfortable position and concentrate passively on verbal formulas suggesting warmth and heaviness in your limbs. Schultz combined some of the autosuggestions of Vogt with some Yoga techniques and in 1932 published his new system in the book entitled *Autogenic Training*.

In its present form, AT not only provides you with the recuperative effects of traditional hypnosis, it also frees you from dependence on a hypnotist. You can learn to induce the feeling of warmth and heaviness whenever you choose.

Schultz's verbal formulas fall into three main kinds of exercises: the standard exercises concentrate on the body, the meditative exercises focus on the mind, and the special exercises are designed to normalize specific problems. This introductory chapter will cover only the standard exercises which deal with the general relaxation and normalization of the body.

The standard exercises are aimed at reversing the "fight or flight" or alarm states that occur when you experience physical or emotional stress. The first standard exercise includes the theme of heaviness. It promotes relaxation of the striped muscles in your body, the voluntary muscles used to move your arms and legs. The second standard exercise brings about peripheral vasodilation. That is, as you say, "My right hand is warm," the smooth muscles which control the diameter of the blood vessels in your hand relax so that more warming blood flows into your hand. This helps reverse the pooling of blood in the trunk and head that is a characteristic of the "fight or flight" reaction to stress.

The third standard exercise focuses on normalizing cardiac activity. It is simply "My heartbeat is calm." The fourth standard exercise regulates the respiratory system. The verbal formula is, "It breathes me." The fifth standard exercise relaxes and warms the abdominal region, as you say, "My solar plexus is warm." The last standard exercise reduces the flow of blood to the head as you say, "My forehead is cool."

Symptom Effectiveness

AT has been found to be effective in the treatment of various disorders of the respiratory tract (hyperventilation and bronchial asthma), the gastrointestinal tract (constipation, diarrhea, gastritis, ulcers and spasms), the circulatory system (racing heart, irregular heartbeat, high blood pressure, cold extremities and headaches), and the endocrine system (thyroid problems). AT is also useful in reducing general anxiety, irritability and fatigue. It can be employed to modify your reaction to pain, increase your resistance to stress, and reduce or eliminate sleeping disorders.

Contraindications

AT is not recommended for children under five years old, persons who lack motivation, or individuals with severe mental or emotional disorders. Prior to beginning AT, it is advised that you have a physical exam and discuss with your medical doctor what physiological effects AT will be likely to have on you. Persons with serious diseases such as diabetes, hypoglycemic conditions or heart conditions should be under the supervision of a medical doctor while in AT. Note that some trainees experience an increase in blood pressure and a few have a sharp drop in blood pressure when they do these exercises. Trainees with high or low blood pressure should check with their medical doctor to be sure that AT is regularizing it. If you feel very anxious or restless during or after AT exercises, or experience recurring disquieting side effects, you should continue AT only under the supervision of a professional AT instructor.

Time for Mastery

AT specialists recommend moving at a slow but sure pace in learning these exercises, taking from four to ten months to master all six exercises.

Begin with one and a half minute sessions five to eight times a day. If you cannot find time for this, do 30 second sessions at least three times a day to get started. As you become more comfortable with AT, you can gradually increase the length of sessions to 30 to 40 minutes twice a day.

Instructions

In doing these exercises, it is essential that you maintain an attitude of passive concentration. That is, experience whatever physical, mental or emotional response you have to the exercises without any expectations. Just let whatever happens happen. Passive concentration does not mean "spacing out" or going to sleep. You remain alert to your experience without analyzing it. This casual attitude is contrasted with active concentration, which occurs when you fix your attention on certain aspects of your experience and have an interest and goal-directed investment in it. Active concentration is essential for such things as preparing a new recipe or fixing a car. Passive concentration is required for relaxation.

Each exercise will introduce a verbal formula that you will keep in mind constantly as you passively concentrate on a particular part of your body. Repeat the formula over and over to yourself, keeping up a steady, silent, verbal stream.

It is very important to keep external stimuli to a minimum. Choose a quiet room where you won't be disturbed. Keep the room temperature at a moderately warm, comfortable level. Turn the lights down low. Wear loose clothing. Let your body be relaxed and your eyes closed before you begin these exercises.

There are three basic AT postures recommended:

1. Sit in an armchair in which your head, back and extremities are comfortably supported and you are as relaxed as possible, or

2. Sit on a stool, slightly stooped over, with your arms resting on your thighs and your hands draped between your knees, or

3. Lie down with your head supported, your legs about eight inches apart, your toes pointed slightly outward and your arms resting comfortably at your sides without touching them.

Scan your body to be sure that the position you choose is tension free. In particular, look for over-extension of limbs such as unsupported arms, head or legs, tightening of the limbs at the joints, or crooked spine.

There are six exercise themes, each with a particular verbal formula. The following is one suggested program for learning them. You may find that you need more or less time than is recommended, so adjust the program to your own pace. The most common mistake made by people just getting started is to become impatient and move too fast, not thoroughly learning each theme. On the other hand, if your body is giving you consistent clear feedback that you are doing the exercise correctly and effectively, move on to the next exercise. If you feel stuck or are experiencing unpleasant side effects over a period of time, move on to the next exercise and postpone the difficult exercise to the end of your training. Perhaps ten percent of all trainees never experience the basic sensations of heaviness or warmth. This does not matter. The formula is used only to bring about a functional change in the body which you may or may not feel. Just focus on doing the exercise correctly.

You will not be able to maintain perfect passive concentration at first. Your mind will wander. That's OK. When you find this happening, just get back to the formula as soon as possible. In addition, you may experience some initial symptoms described as "autogenic discharges" which are normal but distracting. For example, you may sense a change in your weight or temperature, tingling, electric currents, involuntary movements, stiffness, some pain, anxiety, a desire to cry, irritability, headaches, nausea or hallucinations. Whether the autogenic discharges you experience are pleasant or unpleasant, remember that they are transitory, that they are not the purpose of AT and that they will pass as you continue with the program.

When you are ready to stop an AT session, say to yourself, "When I open my eyes, I will feel refreshed and alert." Then open your eyes, breathe a few deep breaths as you stretch and flex your arms. Be sure that you are not still in a trance-like state when you go on to your regular activities.

Standard Exercises for a 12-Week Program

Heaviness Theme

Week 1. Repeat the following verbal formulas for one and a half minutes, five to eight sessions a day. Each time you say a formula, say it slowly, taking about five seconds and then pause about three seconds. Repeat each formula about four times. Always start with your dominant arm. That is, if you write with your right hand, begin with your right arm. Repeat, "My right arm is heavy" four times, and then go on to the next phrase, "My left arm is heavy" and repeat it four times, etc.

My right arm is heavy.
My left arm is heavy.
Both of my arms are heavy.

Week 2. Repeat the following verbal formulas for three minutes, four to seven times a day:

My right arm is heavy.
My left arm is heavy.
Both of my arms are heavy.
My right leg is heavy.
My left leg is heavy.
Both of my legs are heavy.
My arms and legs are heavy.

Week 3. Repeat the following for four minutes, four to seven times a day:

My right arm is heavy.
Both of my arms are heavy.
Both of my legs are heavy.
My arms and legs are heavy.

Note: If you have difficulty achieving a sensation of heaviness using the verbal formulas, you may want to add visual imagery. For example, you might imagine weights attached to your arms and legs gently pulling them down. Or you might want to think of your arms and legs as made of heavy lead sinking into the ground. Think of the heaviness along the entire arm from your shoulder down to the tips of your fingers.

Warmth Theme

Week 4. Repeat the following for five minutes, four to seven times a day:

My right arm is heavy.
My arms and legs are heavy.
My right arm is warm.
My left arm is warm.
Both of my arms are warm.

Week 5. Repeat the following for eight minutes, three to six times a day:

My right arm is heavy.
My arms and legs are heavy.
My right arm is warm.
My left arm is warm.
My right leg is warm.
My left leg is warm.
Both of my legs are warm.
My arms and legs are warm.

Week 6. Repeat the following for ten to fifteen minutes, three to six times a day:

My right arm is heavy.
My arms and legs are heavy.
Both of my arms are warm.
Both of my legs are warm.
My arms and legs are warm.
My arms and legs are heavy and warm.

Week 7. Repeat the following for ten to twenty minutes, three to six times a day:

My right arm is heavy.
My arms and legs are heavy.
My arms and legs are warm.
My arms and legs are heavy and warm.

Note: If you have trouble experiencing a feeling of warmth using the verbal formulas, try visual imagery. For instance, imagine your right arm lying on a warm heating pad. Feel the warmth of the pad through your hand and arm. Imagine yourself in a nice warm shower or bath with the warmth of the water all around you. Imagine your hand submerged in a comfortably warm pan of water. Envision yourself sitting in the sunshine, with the sun falling warmly on your arms and legs. Think about holding a nice, comfortably warm mug of your favorite hot drink in your hand. Think about the blood flowing gently through the fingertips of your hands and through your toes.

Practice the rest of the exercises for ten to forty minutes, one to six times a day. Remember to move at your own pace.

Week 8. Heartbeat Theme. If you have trouble becoming aware of your heartbeat, lie on your back with your right hand resting over your heart. If you experience any discomfort or distress while doing this exercise, move on to the next three themes and do this one in week eleven.

My right arm is heavy.
My arms and legs are heavy and warm.
My heartbeat is calm and regular.

Week 9. Breathing Theme. This enhances the tendency of the previous themes to slow and deepen respiration.

My right arm is heavy and warm.
My arms and legs are heavy and warm.
My heartbeat is calm and regular.
It breathes me.

Week 10. Solar Plexus Theme. Skip this exercise if you have ulcers, diabetes, or any condition involving bleeding from abdominal organs.

My right arm is heavy and warm.
My arms and legs are heavy and warm.
My heartbeat is calm and regular.
It breathes me.
My solar plexus is warm.

Week 11. Forehead Theme. It is best to do this exercise lying on your back, since it may cause dizziness.

My right arm is heavy and warm.
My arms and legs are heavy and warm.
My heartbeat is calm and regular.

It breathes me.
My solar plexus is warm.
My forehead is cool.

Week 12. Special Themes. You can practice *Autogenic Modification* by making up what Schultz called "organ specific formulae" to deal with specific problems. For example, you can develop an indirect formula such as "My feet are warm" or "My shoulders are warm" each time you feel an embarrassing blush coming on. This exercise allows you to passively attend to something other than the problem. At the same time, you move some of the blood from your head that would contribute to the blushing. You might also use a direct formula such as, "My forehead is cool."

When you are troubled by a cough, you may want to use this formula: "My throat is cool, my chest is warm." To cope with asthma, use the same formula and add, "It breathes me, it breathes me calm and regular."

When you are in a very relaxed state toward the end of an AT session, you are highly suggestible. It is a good time to use what Schultz called "Intentional Formulae" to tell yourself to do things that you want to do and are having difficulty with. For example, if you want to stop smoking, say something over and over again such as, "Smoking is a dirty habit, I can do without it." If you want to eat less, say, "I have control over what I eat. I can eat less and be more attractive." The special intentional formulas should be believable, persuasive, and brief.

These additional formulas may be interspersed with the themes of the standard exercises, or said when you are finished saying the standard themes.

I feel quite quiet
My whole body feels quiet, heavy, comfortable and relaxed
My mind is quiet
I withdraw my thoughts from the surroundings and I feel serene and still
My thoughts are turned inward and I am at ease
Deep within my mind, I can visualize and experience myself as relaxed and
    comfortable and still
I feel an inward quietness

Meditative Exercises

These exercises focus on mental rather than physical functions. They are intended to reinforce the effects of the standard exercises. Schultz reserved the Meditative Exercises for trainees who had mastered the Standard Exercises over a period of six to twelve months and who could prolong the Autogenic state for 40 minutes without serious distracting effects.

Schultz's Meditative Exercises are similar to the methods of Psychosynthesis, a program developed at about the same time by the Italian psychiatrist Roberto Assagioli. Both these western physicians sought to duplicate in a predictable way the physical and emotional benefits of eastern meditation without making use of its mystical and religious elements.

The Meditative Exercises stimulate the creative processes and mobilize the resources of both the body and mind toward greater self awareness, problem solving, and emotional and physiological health. They are effective because your mind affects your emotions and your body. If you turn your mental focus away from pain and problems, you will feel better emotionally and physically.

Practice the first stages of the Meditative Exercises twice a day for 20 minutes. When you begin the more complicated visualizations, you will probably want to spend up to an hour at a time. Spend a week on the color and movement exercises, then two to six weeks on the others in turn. Move at your own pace.

Color and Movement

Begin all exercises by assuming your favorite Autogenic posture and running quickly through the standard themes. Then, with your eyes still closed, roll your eyeballs upward. Imagine looking inward at the center of your forehead.

Visualize a static, uniform color filling your mind's eye. Experiment with blue, green, yellow, red, orange and so on until you find a color that is easiest for you to hold in your imagination.

Let darker and lighter shades of your color form. Add movement by letting these vague areas of light and dark color drift around like clouds or shadows.

Add another color in a simple geometric shape. For example, if you have been visualizing blue, see a green triangle superimposed on the blue background. Add other shapes and colors gradually—a yellow square, an orange circle, and so on. Then try changing the color of the background.

Introduce movement by having the geometric shapes move up and down and sideways. Introduce depth by letting them grow larger and smaller. Imagine that the triangles are solid cones, the squares are cubes, and the circles are balls. Stack them up and roll them around.

This exercise gives you practice in forming, controlling, and holding vivid mental images.

Objects

Visualize and hold the image of a specific, unmoving object such as a face, mask, or statue. Let it be light in color against a dark background. Choose an object that comes easily to mind. Concentrate on its details.

If you have trouble getting a clear image or holding it, lengthen your practice sessions up to an hour. With these longer sessions you might need to rest in the middle, or interrupt a disturbing image. Use these cancellation phrases to take a break: "The images gradually recede . . . they have become less clear . . . they have completely disappeared . . . my legs are light . . . my arms are light . . . my heart and breathing normal . . . my forehead temperature normal." Stretch your arms, breathe deeply, and open your eyes. Take a break for a couple of minutes, then start your exercise over from the beginning.

Concepts

Pick an abstract concept such as happiness. Visualize the word printed on a page. Imagine hearing a voice saying "happiness" out loud. Give happiness a color and a shape. Imagine a happy person in a fairy tale or a myth. Tell yourself the story or see it acted out as in a movie or a play. Allow your mind to bring up images, analogies, and associations connected to happiness.

Other abstractions to meditate on in this way are freedom, peace, justice, goodness, and so on.

Fantasy Scenes

Put yourself in a fantasy scene: on top of a mountain, on the moon, seeing a sunrise, flying over clouds, looking out over the ocean, in a palace, or elsewhere. Concentrate on the details of sight, sound, touch, temperature, and movement. Notice if anyone else appears. What do they do or say? See the scene as a "film-strip" in which you are an actor and an active participant.

You may encounter archetypal figures, religious themes, melodrama, or vivid sexual fantasies. Accept and observe whatever comes up. If it becomes disturbing, use your cancellation phrases and take a break.

Real People

Visualize real people. Start with someone like a store clerk or the mailman. It is easier to hold a clear image of someone you don't know well. Next easiest is someone you know and dislike. People you love will probably be the hardest to visualize clearly.

At this stage, the people you visualize may say or do anything, or you may have spontaneous insights about them. You have opened yourself up to messages from your unconscious self, a wellspring of valuable, interesting, and surprising information. What you get when you interrogate your unconscious self is unpredictable. Sometimes you may get images that are alarming. If you do, use the cancellation phrases to terminate the session.

Further Reading

Assagioli, Roberto. *Psychosynthesis.* Hobbs & Dunn, 1965.

Luthe, Wolfgang. "Autogenic Training: Method, Research and Application in Medicine." *American Journal of Psychotherapy.* 1963, vol. 17, 174–95.

Luthe, Wolfgang (ed.). *Autogenic Therapy.* six vols. New York: Grune and Stratton, 1969.

(Note that Wolfgang Luthe, M.D., is a colleague of Schultz's. Luthe practices in Montreal, is Scientific Director of the Oskar Vogt Institute at the medical school of Kyushu University in Japan, and has been the major promoter of Autogenic Training in North America.)

Pelletier, Kenneth R. *Mind as Healer, Mind as Slayer.* New York: Delta, 1977.

9

Thought Stopping

Thought stopping can help you overcome the nagging worry and doubt which stands in the way of relaxation. Thought stopping was first introduced by Bain in 1928 in his book *Thought Control in Everyday Life*. In the late 1950's, it was adapted by Joseph Wolpe and other behavior therapists for the treatment of obsessive and phobic thoughts. Obsessions are repetitive and intrusive trains of thought that are unrealistic, unproductive and often anxiety provoking. A "worry wart" is an example of an obsessive person. Obsessions may take the form of self doubt: "I will never be able to do this job right" or "I'm too plain to get a date." Obsessions may also take the form of fear: "I wonder if something is wrong with my heart" or "If they raise the rent, I'll have to move." Phobias are specific objects or situations which are so frightening that they are avoided if at all possible. Phobic thoughts are also anxiety producing, and may preoccupy the affected individual.

Thought stopping involves concentrating on the unwanted thoughts and, after a short time, suddenly stopping and emptying your mind. The command "stop" or a loud noise is generally used to interrupt the unpleasant thoughts. There are three explanations for the success of thought stopping: 1. The command "stop" serves as a punishment, and behavior which is consistently punished is likely to be inhibited. 2. The command "stop" acts as a distractor, and the imperative self-instruction is incompatible with obsessive phobic thoughts. 3. Thought stopping is an assertive response and can be followed by thought substitutions of reassuring or self-accepting statements. For example, you say, "These big 747's are awfully safe" instead of "Look at that wing shake, I bet it's ready to come off."

It has been well documented that negative and frightening thoughts invariably *precede* negative and frightening emotions. If the thoughts can be controlled, overall stress levels can be significantly reduced.

Symptom Effectiveness

Thought stopping has proved effective with a wide variety of obsessive and phobic thought processes: color naming, sexual preoccupation, hypochondriasis, obsessive thoughts of failure, sexual inadequacy, obsessive memories and frightening reoccurring impulses leading to chronic tension and anxiety attacks. While thought stopping is only effective in approximately 20 percent of cases involving compulsive ritual behavior, it is more than 70 percent effective against phobias such as fear of snakes, driving, the dark, elevators, someone lurking in the house at night, fear of insanity, etc. Thought stopping is recommended when the problem behavior is primarily cognitive, rather than acted out. It is indicated when specific thoughts or images are repeatedly experienced as painful or leading to unpleasant emotional states.

Time for Mastery

For effective mastery, thought stopping must be practiced conscientiously throughout the day for three days to one week.

Instructions

1. *Explore and List Your Stressful Thoughts*
Use the following stressful thoughts inventory to help you assess which recurrent thoughts are the most painful and intrusive.

Stressful Thoughts Inventory
Put a check mark after each item that applies to you. For items which you check, rate them in column A from 1 to 5, based on these statements:

1. *Sensible.* This is quite a sensible and reasonable thing for me to think.
2. *Habit.* This is just a habit. I think it automatically, without really worrying about it.
3. *Not necessary.* I often realize that this thought is not really necessary, but I don't try to stop it.
4. *Try to stop.* I know this thought is not necessary. It bothers me, and I try to stop it.
5. *Try very hard to stop.* This thought upsets me a great deal, and I try very hard to stop it.

For items which you check, rate them in column B from 1 to 4, based on the following statements:

1. *No interference.* This thought does not interfere with other activities.
2. *Interferes a little.* This thought interferes a little with other activities, or wastes a little of my time.
3. *Interferes moderately.* This thought interferes with other activities, or wastes some of my time.
4. *Interferes a great deal.* This thought stops me from doing a lot of things, and wastes a lot of time every day.

	Check here if your answer is yes	A If yes, rate from 1 to 5	B Rate from 1 to 4
Do you worry about being on time?	☐	_____	_____
Do you worry about leaving the lights or the gas on, or whether the doors are locked?	☐	_____	_____
Do you worry about your personal belongings?	☐	_____	_____
Do you worry about keeping the house always clean and tidy?	☐	_____	_____
Do you worry about keeping things in their right place?	☐	_____	_____
Do you worry about your physical health?	☐	_____	_____
Do you worry about doing things in their right order?	☐	_____	_____
Do you ever have to count things several times or go through numbers in your mind?	☐	_____	_____
Are you a person who often has a guilty conscience over quite ordinary things?	☐	_____	_____
Do unpleasant or frightening thoughts or words ever keep going over and over in your mind?	☐	_____	_____
Have you ever been troubled by certain thoughts of harming yourself or others—thoughts which come and go without any particular reason?	☐	_____	_____
Do you worry about household things that might chip or splinter if they were to be knocked over or broken?	☐	_____	_____
Do you ever have persistent ideas that someone you know might be having an accident or that something might have happened to them?	☐	_____	_____
Are you preoccupied with the fear of being raped or assaulted?	☐	_____	_____
Do you go back and think about a task you have already completed, wondering how you could have done it better?	☐	_____	_____
Do you find yourself concerned with germs?	☐	_____	_____
Do you have to turn things over and over in your mind before being able to decide about what to do?	☐	_____	_____
Do you ask yourself questions or have doubts about a lot of things that you do?	☐	_____	_____

	Check here if your answer is yes	A If yes, rate from 1 to 5	B Rate from 1 to 4
Are there any particular things that you try to keep away from or that you avoid doing, because you know that you would be upset by them? ...	☐	_____	_____
Do you worry about money a lot?	☐	_____	_____
Do you frequently think that things will not get better and may, in fact, get worse?	☐	_____	_____
Do you become preoccupied with angry or irritated thoughts when people don't do things carefully or correctly?	☐	_____	_____
Do you ruminate about details?	☐	_____	_____
Do guilt-tinged memories return to you over and over?	☐	_____	_____
Do you have recurring feelings of jealousy, or fear of being left?	☐	_____	_____
Do you feel nervous about heights?	☐	_____	_____
Are you at times preoccupied with desire for things you cannot have?	☐	_____	_____
Do you worry about auto accidents?	☐	_____	_____
Do you find yourself returning to thoughts about your faults?	☐	_____	_____
Do you worry about growing old?	☐	_____	_____
Do you feel nervous when thinking about being alone?	☐	_____	_____
Do you worry about dirt and/or dirty things?	☐	_____	_____
Are you ever worried about knives, hammers, hatchets or other possibly dangerous things?	☐	_____	_____
Do you tend to worry a bit about personal cleanliness or tidiness?	☐	_____	_____
Does a negative feature of your appearance or makeup preoccupy you at times?	☐	_____	_____
Do you worry about getting trapped in crowds, on bridges, elevators, etc.?	☐	_____	_____
Do you think again and again about your failures?	☐	_____	_____
Sometimes do you think about your home burning?	☐	_____	_____
Do you think frequently of certain things of which you are ashamed?	☐	_____	_____
Are you preoccupied with uncomfortable thoughts about sex or sexual adequacy?	☐	_____	_____

(Adapted from the Leyton Scale)

Ask yourself these questions about each stressful thought you checked: Is the thought realistic or unrealistic? Is the thought productive or counter-productive? Is the thought neutral or self-defeating? Is the thought easy or hard to control?

Thought stopping requires consistent motivation. Decide now if you really want to eliminate any of the stressful thoughts you have listed. Select a thought that you feel strongly committed to extinguishing. Column I is the *discomfort* rating for each thought, while column II is the *interference* rating for how disruptive it is to your life. Any thought that has a discomfort rating above three, or an interference rating above two may warrant thought stopping procedures.

2. *Imagine the Thought*

Close your eyes and bring into imagination a situation in which the stressful thought is likely to occur. Try to include normal as well as obsessive thinking. In this way, you can interrupt the stressful thoughts while allowing a continuing flow of healthy thinking.

3. *Thought Interruption*

Thought interruption can be accomplished initially by using one of two "startler" techniques:

Set an egg timer or alarm clock for three minutes. Look away, close your eyes, and ruminate on your stressful thought as described above in step two. When you hear the ring, shout "stop!" You may also want to raise your hand, snap your fingers or stand up. Let your mind empty of all but the neutral and nonanxious thoughts. Set a goal of about 30 seconds after the stop, during which your mind remains blank. If the upsetting thought returns during that time, shout, "stop!" again.

Tape record yourself loudly exclaiming "stop!" at intermittent intervals (e.g. three minutes, two minutes, three minutes, one minute). You may find it useful to repeat the taped stop messages several times at five second intervals. Proceed the same way as with the egg timer or alarm clock. The tape recording shapes and strengthens your thought control.

4. *Unaided Thought Interruption*

Now take control of the thought stopping cue, without the timer or tape recorder. While ruminating on the unwanted thought, shout, "stop!"

When you succeed in extinguishing the thought on several occasions with the shouted command, begin interrupting the thought with "stop" said in a normal voice.

After succeeding in stopping the thought by using your normal speaking voice, start interrupting the thought with "stop" verbalized in a whisper.

When the whisper is sufficient to interrupt stressful thoughts, use the sub-vocal command "stop." Imagine hearing "stop!" shouted inside your mind. Tighten your vocal chords and move your tongue as if you were saying "stop" out loud. Success at this stage means that you can stop thoughts alone or in public, without making a sound or calling attention to yourself.

5. Thought Substitution

The last phase of thought stopping involves thought substitution. In place of the obsessive thought, make up some positive, assertive statements that are appropriate in the target situation. For example, if you are afraid of flying, you might say to yourself, "This is a fantastically beautiful view from way up here." Develop several alternative assertive statements to say to yourself, since the same response may lose its power through repetition.

Example of Successful Thought Stopping

A business executive who did a great deal of traveling developed a fear of sleeping in strange places. He was aware that his obsessive worrying about having to take overnight trips had begun about the time of his divorce. When preparing for bed in the motel, he would think about people entering the room by passkey while he slept. While planning his next business trip at home, he would become very tense anticipating the anxiety he would feel in the strange motel.

Utilizing thought stopping techniques, he allowed himself to visualize unpacking in a strange motel, thinking about plans for the next day, anticipating going to bed. He imagined lying in darkness with the feeling that the door might be swinging slightly ajar. In the middle of these thoughts the egg timer went off—he shouted "stop!" and simultaneously snapped his fingers. If the thought recurred before 30 seconds were up, he shouted "stop!" again.

After succeeding with the shout, he began saying "stop" in a normal voice, and then a whisper. Finally, he was able to shout "stop" silently inside his head. He noted that he had repeated each phrase five or ten times before feeling that he could go on to the next one. During the next three days, he shouted "stop" sub-audibly at the very beginning of each phobic thought. Occasionally he reinforced the command by snapping a rubber band which he kept around his wrist. The thoughts decreased in frequency and only lasted a few moments when they occurred. He had markedly decreased stress on his next trip. He took his tape recorder and set it to say "stop" at intervals of five, ten, three and eight minutes during the time he was preparing for bed. By the end of the trip, he was aware that he wasn't thinking about the terrors of sleeping in strange places, but was much more focused on the challenges of his business.

Special Considerations

1. Failure with your first attempt at thought stopping may mean that you have selected a thought that is very difficult to extinguish. In this situation, select an unwanted thought that is either less intrusive or less frightening than your initial choice. It is helpful to become proficient at the technique before tackling the more stressful obsessive or phobic thoughts.

2. If the sub-vocalized "stop" is not successful for you, and you find it embarrassing to say "stop" aloud in public, you can substitute one of these techniques: Keep a rubber band unobtrusively around your wrist, and when unwanted thoughts occur, snap it. Or pinch yourself when the unwanted thoughts occur. Or finally, you might try pressing your finger nails into the palms of your hands to stop unwanted thoughts.

3. You should be aware that stopping a thought takes time. The thought will return and you will have to interrupt it again. The main effort is to stifle each thought just as it begins, and to concentrate on something else. The thoughts will return less and less readily in most cases, and eventually cease to be a problem.

Further Reading

Lazarus, A. A. *Behavior Therapy and Beyond.* New York: McGraw Hill, 1971.

Rimm, D. C. and Masters, J. C. *Behavior Therapy: Techniques and Empirical Findings.* New York: Academic Press, 1974.

Wolpe, J. *The Practice of Behavior Therapy.* Oxford: Pergamon Press, 1969.

10

Refuting Irrational Ideas

"Man is not disturbed by events, but by the view he takes of them."
—Epictetus

Almost every minute of your conscious life you are engaging in self-talk, your internal thought language. These are the sentences with which you describe and interpret the world. If the self-talk is accurate and in touch with reality, you function well. If it is irrational and untrue, then you experience stress and emotional disturbance. This sentence is an example of irrational self-talk: "I can't bear to be alone." No physically healthy person has ever died merely from being alone. Being alone may be uncomfortable, undesirable and frustrating, but you can live with it, and live through it.

More irrational self-talk: "I should never be cruel to my wife. If I am, I know I'm a rotten person." The words "should never" allow no possibility of flaw or failure. When the inevitable fight occurs, you indict yourself as entirely rotten—all on the basis of a single incident.

Irrational ideas may be based on outright misperceptions ("This person probably won't like me." "When the airplane's wing shakes, I know it's going to fall off.") or perfectionistic shoulds, oughts and musts ('I ought to keep quiet rather than upset anyone."). Inaccurate self-talk such as "I need love" is emotionally dangerous compared to the more realistic "I want love very much, but I don't absolutely need it, and can survive and feel reasonably happy without it." "How terrible to be rejected" is fear-producing in comparison to "I find it unpleasant and momentarily awkward, and feel regretful when I am rejected." Imperatives such as "I've got to be more helpful around the house" can be converted to more rational statements, such as "There would probably be more peace and compatibility if I did a greater share of the work."

Albert Ellis developed a system to attack irrational ideas or beliefs, and replace them with realistic statements about the world. He called his system Rational Emotive Therapy and introduced it first in *A Guide to Rational Living* with co-author Harper in 1961. Ellis' basic thesis is that emotions have nothing to do with actual events. In between the event and the emotion is realistic or unrealistic self-talk. It is the self-talk that produces the emotions. Your own thoughts, directed and controlled by you, are what create anxiety, anger and depression. The following chart shows how it works.

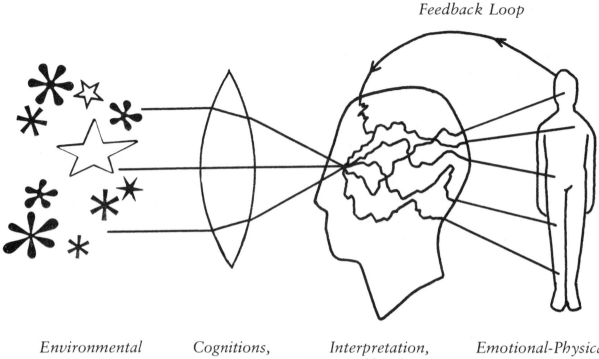

Feedback Loop

| *Environmental Events* | *Cognitions, Perceptions (Sensory Input)* | *Interpretation, Self-Talk (Irrational Ideas)* | *Emotional-Physical System* |

Example

A. Facts and events

A mechanic replaces a fuel pump he honestly believed was malfunctioning, but the car's performance doesn't improve. The customer is very upset and demands that he put the old fuel pump back.

B. Mechanic's self-talk

"He's just a grouch—nothing would please him."
"Why the hell do I get all the tough jobs?"
"I ought to have figured this out by now."
"I'm not much of a mechanic."

C. Emotions

Anger and resentment
Depression

The mechanic may later say to himself, "That guy really made me mad." But it is not the customer or anything that the customer has done which produces the anger—it is the mechanic's own self-talk, his interpretation of reality. This irrational self-talk can be changed, and the stressful emotions changed with it.

Symptom Effectiveness

Rimm and Litvak (1969) found that negative self-talk produced substantial physiological arousal. In other words, your body tenses and becomes stressed when you use such irrational syllogisms as:

> People seem to ignore me at parties.
> It's obvious that I'm either boring or unattractive to them.
> How terrible!

The emotional results of irrational self-talk are anxiety, depression, rage, guilt, and a sense of worthlessness. Rational Emotive Therapy has been shown effective in decreasing the frequency and intensity of these emotions.

Time for Mastery

Assessment of your irrational beliefs, plus homework sufficient to refute one of these beliefs can take approximately 20 minutes a day for two weeks. Rational Emotive Imagery, the process by which you work directly on changing your emotions, also takes about two weeks if you practice ten minutes a day.

Directions—Rational Emotive Therapy

Assessment

This Beliefs Inventory is designed to uncover particular irrational ideas which contribute to unhappiness and stress. Take the test now. Score it and note the sections where your scores are highest.

Beliefs Inventory

It is not necessary to think over any items very long. Mark your answer quickly and go on to the next statement. Be sure to mark how you actually think about the statement, *not* how you think you *should* think.

Agree	Dis-agree	Score	
• ☐	☐	_____	1. It is important to me that others approve of me.
• ☐	☐	_____	2. I hate to fail at anything.
• ☐	☐	_____	3. People who do wrong deserve what they get.
•• ☐	☐	_____	4. I usually accept what happens philosophically.

Dis-
Agree agree Score

•• ☐ ☐ _____ 5. If a person wants to, he can be happy under almost any circumstances.

• ☐ ☐ _____ 6. I have a fear of some things that often bothers me.

• ☐ ☐ _____ 7. I usually put off important decisions.

• ☐ ☐ _____ 8. Everyone needs someone he can depend on for help and advice.

• ☐ ☐ _____ 9. "A zebra cannot change his stripes."

• ☐ ☐ _____ 10. I prefer quiet leisure above all things.

•• ☐ ☐ _____ 11. I like the respect of others, but I don't have to have it.

• ☐ ☐ _____ 12. I avoid things I cannot do well.

• ☐ ☐ _____ 13. Too many evil persons escape the punishment they deserve.

•• ☐ ☐ _____ 14. Frustrations don't upset me.

•• ☐ ☐ _____ 15. People are disturbed not by situations but by the view they take of them

•• ☐ ☐ _____ 16. I feel little anxiety over unexpected dangers or future events.

•• ☐ ☐ _____ 17. I try to go ahead and get irksome tasks behind me when they come up.

• ☐ ☐ _____ 18. I try to consult an authority on important decisions.

• ☐ ☐ _____ 19. It is almost impossible to overcome the influences of the past.

•• ☐ ☐ _____ 20. I like to have a lot of irons in the fire.

• ☐ ☐ _____ 21. I want everyone to like me.

•• ☐ ☐ _____ 22. I don't mind competing in activities in which others are better than I.

• ☐ ☐ _____ 23. Those who do wrong deserve to be blamed.

• ☐ ☐ _____ 24. Things should be different from the way they are.

•• ☐ ☐ _____ 25. I cause my own moods.

• ☐ ☐ _____ 26. I often can't get my mind off some concern.

• ☐ ☐ _____ 27. I avoid facing my problems.

• ☐ ☐ _____ 28. People need a source of strength outside themselves.

•• ☐ ☐ _____ 29. Just because something once strongly affects your life doesn't mean it need do so in the future.

•• ☐ ☐ _____ 30. I'm most fulfilled when I have lots to do.

•• ☐ ☐ _____ 31. I can like myself even when many others don't.

•• ☐ ☐ _____ 32. I like to succeed at something, but I don't feel I have to.

• ☐ ☐ _____ 33. Immorality should be strongly punished.

• ☐ ☐ _____ 34. I often get disturbed over situations I don't like.

•• ☐ ☐ _____ 35. People who are miserable have usually made themselves that way.

•• ☐ ☐ _____ 36. If I can't keep something from happening, I don't worry about it.

•• ☐ ☐ _____ 37. I usually make decisions as promptly as I can.

• ☐ ☐ _____ 38. There are certain people that I depend on greatly.

•• ☐ ☐ _____ 39. People overvalue the influence of the past.

•• ☐ ☐ _____ 40. I most enjoy throwing myself into a creative project.

Agree	Dis-agree	Score

•• ☐ ☐ _____ 41. If others dislike me, that's their problem, not mine.

• ☐ ☐ _____ 42. It is highly important to me to be successful in everything I do.

•• ☐ ☐ _____ 43. I seldom blame people for their wrongdoings.

•• ☐ ☐ _____ 44. I usually accept things the way they are, even if I don't like them.

•• ☐ ☐ _____ 45. A person won't stay angry or blue long unless he keeps himself that way.

• ☐ ☐ _____ 46. I can't stand to take chances.

• ☐ ☐ _____ 47. Life is too short to spend it doing unpleasant tasks.

•• ☐ ☐ _____ 48. I like to stand on my own two feet.

• ☐ ☐ _____ 49. If I had had different experiences I could be more like I want to be.

• ☐ ☐ _____ 50. I'd like to retire and quit working entirely.

• ☐ ☐ _____ 51. I find it hard to go against what others think.

•• ☐ ☐ _____ 52. I enjoy activities for their own sake, no matter how good I am at them.

• ☐ ☐ _____ 53. The fear of punishment helps people be good.

•• ☐ ☐ _____ 54. If things annoy me, I just ignore them.

• ☐ ☐ _____ 55. The more problems a person has, the less happy he will be.

•• ☐ ☐ _____ 56. I am seldom anxious over the future.

•• ☐ ☐ _____ 57. I seldom put things off.

•• ☐ ☐ _____ 58. I am the only one who can really understand and face my problems.

•• ☐ ☐ _____ 59. I seldom think of past experiences as affecting me now.

•• ☐ ☐ _____ 60. Too much leisure time is boring.

•• ☐ ☐ _____ 61. Although I like approval, it's not a real need for me.

• ☐ ☐ _____ 62. It bothers me when others are better than I am at something.

• ☐ ☐ _____ 63. Everyone is basically good.

•• ☐ ☐ _____ 64. I do what I can to get what I want and then don't worry about it.

•• ☐ ☐ _____ 65. Nothing is upsetting in itself—only in the way you interpret it.

• ☐ ☐ _____ 66. I worry a lot about certain things in the future.

• ☐ ☐ _____ 67. It is difficult for me to do unpleasant chores.

•• ☐ ☐ _____ 68. I dislike for others to make my decisions for me.

• ☐ ☐ _____ 69. We are slaves to our personal histories.

• ☐ ☐ _____ 70. I sometimes wish I could go to a tropical island and just lie on the beach forever.

• ☐ ☐ _____ 71. I often worry about how much people approve of and accept me.

• ☐ ☐ _____ 72. It upsets me to make mistakes.

• ☐ ☐ _____ 73. It's unfair that "the rain falls on both the just and the unjust."

•• ☐ ☐ _____ 74. I am fairly easygoing about life.

• ☐ ☐ _____ 75. More people should face up to the unpleasantness of life.

• ☐ ☐ _____ 76. Sometimes I can't get a fear off my mind.

•• ☐ ☐ _____ 77. A life of ease is seldom very rewarding.

• ☐ ☐ _____ 78. I find it easy to seek advice.

	Dis-		
Agree	agree	Score	

• ☐ ☐ _____ 79. Once something strongly affects your life, it always will.

• ☐ ☐ _____ 80. I love to lie around.

• ☐ ☐ _____ 81. I have considerable concern with what people are feeling about me.

• ☐ ☐ _____ 82. I often become quite annoyed over little things.

•• ☐ ☐ _____ 83. I usually give someone who has wronged me a second chance.

• ☐ ☐ _____ 84. People are happiest when they have challenges and problems to overcome.

•• ☐ ☐ _____ 85. There is never any reasons to remain sorrowful for very long.

•• ☐ ☐ _____ 86. I hardly ever think of such things as death or atomic war.

•• ☐ ☐ _____ 87. I dislike responsibility.

•• ☐ ☐ _____ 88. I dislike having to depend on others.

• ☐ ☐ _____ 89. People never change basically.

• ☐ ☐ _____ 90. Most people work too hard and don't get enough rest.

•• ☐ ☐ _____ 91. It is annoying but not upsetting to be criticized.

•• ☐ ☐ _____ 92. I'm not afraid to do things which I cannot do well.

•• ☐ ☐ _____ 93. No one is evil, even though his deeds may be.

•• ☐ ☐ _____ 94. I seldom become upset over the mistakes of others.

•• ☐ ☐ _____ 95. Man makes his own hell within himself.

• ☐ ☐ _____ 96. I often find myself planning what I would do in different dangerous situations.

•• ☐ ☐ _____ 97. If something is necessary, I do it even if it is unpleasant.

•• ☐ ☐ _____ 98. I've learned not to expect someone else to be very concerned about my welfare.

•• ☐ ☐ _____ 99. I don't look upon the past with any regrets.

• ☐ ☐ _____ 100. I can't feel really content unless I'm relaxed and doing nothing.

Scoring the Beliefs Inventory

A. Single dot items

If the item has one dot (.) and you checked the "agree" box, give yourself one point in the space provided next to the item.

B. Double dot items

If the item has two dots (..) and you checked the "disagree" box, give yourself a point in the space provided next to the item.

C. Add up your points for items:

1, 11, 21, 31, 41, 51, 61, 71, 81, and 91, and enter the total here: _____
The higher the total, the greater your agreement with the irrational idea that *it is an absolute necessity for an adult to have love and approval from peers, family and friends.*

2, 12, 22, 32, 42, 52, 62, 72, 82, and 92, and enter the total here: _____
The higher the total, the greater your agreement with the irrational idea that *you must be unfailingly competent and almost perfect in all you undertake.*

3, 13, 23, 33, 43, 53, 63, 73, 83, and 93, and enter the total here: _____
The higher the total, the greater your agreement with the irrational idea that *certain people are evil, wicked and villainous, and should be punished.*

4, 14, 24, 34, 44, 54, 64, 74, 84, and 94, and enter the total here: _____
The higher the total, the greater your agreement with the irrational idea that *it is horrible when things are not the way you would like them to be.*

5, 15, 25, 35, 45, 55, 65, 75, 85, and 95, and enter the total here: _____
The higher the total, the greater your agreement with the irrational idea that *external events cause most human misery—people simply react as events trigger their emotions.*

6, 16, 26, 36, 46, 56, 66, 76, 86, and 96, and enter the total here: _____
The higher the total, the greater your agreement with the irrational idea that *you should feel fear or anxiety about anything that is unknown, uncertain or potentially dangerous.*

7, 17, 27, 37, 47, 57, 67, 77, 87, and 97, and enter the total here: _____
The higher the total, the greater your agreement with the irrational idea that *it is easier to avoid than face life difficulties and responsibilities.*

8, 18, 28, 38, 48, 58, 68, 78, 88, and 98, and enter the total here: _____
The higher the total, the greater your agreement with the irrational idea that *you need something other or stronger or greater than yourself to rely on.*

9, 19, 29, 39, 49, 59, 69, 79, 89, and 99, and enter the total here: _____
The higher the total, the greater your agreement with the irrational idea that *the past has a lot to do with determining the present.*

10, 20, 30, 40, 50, 60, 70 80, 90, and 100, and enter the total here: _____
The higher the total, the greater your agreement with the irrational idea that *happiness can be achieved by inaction, passivity and endless leisure.*

Irrational Ideas

At the root of all irrational thinking is the assumption that things are done to you: "That really got me down . . . She makes me nervous . . . Places like that scare me . . . Being lied to makes me see red." Nothing is done to you. Events happen in the world. You experience those events (A), engage in self-talk (B), and then experience an emotion (C) resulting from the self-talk. *A* does not cause *C* — *B* causes *C*. If your self-talk is irrational and unrealistic, you create unpleasant emotions.

Two common forms of irrational self-talk are statements that "awfulize" and "absolutize." You awfulize by making catastrophic, nightmarish interpretations of your experience. A momentary chest pain is a heart attack, the grumpy boss intends to fire you, your mate takes a night job and the thought of being alone is unthinkably terrible. The emotions that follow awfulizing self-talk tend themselves to be awful— you are responding to your own description of the world.

Irrational self statements that "absolutize" often include words such as "should, must, ought, always and never." The idea is that things have to be a certain way, or you have to be a certain way. Any deviation from that particular value or standard is bad. The person who fails to live up to the standard is bad. In reality, it is the standard that is bad, because it is irrational.

Albert Ellis has suggested ten basic irrational ideas, which are listed below. To these we have added some additional common self statements which are highly unrealistic. Based on your scores on the Beliefs Inventory, and your knowledge of the situations in which you characteristically experience stress, check the ones that seem to apply to you:

☐ 1. **It is an absolute necessity for an adult to have love and approval from peers, family and friends.**
In fact, it is impossible to please all the people in your life. Even those who basically like and approve of you will be turned off by some behaviors and qualities. This irrational belief is probably the single greatest cause of unhappiness.

☐ 2. **You must be unfailingly competent and almost perfect in all you undertake.**
The results of believing you must behave perfectly are self blame for inevitable failure, lowered self esteem, perfectionistic standards applied to mate and friends, and paralysis and fear at attempting anything.

☐ 3. **Certain people are evil, wicked and villainous, and should be punished.**
A more realistic position is that they are behaving in ways which are anti-social or inappropriate. They are perhaps stupid, ignorant or neurotic, and it would be well if their behavior could be changed.

☐ 4. **It is horrible when people and things are not the way you would like them to be.**
This might be described as the spoiled child syndrome. As soon as the tire goes flat the self-talk starts: "Why does this happen to me? Damn, I can't take this. It's awful, I'll get all filthy." Any inconvenience, problem or failure to get your way is likely to be met with such awfulizing self statements. The result is intense irritation and stress.

☐ 5. **External events cause most human misery—people simply react as events trigger their emotions.**
A logical extension of this belief is that you must control the external events in order to create happiness or avoid sorrow. Since such control has limitations and we are at a loss to completely manipulate the wills of others, there results a sense of helplessness and chronic anxiety. Ascribing unhappiness to events is a way of avoiding reality. Self statements *interpreting* the event caused the unhappiness. While you may have only limited control over others, you have enormous control over your emotions.

☐ 6. **You should feel fear or anxiety about anything that is unknown, uncertain or potentially dangerous.**
Many describe this as, "a little bell that goes off and I think I ought to start worrying." They begin to rehearse their scenarios of catastrophy. Increasing the fear or anxiety in the face of uncertainty makes coping more difficult and adds to stress. Saving the fear response for actual, perceived danger allows you to enjoy uncertainty as a novel and exciting experience.

☐ 7. **It is easier to avoid than to face life difficulties and responsibilities.**
There are many ways of ducking responsibilities: "I should tell him/her I'm no longer interested—but not tonight . . . I'd like to get another job, but I'm just too tired on my days off to look . . . A leaky faucet won't hurt anything . . . We could shop today, but the car is making a sort of funny sound."
If you have checked this idea, please add your standard excuses to avoid responsibility here:

Area of responsibility   *Method of Avoidance*

_____   _____

_____   _____

_____   _____

_____   _____

_____   _____

☐ 8. **You need something other or stronger or greater than yourself to rely on.**
This belief becomes a psychological trap in which your independent judgment, and the awareness of your particular needs are undermined by a reliance on higher authority.

☐ 9. **The past has a lot to do with determining the present.**
Just because you were once strongly affected by something, that does not mean that you must continue the habits you formed to cope with the original situation. Those old patterns and ways of responding are just decisions made so many times they have become nearly automatic. You can identify those old decisions and start changing them *right now*. You can learn from past experience, but you don't have to be overly attached to it.

☐ 10. **Happiness can be achieved by inaction, passivity and endless leisure.**
This is called the Elysian Fields syndrome. There is more to happiness than perfect relaxation.

Other irrational ideas

☐ 11. **You are helpless and have no control over what you experience or feel.**
This belief is at the heart of much depression and anxiety. The truth is we not only exercise considerable control over interpersonal situations, we control how we interpret and emotionally respond to each life event.

☐ 12. **People are fragile and should never be hurt.** (Farquhar and Lowe)
This irrational belief results in failure to openly communicate important feelings, and in self sacrifice that gives up what is nourishing and pleasurable. Since everything you need or want seems to hurt or deprive someone else, you feel frustration, helplessness and depression. Relationships become full of dead space where conflicts developed and nothing was said.

☐ 13. **Good relationships are based on mutual sacrifice and a focus on giving.**
This belief rests on the assumption that it is better to give than to receive. It is expressed in a reluctance to ask for things, and the anticipation that your hidden needs will be divined and provided for. Unfortunately, constant self denial usually results in bitterness and withdrawal.

☐ 14. **If you don't go to great lengths to please others, they will abandon or reject you.**
This belief is a by-product of low self esteem. You usually run less risk of rejection if you offer others your true unembellished self. They can take it or leave it. But if they respond to the real you, you don't have to worry about slacking off, letting down your guard, and being rejected later.

☐ 15. **When people disapprove of you, it invariably means you are wrong or bad.** (Farquhar and Lowe)
This extremely crippling belief sparks chronic anxiety in most interpersonal situations. The irrationality is contained in the generalization of one specific fault or unattractive feature to a total indictment of the self.

☐ 16. **Happiness, pleasure and fulfillment can only occur in the presence of others, and being alone is horrible.** (Farquhar and Lowe)
Pleasure, self worth and fulfillment can be experienced alone as well as with others. Being alone is growth-producing and desirable at times.

☐ 17. **There is a perfect love, and a perfect relationship.**
Subscribers to this belief often feel resentful of one close relationship after another. Nothing is quite right because they are waiting for the perfect fit. It never comes.

☐ 18. **You shouldn't have to feel pain, you are entitled to a good life.**
The realistic position is that pain is an inevitable part of human life. It frequently accompanies tough, healthy decisions and the process of growth. Life is not fair, and sometimes you will suffer no matter what you do.

☐ 19. **Your worth as a person depends on how much you achieve and produce.** (Farquhar and Lowe, 1974)
A more rational assessment of your real worth would depend on such things as your capacity to be fully alive, feeling everything it means to be human.

☐ 20. **Anger is automatically bad and destructive.** (Farquhar and Lowe)
Anger is frequently cleansing. It can be an honest communication of current feelings, without attacking the personal worth and security of others.

☐ 21. **It is bad or wrong to be selfish**
The truth is that no one knows your needs and wants better than you, and no one else has as great an interest in seeing them fulfilled. Your happiness is your responsibility. Being selfish means you are accepting that responsibility.

It is quite probable that you could add other irrational ideas to this list. Please do. The best way to uncover your own irrational ideas is to think of situations in which you experience anxiety, depression, anger, guilt or a sense of worthlessness. Behind each of these emotions, particularly if they are chronic, is irrational self-talk.

Your other irrational ideas: _____

_____

_____

Much of the difficulty in uncovering irrational self-talk results from the speed and invisibility of thoughts. They may be lightning quick and barely on the edge of awareness. You will rarely be conscious of a complete sentence, as in the irrational statements above. Because self-talk has a reflexive, automatic quality, it is easy to keep the illusion that feelings arise spontaneously from events. However, once the thoughts are slowed down like a slow motion film, frame by frame, the millisecond it takes to say, "I'm falling apart" is exposed for its malignant influence. The thoughts that create your emotions may frequently appear in a kind of shorthand: "no good . . . crazy . . . feeling sick . . . dumb," etc. That shorthand has to be stretched out into the original sentence from which it was extracted. The sentence can then be challenged with methods you'll learn in the section on refuting irrational ideas.

Rules to Promote Rational Thinking

Evaluate your self statements against these six rules or guidelines for rational thinking (from David Goodman's *Emotional Well Being Through Rational Behavior Training.*

It doesn't do anything to me.
The situation doesn't make me anxious or afraid. I say things to myself that produce anxiety and fear.

Everything is exactly the way it should be.
The conditions for things or people to be otherwise don't exist. To say things should be other than what they are is to believe in magic. They are what they are because of a long series of causal events, including interpretations, responses from irrational self-talk, etc. To say things should be different is to throw out causality.

All humans are fallible creatures.
This is inescapable. If you haven't set reasonable quotas of failure for yourself and others, you increase the prospects for disappointment and unhappiness. It becomes all too easy to attack yourself and others as worthless, bad, etc.

It takes two to have a conflict.
Before beginning a course of accusation and blame, consider the 30 percent rule. Any party to a conflict is contributing at least 30 percent of the fuel to keep it going.

The original cause is lost in antiquity.
It is a waste of time to try to discover who did what first. The search for the original cause of chronic painful emotions is extremely difficult. The best strategy is to make decisions to change your behavior *now*.

We feel the way we think.
This is the positively stated principle behind the first statement in this list. It reinforces the idea that events don't cause emotions—our interpretation of events cause emotions.

Refuting Irrational Ideas

There are five steps (A through E) to disputing and eliminating irrational ideas. Start by selecting a situation that consistently generates stressful emotions in you.

A. **Write down the facts** of the event as they occurred at the time you were upset. Be certain to include only the *objective* facts, not conjecture, subjective impressions or value judgments.

B.   Write down your self-talk about the event. State all your subjective value judgments, assumptions, beliefs, predictions and worries. Note which self statements have been previously described as irrational ideas.

C.   Focus on your emotional response. Make a clear one or two word label such as angry, depressed, felt worthless, afraid, etc.

D.   Dispute and change the irrational self-talk identified at step B. Here's how it is done, according to Ellis:

1.   **Select the irrational idea** that you wish to dispute. As an illustration, we will use the irrational idea, "It's not fair that I have to suffer with such a problem."

2.   **Is there any rational support for this idea?** Since everything is as it should be, given long chains of cause and effect, the answer is no. The problem must be endured and dealt with because it happened. It happened because all the conditions existed necessary to make it happen.

3.   **What evidence exists for the falseness of this idea?**
    a.   There are no laws of the universe that say I shouldn't have pain or problems. I can experience any problem for which the necessary conditions exist.

    b.   Life is not fair. Life is just a sequence of events, some of which bring pleasure and some of which are inconvenient and painful.

    c.   If problems occur, it is up to me to solve them.

    d.   Trying to keep a problem from developing is adaptive, but resenting and not facing it once it exists is a dangerous strategy.

    e.   No one is special. Some go through life with relatively less pain than I do. This is due to one of two things: Luck of the draw, or decisions I have made that contributed to the necessary conditions for my problems.

    f.   Just because I have a problem doesn't mean I have to suffer. I can take pride in the challenge of a creative solution. This may be an opportunity to increase my self esteem.

4.   **Does any evidence exist for the truth of this idea?**
    No, my suffering is due to my self-talk, how I have interpreted this event. I have convinced myself that I should be unhappy.

5.   **What is the worst thing that could happen to me** if what I want to happen doesn't, or what I don't want to happen does?

   a.   I could be deprived of various pleasures while I deal with the problem.

   b.   I might feel inconvenienced.

   c.   I might never solve the problem, and experience myself as ineffective in this particular area.

   d.   I might have to accept the consequences of failure.

   e.   Others might not approve of how I am behaving, I might be rejected as incompetent.

   f.   I might feel more stress, tension and a sense of being up against it.

6.   **What good things might occur** if what you want to happen doesn't, or what you don't want to happen does?

   a.   I might learn to tolerate frustration better.

   b.   I might improve my coping skills.

   c.   I might become more responsible.

E.   **Substitute alternative self-talk,** now that you have clearly examined the irrational idea and compared it with rational thinking.

   1.   There's nothing special about me. I can accept painful situations when they emerge.

   2.   Facing the problem is more adaptive than resenting it or running away from it.

   3.   I feel what I think. If I don't think negative thoughts, I won't feel stressful emotions. At worst I will experience inconvenience, regret and annoyance—not anxiety, depression and rage.

Homework

To succeed in your war against irrational ideas, you need a daily commitment to homework. Use the homework sheet below as a model. Fill one out at least once a day.

Here is an example of a homework sheet completed by a woman who had a date with a friend cancelled:

A.   **Activating Event:**

   A friend cancelled a date with me.

B. **Rational Ideas:**

I know he's under a lot of time pressure right now . . . I'll do something by myself.

Irrational Ideas:

I'll feel terribly alone tonight . . . The emptiness is setting in . . . He doesn't really care for me . . . No one really wants to spend time with me . . . I'm falling apart.

C. **Consequences** of the irrational ideas:

I was depressed . . . I was moderately anxious.

D. **Disputing** and challenging the irrational ideas:

1. **Select the irrational idea:**

   I'll feel terribly alone tonight . . . I'm falling apart.

2. **Is there any rational support for this idea?**

   No.

3. **What evidence exists for the falseness of the idea?**

   Being alone is not as pleasurable as having a date, but I can find pleasure in an alternate activity.

   I usually enjoy being alone, and I will tonight as soon as I face the disappointment.

   I'm mislabelling frustration and disappointment as "falling apart."

4. **Does any evidence exist for the truth of the idea?**

   No, only that I've talked myself into feeling depressed.

5. **What is the worst thing that could happen to me?**

   I could continue to feel disappointed and not find anything really pleasurable to do tonight.

6. **What good things might occur?**

   I might feel more self reliant, and realize that I do have inner resources.

E. **Alternative thoughts:**

   I'm OK. I'll get out my detective novel. I'll treat myself to a good Chinese dinner. I'm good at being alone.

   Alternative emotions:

   I feel quiet, a little disappointed, but I'm anticipating a good meal and a good book.

Use this format with all the stressful events you experience. Spend at least 20 minutes a day on the homework. When possible, do the homework right after the event has occurred. Use a separate sheet for each event, and save them as a record of your growth.

Homework Sheet

A. **Activating Event:**

B. **Rational Ideas:**

   Irrational Ideas:

C. **Consequences** of the irrational ideas:

D. **Disputing** and challenging the irrational ideas:

   1. Select the irrational idea:

   2. Is there any rational support for this idea?

   3. What evidence exists for the falseness of the idea?

   4. Does any evidence exist for the truth of the idea?

   5. What is the worst thing that could happen to me?

   6. What good things might occur?

E. **Alternative thoughts:**

   Alternative emotions:

Special Considerations

If you have difficulty making headway with Rational Emotive Therapy, one of three factors may be at influence:

1. You remain unconvinced that thoughts cause emotions. If this is the case, confine your work initially to the following technique of Rational Emotive Imagery. If you then find that changes in your self-talk can push you toward less stressful emotions, the theorem that thoughts cause emotions may become more believable.

2. Your irrational ideas and self-talk are so lightning swift that you have difficulty catching them. You need to keep a journal while undergoing intense emotions. Put down everything that flows through your mind: scenes, images, single words, vague half-formed thoughts, names, sounds, sentences, etc.

3. You have difficulty remembering your thoughts. If this is the case, don't wait till after the fact. Use a journal to write everything down just as it is happening.

Rational Emotive Imagery

Dr. Maxie Maultsby introduced Rational Emotive Imagery in an article entitled "Systematic Written Homework in Psychotherapy." It will help you develop strategies to change stressful emotions. The technique works as follows:

1. Imagine an event that is stressful, and usually is accompanied by unpleasant emotions. Notice all the details of the situation: sight, smell, sound, how you are dressed, what is being said.

2. As you clearly imagine the event, let yourself feel uncomfortable. Let in the emotions of anger, anxiety, depression, worthlessness or shame. Don't try to avoid it—feel it.

3. After experiencing the stressful emotion, *push* yourself to change it. You can fundamentally alter this emotion so that anxiety, depression, rage and guilt can be replaced by keenly felt concern, disappointment, annoyance or regret. If you think you can't do this, you are only fooling yourself. Everybody can push themselves to change a feeling, if only for a few moments.

4. Having contacted the stressful feeling, and pushed it, however briefly, into a more appropriate emotion, you can examine how you did it. What happened inside your head that altered your original depression, anxiety, rage, etc.? You will find that you altered, in some way, your belief system.

5. Instead of saying, "I can't handle this . . . This will drive me crazy," you might now be saying, "I've dealt successfully with situations like this before." You have changed your beliefs, your interpretations of experience.

Once you know how you changed the stressful emotion to a more appropriate one, you can substitute the new, adaptive beliefs any time you want. Become deeply aware of how the new beliefs lead you away from stress and produce more bearable emotions.

Example. Rational Emotive Imagery was practiced by a housewife who became depressed whenever her husband turned on the television in the evening. During the day, she conjured the situation up in her imagination: her husband wiping his mouth, getting up from the table, taking the plates to the sink, and leaving the room. She could imagine a few moments later the sound of the television coming on, the changing of channels, voices from his favorite situation comedy. As she went through the sequence, she sank into despondency.

After becoming fully in contact with the stressful emotion, she pushed herself to change the feeling into one of disappointment and irritation. It felt like shoving a huge rock, and it took 15 minutes of effort before she could get even momentary contact with the more appropriate emotions. Practicing at hourly intervals, she was soon able to push the depression into irritation or disappointment for several minutes.

She was ready to examine how she had changed her thoughts (self-talk) in order to change her emotions. She found she could change depression into irritation by saying "I don't have to feel helpless. If he wants to spend his time with TV, I can do something that feels good to me." Other thoughts included: "It's his life. He can waste it if he wants to. I'm not going to waste mine. There are people that I don't visit because I think I should stay home with him. I'm going to take care of myself. He may be displeased if I don't stay home, but this is not fulfilling for me."

Developing Alternative Emotional Responses

Here is a list of sample situations and alternative emotional responses:

Situation	Stressful Emotion	Appropriate Emotion
Fight with mate	Rage	Annoyance, irritation
Failure to meet work deadline	Anxiety	Concern
Cruelty toward your child	Intense guilt	Regret
Something you enjoy very much is cancelled	Depression	Disappointment
Criticized	Worthless	Annoyance, concern
A public mistake	Shame	Irritation

Now fill in your own stressful situations, including the stressful emotions you feel, and the more appropriate emotions you would like to feel.

Situation	Stressful Emotion	Appropriate Emotion

You can use Rational Emotive Imagery in each of these situations. If the stressful emotions do not change right away, let yourself keep feeling them until they do change. It is an absolute certainty that you can alter these emotions by merely pushing yourself to do so. Afterwards, you will isolate the key thoughts and phrases that made the new, more appropriate emotion possible. Changing your self-talk to include these more adaptive thoughts, beliefs and ideas will make it increasingly easy to change the emotion. For best results, practice this technique ten minutes a day for at least two weeks.

Insight

It is important to recognize that there are three levels of insight necessary to change:

1. Knowledge that you have a problem, and awareness of some of the events that may have caused the problem.

2. Seeing clearly that the irrational ideas which you acquired early in life are creating the emotional climate you live in now, and that consciously or unconsciously you work fairly hard to perpetuate them.

3. The strong belief that after discovering these two insights, you will still find no way of eliminating the problem other than steadily, persistently and vigorously working to change your irrational ideas.

Without a commitment to this last insight, it will be very difficult to alter your habitual emotional responses.

If you think this technique could be useful to you, but you are unable to master it, contact a rational emotive therapist or center for consultation.

Further Reading

Beck, A. T. *Depression: Clinical, Experimental and Theoretical Aspects*. New York: Hoeber, 1967.

Beck, A. T. "Cognitive Therapy: Nature and Relation to Behavior Therapy." *Behavior Therapy*. 1970, 1, 184–200.

Ellis, A. *Growth Through Reason*. Palo Alto: Science and Behavior Books, 1971.

Ellis, A. "Emotional Disturbance and its Treatment in a Nutshell." *Canadian Counselor*. 1971, 5 (3), 168–71.

Ellis, A. *A New Guide to Rational Living*. North Hollywood, California: Wilshire Books, 1975.

Ellis, A. and Harper, R. *A Guide to Rational Living*. North Hollywood, California: Wilshire Books, 1961.

Farquhar, W. and Lowe, J. "A List of Irrational Ideas." reported by Tosi, D. J. in *Youth Toward Personal Growth, a Rational Emotive Approach*. Columbus, Ohio: Charles E. Merrill, 1974.

Goodman, D. S. *Emotional Well-Being Through Rational Behavior Training*. Springfield, Illinois: Charles C. Thomas, 1974.

Lazarus, A. A. *Behavior Therapy and Beyond*. New York: McGraw Hill, 1971.

Maultsby, M. "Rational Emotive Imagery." *Rational Living*. 6, 1971, 16–23.

Rimm, D. C. and Litvak, S. B. "Self-verbalization and Emotional Arousal." *Journal of Abnormal Psychology*. 74, 1969, 181–7.

11

Coping Skills Training

Coping skills training teaches you to relax away anxiety and stress reactions. It provides a greater ability for self control in the particular situation which you find anxiety provoking. The basic procedures were formulated by Marvin Goldried in 1973 and by Suinn and Richardson in 1971 as outgrowths of Wolpe's work with deep muscle relaxation and systematic desensitization. These techniques were later expanded by Meichenbaum and Cameron in 1974 in a treatment program they called "stress inoculation."

It is not necessary, just because you are in a stressful situation, to feel nervous and upset. You have merely *learned* to react that way. Coping skills training involves learning, instead, to relax using progressive muscle relaxation, so that whenever or wherever you are experiencing stress, you can let go of the tension. The first step is to construct a personal list of stressful situations, and arrange the list vertically from the least anxious to most anxious situation. Using your imagination, you can call up each of those situations and learn to relax away any stress you feel. The second step is the creation of a private arsenal of stress coping remarks. These will be used to get you through the periods when you are saying to yourself, "I can't do this . . . I'm not strong enough . . . They seem so much smarter than I am," etc.

Coping skills training provides rehearsal in imagination for the real life events you find distressing. You learn to relax in the imagined scenes, and are thereafter prepared to relax away tension when under fire, when facing deadlines, when problem solving, etc. Eventually, self relaxation procedures and stress coping thoughts become automatic in any stressful situation.

Symptom Effectiveness

Coping skills training has been shown to be effective in the reduction of general anxiety, as well as interview, speech and test anxiety. It appears to be useful in the treatment of phobias, particularly the fear of heights. The control of specific and generalized anxiety has long term effects: Two year follow-ups of hypertense, post cardiac patients showed that 89 percent were still able to achieve general relaxation using coping skills training, 79 percent could still generally control tension, and 79 percent were able to fall asleep sooner and sleep more deeply.

Time for Mastery

Assuming you have already learned progressive relaxation, which takes one to two weeks, initial mastery of coping skills training can be achieved in approximately one week. Once able to relax away tension in situations conjured up in the imagination, it is a matter of putting the skill to work during actual stressful events. This is a *habit* that takes time and practice, and the time very much depends on the amount of practice and commitment.

Instructions

Learning To Relax Efficiently

The foundation stone of coping skills training is knowing how to relax. First, you need to have learned progressive relaxation (see chapter three) sufficiently well so that deep muscle relaxation can be achieved in a minute or two. This relaxation procedure should be "over learned" so it can be done almost automatically, at a moment's notice. The sequences of tensing and relaxing muscles can then be gone through with the same unconscious coordination with which you drive a car or tie your shoelaces.

The second component of relaxation is deep breathing, sometimes called "belly breathing." To achieve deep breathing, place both hands on your belly, just above the pubic area. Breathe in so that the air expands your belly and pushes your hands. Direct all the air downward into your abdomen to push your hands as much as feels comfortable. Let each breath be deep, at a rhythm that feels right to you, and let it gently push your hands. Exhale with a sigh, and imagine that the tension is flowing out of your body as you let go of each breath. For a more elaborate explanation, see the chapter on breathing.

Making a Stressful Events Hierarchy

You are now ready to make a list of all your current life situations which trigger anxiety. Include any stressful event that you are likely to encounter in the relatively near future. Be specific, including the setting and the persons involved. Get as close to 20 items on your list as possible, and let them run the full gambit from very mild discomfort to your most dreaded experiences.

Your list can be turned into a hierarchy by ranking the stressful experiences in order, from the least to the most anxiety producing. Each item on the list should represent an increase in stress over the last item, and the increases should be in approximately equal increments. To accomplish this, Wolpe has devised a rating system based on *Subjective Units of Distress* [suds]. Total relaxation is zero suds, while the most stressful situation on your hierarchy is rated at 100 suds. All the other items fall somewhere in between, and are assigned suds scores based on your subjective impression of where each situation falls relative to your most relaxed or most anxious states. For example, if the most stressful item on your hierarchy, "making conversation with attractive members of the opposite sex" is ranked at 100 suds, then "working right up to a deadline" might be ranked 65 suds, and "speech at PTA meeting" might fall down around 35 suds. You are the expert on how you react to each situation, and you therefore must decide where each stressful event fits, relative to the others. It is advisable, on a list of 20 items, to separate them by increments of five suds. In that way, the items will progress in relatively equal steps from one to twenty. The following sample hierarchy was constructed by a school teacher:

Rank	Item	Suds (Subjective Units of Distress)
1	Running cub scouts meeting Wednesday afternoons	5
2	Rushing to get son to violin lesson	10
3	Doctor's appointment, etc.	15
4	Gynecological exam	20
5	Yard duty in cold weather	25
6	Catching up on Saturday with housework and bills and correcting papers	30
7	Fatigued at end of day, but still needing to shop and cook	35
8	Disagreement with husband over bills, spending on dresses, etc.	40
9	Deadline for written evaluation of student teacher, problem child, etc.	45
10	Preparing house for social occasion	50
11	Having to work late at school, and going home after dark	55
12	Extra work assignment when tired: hall displays, report to school psychologist	60
13	Preparation for observation by principal	65
14	Being alone at night because husband is working late	70

Rank	Item	Suds (Subjective Units of Distress)
15	Evening consultation meetings with parents	75
16	Principal criticizes something in which a lot of work has been invested	80
17	Complaints from parents	85
18	Husband announces a business trip	90
19	Fit of worrying about health brought on by intense menstrual symptoms	95
20	Asthmatic son sick at home while working	100

A good hierarchy is a mixture of many different concerns. Its focus is not limited to one particular fear or problem in your life. The described situations are succinct, but clear enough to reconstruct the scene in imagination.

Applying Relaxation Techniques to Your Hierarchy

Your hierarchy can now be used for learning how to relax while experiencing stress. Start with the first scene (lowest suds) and build a clear picture of the situation in your imagination. Hold onto the stressful image for 30 to 40 seconds. Notice the beginning of any tension in your body, any sense of anxiety. Use the sensation of tension as a signal for deep muscle relaxation and deep breathing. Tightening in your body is like an early warning system of what later will be real emotional discomfort. You can relax away this tension, even as you imagine the stressful situations.

When you have twice imagined a particular scene without tension or anxiety, holding the clear image 20 seconds each time, go on to the next item in your hierarchy. In the next few days, move through your entire hierarchy of stressful situations using this same procedure, progressing from the least to most difficult. At the end, you will have a more profound awareness of how and where tension builds in your body. You will welcome early signs of tension as your signal to relax. Mastery of those items with the highest suds provides a degree of confidence that stress reduction is possible, even in the most threatening situations.

Learning relaxation in the face of fear requires that each scene be vivid and real to you. You have to be able to call up the sounds, smells, sights and textures of the situation. The first few times you may not feel "in it" at all. However, the more you practice putting yourself in the picture, letting the scene touch each of your senses, the easier it will be to really feel what it's like to be there. If you have trouble evoking the scene, describe it vividly and completely into a tape recorder. Play it back with eyes closed, letting the words call up the sense impressions of your problem situation. Include on the tape all dialogues and statements by others that you find distressing, describe your body movements. As soon as you are successful at visualizing the scene, notice any physical tension and begin the relaxation response. Rather than a signal for anxiety, physical tension is now your signal to relax.

The first day you begin practicing relaxation with your hierarchy, don't push much beyond three or four scenes. Stop before you get tired or turned off by the procedure. By the end of four days, you should have made it through your entire hierarchy. After you have relaxed your way through the list two or three times, you may expect a feeling of greater confidence when confronting the same problem situations in real life.

Stress Coping Thoughts

Having mastered relaxation skills using the hierarchy, you are ready to create a personal list of stress coping thoughts. Stress coping thoughts can short circuit painful emotions. To understand how they work, you must consider the four components of an emotional response:

1. *The stimulus situation:* Your supervisor has just gotten angry at you for forgetting an appointment.

2. *Physical reactions:* Your autonomic nervous system produces symptoms such as hand tremor, tightness in the stomach, sweating, palpitations, light headedness, etc.

3. *Behavioral response:* You attempt to deal with the situation by apologizing and getting away as quickly as possible.

4. *Thoughts:* Your interpretations of the situation, predictions and self evaluations are what create emotions. If, at this point, you say to yourself, "I can't stand this . . . It's too much for me . . . I'm falling apart," then the emotional response will be fear. If your self statements are, "I've had it with him riding me all the time . . . He's a real sadist," then your emotional response is likely to be anger.

Your interpretation of the incident, how you imagine it will affect the future, and what you say to yourself about your own worth are the ways you select and intensify the emotions you will feel.

If you say to yourself, "I'm going to fail (prediction), I'm too nervous and disorganized for this kind of job (self evaluation), I know he wants to get rid of me (interpretation)," then your physiological response will probably be sweating, tremor and a knot in your stomach. Noticing the physical reactions, you then might think, "I'm panicking, I can't do this anymore, I've got to go home." These self statements in turn increase the physiological symptoms and the tendency to make poor decisions.

The feedback loop from thoughts to physical reactions to behavioral choices to more negative thoughts can continue unbroken into a state of chronic stress.

Your thoughts don't have to intensify fear. Instead, they can act as tranquilizers for a tense stomach, calming you and pushing away panic. The feedback loop can work for you as well as against you. Stress coping thoughts tell your body there is no need for arousal—it can relax. In the middle of any stressful situation, you can begin saying to yourself a series of fear conquering statements such as, "Stay calm . . . You've dealt with this before . . . Relax now . . . He/she can't really hurt me."

The more attention you give to your coping monologue, the quicker will come relief from physiological arousal and what was described in chapter one as the "fight or flight" reaction. Make your own list of stress coping thoughts, and memorize them. Meichenbaum and Cameron's stress inoculation program suggested the following categories for stress coping statements:

1. Preparation

There's nothing to worry about.
I'm going to be all right.
I've succeeded with this before.
What exactly do I have to do?
I know I can do each one of these tasks.
It's easier once you get started.
I'll jump in and be all right.
Tomorrow I'll be through it.
Don't let negative thoughts creep in.

2. Confronting the stressful situation

Stay organized.
Take it step by step, don't rush.
I can do this, I'm doing it now.
I can only do my best.
Any tension I feel is a signal to use my coping exercises.
I can get help if I need it.
If I don't think about fear I won't be afraid.
If I get tense, I'll take a breather and relax.
It's OK to make mistakes.

3. Coping with fear

Relax now!
Just breathe deeply.
There's an end to it.
Keep my mind on right now, on the task at hand.
I can keep this within limits I can handle.
I can always call _____.
I am only afraid because I decided to be. I can decide not to be.
I've survived this and worse before.
Being active will lessen the fear.

4. Reinforcing success

I did it!
I did all right. I did well.
Next time I won't have to worry so much.
I am able to relax away anxiety.
I've got to tell _____ about this.
It's possible not to be scared. All I have to do is stop thinking I'm scared.

Adapted from "The Clinical Potential of Modifying What Clients Say to Themselves" by D. Meichenbaum and R. Cameron. In M. J. Mahoney and C. E. Thoresen, *Self-Control: Power to the Person.* Copyright © 1974 by Wadsworth, Inc. Reprinted by permission.

Some of these stress coping thoughts may work for you, but your best ones will probably be those you write yourself. Memorize a number of them for each of the four stages of coping: preparation for stress, facing the challenge, feeling the rising fear, and self congratulation. Make the coping statements meaningful to *you,* and change them if they begin to lose their power. Keep the list handy: scotch tape some of the most useful stress coping thoughts on your nightstand, over the kitchen sink, on the inside flap of your briefcase. Slip them inside the cellophane of your cigarettes. Let them become second nature.

A note of caution: some people are afraid to tempt fate by congratulating themselves for any achievement. They harbor the superstition that self praise *causes* disaster. What this really means is that something else, such as fate or luck, is also given credit for their successes. Taking credit for coping means that *you* are responsible for how things turn out, and you have power to limit painful emotions.

Coping "In Vivo"

The final step in the training is applying coping skills in real life situations. When encountering stress, body tension is used as a cue to relax away tightness. At the same time, stress coping thoughts flow in a constant stream as you prepare for and confront the situation, limit the fear, and praise yourself for meeting the challenge.

It is expected that using coping skills *in vivo* will be more difficult than relaxing away stress in the imagined scenes. Some setbacks are inevitable. Practice, however, will make relaxation and stress coping thoughts so natural that they will automatically begin at the first clutch of tension.

Example

A kitchen remodeling contractor, who felt shy and worried excessively about his business, made the following hierarchy:

Rank	Item	Suds (Subjective Units of Distress)
1	Attempting to figure out the bills	5
2	Repair or maintenance of the car	10
3	Read about falling construction market and tight money. Concerned about drop in business	15
4	Going camping to Yosemite alone	20
5	Waking up Saturday morning with absolutely no planned activities for the weekend	25
6	Measurement is off and produces a noticeably poor fit	30
7	Dental visit	35
8	Having a small group over to the apartment for dinner. Friends from the singles group	40
9	Past 2:00 A.M. and still not able to sleep	45
10	Construction materials on order do not arrive, delaying work	50
11	Going to dinner party including new woman friend's sister and ex-roommate from college. Strangers	55
12	Bouts of worry during layoff period between jobs	60
13	Striking up a conversation at a party for singles	65
14	First evening with a new woman friend. Dinner, dancing	70

Rank	Item	Suds (Subjective Units of Distress)
15	Required to make presentation of remodeling options to a prospective customer	75
16	First sexual overtures to a new woman friend	80
17	Coldly turned down for a date	85
18	Customer is quite displeased with kitchen cabinets, workmanship, etc.	90
19	Visit to father, whose worsening heart condition leaves him observedly more frail	95
20	Cost of a job is running over the original bid to do the work	100

Following mastery of relaxation procedures and construction of the hierarchy, an attempt was made to call into imagination the first stressful situation (5 suds). He had difficulty, however, visualizing the scene. Bills were usually made out in a small den, furnished with desk and easy chair. He went to the den and wrote down his sense impressions: "Window looking out on lamp pole and street, green desk blotter, hum of fluorescent light, squeak of swivel chair, rustle of shuffling papers, aftertaste from licking stamps and envelopes." The elements of the scene were tape recorded and played back. He repeated the tape until he could construct a vivid image of the setting in imagination. The effort invested in sharpening his imagination in the first scene paid off with the others. They were easier, and he knew he could tape record a vivid picture if there was any difficulty.

Moving through the hierarchy, he learned to watch for the first signs of tension—usually in his diaphragm and upper abdomen. These became the signal to relax away stress. Holding the image of a scene for 30–40 seconds, he "listened" to his body, focusing on deep breathing and progressive relaxation. After visualizing a scene twice, for at least 20 seconds each time, without tension or anxiety, he proceeded to the next item on the hierarchy. Sometimes, he would have to visualize a situation six or more times before the image held no anxiety.

Practice was scheduled mornings and evenings for 15 minutes. He was able to successfully relax away tension in four to five scenes per day, and within five days he completed the hierarchy. The hierarchy was then repeated, start to finish, one additional time.

During this same period, he had also been working on writing his list of stress coping thoughts. They were as follows:

1. Preparation

I've done this before.
This is a good time to make a definite plan.
Turn off the worry and *do* something.
Stay focused on what I have to do.
It can't ruin me, worse things have happened.
Embarrassment is just throwing away my self acceptance.

2. Confronting

No fear thoughts.
It doesn't matter what others think; do it.
I'll take care of myself.
It only lasts a little while.
I'll feel very good when this goes well.
I have a specific proposal for solving this problem.

3. Coping with fear

How much fear do I feel? Watch it go down as I relax.
Deep breathing really works.
Concentrate on breathing.
I can keep my stomach tension free.
It will be pleasant later at home.
If I think of what I have to do, I can crowd out fear thoughts.

4. Reinforcing success

I dealt with that and felt a lot more comfortable than usual.
I'm getting healthier.
I can really relax now.
It's easier to turn off worry.
Problems don't have to flatten me anymore.

He typed a file card with the phrase, "Turn off the worry and *do* something," and taped it to the inside of the front door. Other signs went on the shaving mirror, the truck dash, etc. In each real life stressful situation, he began to apply the relaxing skills and to select appropriate stress coping thoughts. For the first two weeks he was plagued by the problem of forgetting his training, and sometimes became overwhelmed by the intensity of the situation. After a time, he developed the capacity to spot stress coming, and to start tuning into any physical tension. The process of "checking in" with his body and starting coping skills was becoming automatic.

Further Reading

Goldfried, M. R. "Reduction of Generalized Anxiety Through a Variant of Systematic Desensitization." in *Behavior Change Through Self-Control* by Goldried, M. R. and Merbaum, M. (eds.). New York: Holt, Rinehart and Winston, 1973.

Meichenbaum, D. "Self Instructional Methods." in *Helping People Change* by Kanfur, F. K. and Goldstein, A. P. (eds.). New York: Pergamon Press, 1974.

Meichenbaum, D. and Cameron, R. "Modifying What Clients Say to Themselves." in *Self-Control: Power to the Person* by Mahoney, M. J. and Thoresen, C. E. Monterey, California: Brooks/Cole, 1974.

Suinn, R. M. and Richardson, F. "Anxiety Management Training: A Non-Specific Behavior Therapy Program for Anxiety Control." *Behavior Therapy.* 1971, 2, 498–510.

12

Assertiveness Training

How you interact with others can be a source of considerable stress in your life. Assertiveness training can reduce that stress by teaching you to stand up for your legitimate rights, without bullying others or letting them bully you.

Before reading any further, it will be useful to write down how you would typically respond to the following problem situations:

1. You buy your favorite beverage in the market, and after you walk out you discover that the change is a dollar short.

   I would _____

   _____

   _____

2. You order a steak rare and it arrives medium-well.

   I would _____

   _____

   _____

3. You're giving a friend a lift to a meeting. The friend keeps puttering around for half an hour so that you will arrive late.

   I would _____

   _____

   _____

4. You ask for $5 worth of gas at a service station. The attendant fills up your tank and asks you for $9.50.

   I would _____

   _____

   _____

5. You are relaxing with the paper after a long day. Your spouse pops in, list in hand, and says, "I never thought you'd get here, Quick, pick these up from the store."

   I would _____

   _____

   _____

6. While you wait for the clerk to finish with the customer ahead of you, another customer comes in and the clerk waits on him before you.

   I would _____

   _____

   _____

After you have written down what you would do in these problem situations, set your responses aside. They will be put to use shortly.

Assertiveness was initially described as a personality trait by Andrew Salter in 1949. It was thought that some people had it, and some people didn't, just like extroversion or stinginess. But Wolpe (1958) and Lazarus (1966) redefined assertiveness as "expressing personal rights and feelings." They found that nearly everybody could be assertive in some situations, and yet be totally ineffectual in others. The goal of assertiveness training is to increase the number and variety of situations in which assertive behavior is possible, and decrease occasions of passive collapse or hostile blow-up.

You are assertive when you stand up for your rights in such a way that the rights of others are not violated. Beyond just demanding your rights, you can express your personal likes and interests spontaneously, you can talk about yourself without being self-conscious, you can accept compliments comfortably, you can disagree with someone openly, you can ask for clarification, and you can say no. In short, when you are an assertive person, you can be more relaxed in interpersonal situations.

Some people think that assertiveness training turns nice people into irascible complainers or calculating manipulators. Not so. It's your right to protect yourself when something seems unfair. You are the one who best knows your discomfort and your needs.

Invesitgators such as Jakubowski-Spector (1973) and Alberti and Emmons (1970) discovered that people who show relatively little assertive behavior do not believe that they have a right to their feelings, beliefs, or opinions. In the deepest sense, they reject the idea that we are created equal and are to treat each other as equals. As a result, they can't find grounds for objecting to exploitation or mistreatment. It is likely that they learned as children traditional assumptions that implied that their perceptions, opinions, feelings, and wants were less important or correct than those of others. They grew up doubting themselves and looking to others for validation and guidance.

You did not have much choice about which traditional assumptions you were taught as a child. Now, however, you have the option of deciding whether to continue behaving according to assumptions that keep you from being an assertive adult. Each of these mistaken assumptions violates one of your legitimate rights as an adult:

Mistaken Traditional Assumptions

1. It is selfish to put your needs before others' needs.

2. It is shameful to make mistakes. You should have an appropriate response for every occasion.

3. If you can't convince others that your feelings are reasonable, then they must be wrong, or maybe you are going crazy.

4. You should respect the views of others, especially if they are in a position of authority. Keep your differences of opinion to yourself. Listen and learn.

5. You should always try to be logical and consistent.

6. You should be flexible and adjust. Others have good reasons for their actions and it's not polite to question them.

7. You should never interrupt people. Asking questions reveals your stupidity to others.

8. Things could get even worse, don't rock the boat.

9. You shouldn't take up others' valuable time with your problems.

10. People don't want to hear that you feel bad, so keep it to yourself.

Your Legitimate Rights

You have a right to put yourself first sometimes.

You have a right to make mistakes.

You have a right to be the final judge of your feelings and accept them as legitimate.

You have a right to have your own opinions and convictions.

You have a right to change your mind or decide on a different course of action.

You have a right to protest unfair treatment or criticism.

You have a right to interrupt in order to ask for clarification.

You have a right to negotiate for change.

You have a right to *ask* for help or emotional support.

You have a right to feel and express pain.

11. When someone takes the time to give you advice, you should take it very seriously. They are often right.

You have a right to ignore the advice of others.

12. Knowing that you did something well is its own reward. People don't like show-offs. Successful people are secretly disliked and envied. Be modest when complimented.

You have a right to receive formal recognition for your work and achievements.

13. You should always try to accommodate others. If you don't, they won't be there when you need them.

You have a right to say "no."

14. Don't be anti-social. People are going to think you don't like them if you say you'd rather be alone instead of with them.

You have a right to be alone, even if others would prefer your company.

15. You should always have a good reason for what you feel and do.

You have a right not to have to justify yourself to others.

16. When someone is in trouble, you should help them.

You have a right not to take responsibility for someone else's problem.

17. You should be sensitive to the needs and wishes of others, even when they are unable to tell you what they want.

You have a right not to have to anticipate others' needs and wishes.

18. It's always a good policy to stay on people's good side.

You have a right not to always worry about the goodwill of others.

19. It's not nice to put people off. If questioned, give an answer.

You have a right to choose not to respond to a situation.

As you continue through this chapter, keep in mind that assertive communication is based on the assumption that you are the best judge of your thoughts, feelings, wants, and behavior. Nobody is better informed than you regarding how your heredity, history, and current circumstances have shaped you into a unique human being. Therefore, you are the best advocate for expressing your positions on important issues. Because of your uniqueness, there are many times when you differ with significant people in your life. Rather than overpower the meek or give in to the aggressive, you have the right to express your position and try to negotiate your differences.

Symptom Effectiveness

Assertiveness training has been found to be effective in dealing with depression, anger, resentment, and interpersonal anxiety, especially when these symptoms have been brought about by unfair circumstances. As you become more assertive, you begin to lay claim to your right to relax, and are able to take time for yourself.

Time for Mastery

Some people master assertiveness skills sufficiently for symptom relief with just a few weeks of practice. For others, several months of step-by-step work are necessary to experience significant change.

Instructions

1. *Three Basic Interpersonal Styles*

The first step in assertiveness training is to identify the three basic styles of interpersonal behavior.

Aggressive Style. Typical examples of aggressive behavior are fighting, accusing, threatening, and generally stepping on people without regard for their feelings. The advantage of this kind of behavior is that people do not push the aggressive person around. The disadvantage is that people do not want to be around him or her.

Passive Style. A person is behaving passively when he lets others push him around, when he does not stand up for himself, and when he does what he is told, regardless of how he feels about it. The advantage of being passive is that you rarely experience direct rejection. The disadvantage is that you are taken advantage of, and you store up a heavy burden of resentment and anger.

Assertive Style. A person is behaving assertively when he stands up for himself, expresses his true feelings, and does not let others take advantage of him. At the same time, he is considerate of others' feelings. The advantage of being assertive is that you get what you want, usually without making others mad. If you are assertive, you can act in your own best interest and not feel guilty or wrong about it. Meekness and withdrawal, attack and blame are no longer needed with the mastery of assertive behavior. They are seen for what they are—sadly inadequate strategies of escape that create more pain and stress than they prevent. Before you can achieve assertive behavior, you must face the fact that the passive and aggressive styles have often failed to get you what you want.

To test your ability to distinguish interpersonal styles, lable person A's behavior in the following scenes as aggressive, passive, or assertive:

Scene 1

A: *Is that a new dent I see in the car?*

B: *Look, I just got home, it was a wretched day and I don't want to talk about it now.*

A: *This is important to me, and we're going to talk about it now!*

B: *Have a heart.*

A: *Let's decide now who is going to pay to have it fixed, when and where.*

B: *I'll take care of it. Now leave me alone, for heaven's sake!*

A's behavior is ☐ Aggressive ☐ Passive ☐ Assertive

Scene 2

A: *You left me so by myself at that party . . . I really felt abandoned.*

B: *You were being a party pooper.*

A: *I didn't know anybody—the least you could have done is introduce me to some of your friends.*

B: *Listen, you're grown up. You can take care of yourself. I'm tired of your nagging to be taken care of all the time.*

A: *And I'm tired of your inconsiderateness.*

B: *Okay, I'll stick to you like glue next time.*

A's behavior is ☐ Aggressive ☐ Passive ☐ Assertive

Scene 3

A: *Would you mind helping me for a minute with this file?*

B: *I'm busy with this report. Catch me later.*

A: *Well, I really hate to bother you, but it's important.*

B: *Look, I have a four o'clock deadline.*

A: *Okay, I understand. I know it's hard to be interrupted.*

A's behavior is ☐ Aggressive ☐ Passive ☐ Assertive

Scene 4

A: *I got a letter from Mom this morning. She wants to come and spend two weeks with us. I'd really like to see her.*

B: *Oh no, not your mother! And right on the heels of your sister. When do we get a little time to ourselves?*

A: *Well, I do want her to come, but I know you need to spend some time without inlaws under foot. I'd like to invite her to come in a month, and instead of two weeks, I think one week would be enough. What do you say to that?*

B: *That's a big relief to me.*

A's behavior is ☐ Aggressive ☐ Passive ☐ Assertive

Scene 5

A: *Boy, you're looking great today!*

B: *Who do you think you're kidding? My hair is a fright and my clothes aren't fit for the Goodwill box.*

A: *Have it your way.*

B: *And I feel just as bad as I look today.*

A: *Right. I've got to run now.*

A's behavior is   ☐ Aggressive   ☐ Passive   ☐ Assertive

Scene 6

(While at a party, A is telling her friends how much she appreciates her boyfriend taking her out to good restaurants and to the theater. Her friends criticize her for being unliberated.)

A: *Not so. I don't make nearly as much as a secretary as he does as a lawyer. I couldn't afford to take us both out or pay my own way to all the nice places we go. Some traditions make sense, given the economic realities.*

A's behavior is   ☐ Aggressive   ☐ Passive   ☐ Assertive

Now that you have labeled person A's responses in these scenes as aggressive, passive, or assertive, it may be useful to compare your assessment with ours:

Scene 1. A is aggressive. A's initial hostile statement produces resentment and withdrawal.

Scene 2. A is aggressive. The tone is accusing and blaming. B is immediately placed on the defensive and no one wins.

Scene 3. A is passive. A's timid opening line is followed by complete collapse. The file problem must now be dealt with alone.

Scene 4. A is assertive. The request is specific, non-hostile, open to negotiation and successful.

Scene 5. A is passive. A allows the compliment to be rebuffed and surrenders to B's rush of negativity.

Scene 6. A is assertive. She stands up to the prevailing opinion of the group and achieves a clear, non-threatening statement of her position.

The Assertiveness Questionnaire

(Adapted from Sharon and Gordon Bower's *Asserting Your Self*.)

Step two in assertiveness training is to identify those situations in which you want to be more effective. Having clarified the three interpersonal styles, now re-examine your responses to the six problem situations you responded to at the beginning of this chapter. Label your responses as falling primarily in the aggressive, passive, or assertive style. This is a start in objectively analyzing your own behavior and finding out where assertiveness training can most help you.

To further refine your assessment of the situations in which you need to be more assertive, complete the following questionnaire. Put a check mark in column "A" by the items that are applicable to you and then rate those items in column "B" as:

1. Comfortable
2. Mildly uncomfortable
3. Moderately uncomfortable
4. Very uncomfortable
5. Unbearably threatening

(Note that the varying degrees of discomfort can be expressed whether your inappropriate reactions are hostile or passive.)

A *Check here if the item applies to you*	B *Rate from 1–5 for discomfort*	
		WHEN do you behave non-assertively?
_____	_____	asking for help
_____	_____	stating a difference of opinion
_____	_____	receiving and expressing negative feelings
_____	_____	receiving and expressing positive feelings
_____	_____	dealing with someone who refuses to cooperate
_____	_____	speaking up about something that annoys you
_____	_____	talking when all eyes are on you
_____	_____	protesting a rip-off
_____	_____	saying "no"
_____	_____	responding to undeserved criticism

_____	_____	making requests of authority figures
_____	_____	negotiating for something you want
_____	_____	having to take charge
_____	_____	asking for cooperation
_____	_____	proposing an idea
_____	_____	taking charge
_____	_____	asking questions
_____	_____	dealing with attempts to make you feel guilty
_____	_____	asking for service
_____	_____	asking for a date or appointment
_____	_____	asking for favors
_____	_____	other _____

WHO are the people with whom you are non-assertive?

_____	_____	parents
_____	_____	fellow workers, classmates
_____	_____	strangers
_____	_____	old friends
_____	_____	spouse or mate
_____	_____	employer
_____	_____	relatives
_____	_____	children
_____	_____	acquaintances
_____	_____	sales people, clerks, hired help
_____	_____	more than two or three people in a group
_____	_____	other _____

WHAT do you want that you have been unable to achieve with non-assertive styles?

_____	_____	approval for things you have done well
_____	_____	to get help with certain tasks

_____	_____	more attention, or time with your mate
_____	_____	to be listened to and understood
_____	_____	to make boring or frustrating situations more satisfying
_____	_____	to not have to be nice all the time
_____	_____	confidence in speaking up when something is important to you
_____	_____	greater comfort with strangers, store clerks, mechanics, and so on
_____	_____	confidence in asking for contact with people you find attractive
_____	_____	to get a new job, ask for interviews, raises, and so on
_____	_____	comfort with people who supervise you, or work under you
_____	_____	to not feel angry and bitter a lot of the time
_____	_____	to overcome a feeling of helplessness and the sense that nothing ever really changes
_____	_____	to initiate satisfying sexual experiences
_____	_____	to do something totally different and novel
_____	_____	to have time by yourself
_____	_____	to do things that are fun or relaxing for you
_____	_____	other _____

Evaluating Your Responses

Examine your answers, and analyze them for an overall picture of what situations and people threaten you. How does non-assertive behavior contribute to the specific items you checked on the "What" list? In constructing your own assertiveness program, it will be initially useful to focus on items you rated as falling in the 2–3 range. These are the situations that you will find easiest to change. Items that are very uncomfortable or threatening can be tackled later.

3. Describing Your Problem Scenes

Step three in assertiveness training, according to Sharon and Gordon Bower, is to describe your problem scenes. Select a mildly to moderately uncomfortable situation that suggests itself from items on the Assertiveness Questionnaire. Write out a description of the scene, being certain to include _who_ the person involved is, _when_ it takes place (time and setting), *what* bothers you, *how* you deal with it, your *fear* of what will take place if you are assertive, and your *goal*. Always be specific! Generalizations will make it difficult later on to write a script that will make assertive behavior possible in this situation. The following is an example of a poor scene description.

I have a lot of trouble persuading some of my friends to listen to *me* for a change. They never stop talking, and I never get a word in edgewise. It would be nice for me if I could participate more in the conversation. I feel that I'm just letting them run over me.

Notice that the description doesn't specify *who* the particular friend is, *when* this problem is most likely to occur, *how* the non-assertive person acts, what *fears* are involved in being assertive, and a specific *goal* for increased involvement in the conversation. The scene might be rewritten as follows:

My friend Joan (*who*), when we meet for a drink after work (*when*), often goes on nonstop about her marriage problems (*what*). I just sit there and try to be interested (*how*). If I interrupt her, I'm afraid she'll think I just don't care (*fear*). I'd like to be able to change the subject and talk sometimes about my own life (*goal*).

Here is a second poor scene description:

A lot of times I want to strike up a conversation with people, but I worry that maybe they don't want to be disturbed. Often I notice someone who seems interesting, but I can't imagine how to get their attention.

Once again there is a lack of detail. No clear statement is made as to *who* these people are, *when* the experience takes place, *how* the non-assertive person behaves, or the specific *goal*. The described scene will become much more useful by including these elements:

There is an attractive girl who always brings a bag lunch (*who*) and often sits at my table in the cafeteria (*when*). I would like to start a conversation by asking about her boss, who has a very hard-to-get-along-with reputation (*what*), but she looks so intent on her book I'm afraid she would be put out if I interrupted (*how, fear*). I'd like to start a conversation with her tomorrow (*goal*).

Write three or four problem scenes, and for each scene try to relive your thoughts and feelings when you were actually experiencing it. You might notice, for example, that in each problem scene you gun yourself down with negative thoughts ("I can't do it, I'm blowing it again, boy do I look stupid," and so on), or you usually feel tense in the stomach and seem to be breathing way up in your chest. Strategies in other chapters of this workbook will help you cope with habitual thoughts and physical reactions that make you uncomfortable when you act assertively. Coping skills training, deep muscle relaxation, breathing exercises, and so on should all be useful with these uncomfortable thoughts and feelings. At this point, however, we will concern ourselves with behavior—changing your habitual way of dealing with these problem situations.

4. *Your Script for Change*

The fourth step in assertiveness training is writing your script for change. A script is a working plan for dealing with the problem scene assertively. There are six elements in a script:

1. Look at your rights, what you want, what you need, and your feelings about the situation. Let go of blame, the desire to hurt, and self pity. Define your goal and keep it in mind when you negotiate for change.

2. Arrange a time and place to discuss your problem that is convenient for you and for the other person. This step may be excluded when dealing with spontaneous situations in which you choose to be assertive, such as when a person cuts ahead of you in line.

3. Define the problem situation as specifically as possible. This is essential for focusing the discussion. Here is your opportunity to state the facts as you see them and share your opinion and beliefs. For example: "It's time to make a decision about where we're going to eat tonight. I know you love Mexican food, but we've eaten at Tijuana Joe's the last three times we've gone out for dinner. We're in a rut!"

4. Describe your feelings so that the other person has a better understanding of how important an issue is to you. Once they are expressed, your feelings can often play a major role in helping you get what you want, especially when your opinion differs markedly from that of your listener. If nothing else, the listener may be able to relate to and understand your feelings about an issue even when he totally disagrees with your perspective. When you share your feelings, you become less of an adversary.
There are three important rules to remember when assertively expressing your feelings:

1. Do not substitute an opinion for a feeling ("I feel that Mexican food should be abolished!") The more accurate feeling statement is, "I hate Mexican food!"

2. Use "I messages" that express your feelings without evaluating or blaming others. Rather than saying "You are inconsiderate" or "You hurt me," the I message would be, "I feel hurt."

3. "I messages" connect the feeling statement with specific behaviors of the other person. For example, "I feel hurt when you ignore my wishes about where we eat." Contrast the clarity of this message with the vague blame statement, "I feel hurt because you are inconsiderate."

5. Express your request in one or two easy-to-understand sentences. Be specific and firm! Instead of expecting others to read your mind and magically meet your needs, as in the case of the passive individual, you state clearly your wishes and needs. Rather than assuming that you are always right and entitled to getting your way, as an aggressive person might, you state your wants as preferences, not commands. Example: "I would really like to go to a French restaurant tonight."

6. Reinforce the other person to give you what you want. The best reinforcement is to describe positive consequences. "We'll save money . . . We'll have more time together . . . I'll give you a backrub . . . My mother will only stay a week . . . I'll be less tired and more fun to be with . . . I'll be able to get my work in on time . . . Little Julia will do better in school, and so on."

When you're dealing with someone who has a history of being resistant and uncooperative, positive reinforcement may not be terribly motivating. Consider, instead, describing some negative consequences for failure to cooperate. The most effective negative consequences are descriptions of the alternative way you will take care of yourself if your wishes aren't accommodated.

- If we can't leave on time, I'll have to leave without you. Then you'll have to drive over later on your own.

- If you can't clean the bathroom, I'll hire someone to do it once a week and add it to your rent.

- If you won't fold and put away your clothes, I'll just leave them in this box. I guess you can sort through it whenever you need something.

- If you keep talking in this loud, attacking way, I'll leave. We can talk again tomorrow.

- If you drink heavily again at these office functions, I won't go with you.

- If your check bounces again, we'll have to work on a cash basis only.

- If you keep talking during the movie, I'm going to ask the manager to come in here.

- If you can't give me an accurate idea of when you'll be home, I'm not going to cook and keep things warm for you.

Notice that these examples are different from threats. The consequence of noncooperation is that the speaker takes care of his or her interests. The consequences are not designed to hurt, merely to protect. Threats usually don't work because they make people so angry. If you do make a threat (You won't go to my sister's wedding? I won't go to your family reunion"), make sure you are willing and able to back it up. Even then it will often do more harm than good.

The first letters of each script element combine to spell "LADDER." You may find this a useful mnemonic device to recall the steps toward assertive behavior. The

LADDER script can be used to rewrite your problem scenes so that you can assert what you want. Initially, LADDER scripts should be written out and practiced well in advance of the problem situation for which they are created. Writing the script forces you to clarify your needs and increases your confidence in success.

As an example of a ladder script, let's say that Jean wants to assert her right to half an hour each day of uninterrupted peace and quiet while she does her relaxation exercises. Frank often interrupts with questions and attention-getting maneuvers. Jean's script goes like this:

Look at your rights, what you want, and what you need.

> *It's my responsibility to make sure Frank respects my needs, and I am certainly entitled to some time to myself.*

Arrange a time and a place to discuss the situation.

> *I'll ask him if he's willing to discuss this problem when he gets home tonight. If he isn't, we'll set a time and place to talk about it in the next day or two.*

Define the problem specifically.

> *At least once, and sometimes more often, I'm interrupted during my relaxation exercises—even though I've shut the door and asked for the time to myself. My concentration is broken and it becomes harder to achieve the relaxation.*

Describe your feelings using "I messages."

> *I feel angry when my time alone is broken into and frustrated that the exercises are then made more difficult.*

Express your request simply and firmly.

> *I would like not to be interrupted except in dire emergency, when my door is closed. As long as it is closed, assume that I am still doing the exercises and want to be alone.*

Reinforce the possibility of getting what you want.

> *If I'm not interrupted, I'll come in afterward and chat with you. If I am interrupted, it will increase the time I take doing the exercises.*

In another example, Harold has felt very reluctant to approach his boss to find out why he was turned down for a promotion. He's received no feedback about the reasons for the decision, and Harold is now feeling somewhat negative toward the company, and his boss in particular. Harold's script is as follows:

Look at: *Resentment won't solve this. I need to assert my right to reasonable feedback from my employer*

Arrange: *I'll send him a memo tororrow morning asking for time to discuss this problem.*

Define: *I haven't gotten any feedback about the promotion. The position I applied for has been filled by someone else, and that's all I know.*

Describe: *I felt uncomfortable not knowing at all why I didn't get it and how the decision was made.*

Express: *So I'd like to get some feedback from you about how my performance is seen, and what went into the decision.*

Reinforce: *I think your feedback will help me do a better job.*

These scripts, like the problem scenes earlier, are specific and detailed. The statement of the problem is clear and to the point, without blaming, accusing, or being passive. The feelings are expressed with "I messages" and are linked to specific events or behaviors, not to evaluation of Jean's husband or Harold's boss. "I messages" provide a tremendous amount of safety for the assertive individual because they usually keep the other person from getting defensive and angry. You are not accusing anyone of being a bad person, you are merely stating what you want or feel entitled to.

Successful LADDER scripts do the following:

1. When appropriate, establish a mutually agreeable time and place to assert your needs.

2. Describe behavior objectively, without judging or devaluing.

3. Describe clearly, using specific references to time, place and frequency.

4. Express feelings calmly and directly.

5. Confine your feeling response to the specific problem behavior, not the whole person.

6. Avoid delivering put-downs disguised as "honest feelings."

7. Ask for changes that are reasonably possible, and small enough not to incur a lot of resistance.

8. Ask for no more than one or two very specific changes at a time.

9. Make the reinforcements explicit, offering something that is really desirable to the other person.

10. Avoid threats or negative consequences that you're not willing or able to do.

11. Keep your mind on your rights and goals when being assertive.

Using these rules, we can now distinguish between good and bad scripts. For example, for several semesters running, Julie has wanted to take a night class in ceramics. Each time, her husband has an excuse for why he can't watch the children on the class night. Julie's script:

L	*I'm sick of being pushed around,*
A	*so I'm going to tell him tonight.*
D	*A year is long enough to wait.*
D	*He's too selfish to help*
E	*but he's just going to have to suffer every Wednesday night.*
R	*If he doesn't like it, he can just kiss this marriage goodbye.*

Julie has violated rule number:

1. by not getting agreement on the time and place for the discussion,

2. by using non-specific and accusing phrases such as "pushed around,"

3. by failing to specify exactly what the problem is,

5. by describing her husband as selfish, rather than expressing her own feelings about specific behaviors,

8. by not specifying times, or duration of the semester,

9. by threatening negative consequences that she isn't willing or able to carry out.

Julie's script could be successfully rewritten as follows:

L	*It is vital for me to have time to myself during which I can pursue interests of my own.*
A	*I'll ask him to discuss it after breakfast Saturday morning, or as soon afterwards as possible.*
D	*I've missed two previous ceramics classes because you weren't available for babysitting on the class night. I've waited a year and I would like to enroll this time.*
D	*I feel frustrated that I haven't been able to explore something that really excites me. I also feel hurt when you do other things rather than help me take the class.*

> E   *I'd like you to look after the children on Wednesday nights between 6:30 and 9:00. The semester ends June 2nd.*
>
> R   *If you're willing, I'll cook my special meatloaf for you on Wednesdays, but if you're not, we'll have the expense of a babysitter.*

The described problem behavior has become specific, the expressed feelings non-threatening. Julie's reinforcements are realistic and explicit. It should be noted that negative reinforcement is often not necessary, and that positive reinforcement may require no more than the assurance that you will feel good if a certain behavior change is made. Elaborate promises can usually be avoided.

You can now write your own LADDER scripts. Using your written scripts, rehearse in front of a mirror. If possible, tape record your rehearsals to further refine your assertive style. It is helpful to rehearse scripts with a friend, and get immediate feedback. Let yourself imagine, or better yet, act out, the worst possible response that could be made to your assertive request. Get desensitized to the "nightmare" response by facing it, and then preparing your own countermeasures.

Short Form Assertiveness Technique

The short form assertiveness technique is designed for situations where you lack the time or energy to prepare an entire LADDER script. Assertiveness can be condensed to three basic statements:

1. *Your thoughts* about the problematic situation. This is a non-blaming, non-pejorative description of the problem as you see it. You stick as closely as possible to objective facts, making no inferences about the motives or feelings of others.

2. *Your feelings.* These are "I statements" about your emotional reaction to the problem. Try to avoid the implication that you're holding the other person responsible for your feelings. You're angry, sad, hurt, or disappointed. But your main message should be that you are trying to solve a problem, not blame or prove the other person wrong.

3. *Your wants.* As in the LADDER script, make your request specific and behavioral. Don't ask your tardy spouse to be "more considerate." Request specifically that he or she call if more than 15 minutes late.

Whenever you're in a situation that requires an assertive response, quickly run through the three short form components in your mind.

I think . . . we've been working every night for two weeks on our bathroom remodel.

I feel . . . tired, grumpy, and pressured by your desire that it be done in one month's time.

I want . . . not to work more than three nights without one night off.

Make sure you've developed some idea of what you think, feel, and want before starting to speak. Try to express each component of your assertive statement in order. finish one part before going on to the next.

Make the greatest effort to follow the rules about being non-blaming and making "I" statements. If you stick to these two, simple rules, you'll find the other person far less defensive and far more cooperative. Stay away from attempts to prove that your needs are more important or more legitimate than the other person's. Just keep on track with a statement of facts, feelings, and a specific request for change.

Annie invariably ate lunch with her co-worker, Marge. Once or twice a week Marge asked Annie to drop her by a bank or store on the way to eat. Annie finally reached the boiling point when Marge had her driving 40 minutes to get something notarized. Annie quickly reviewed the three statements in short form assertiveness.

I think . . . Once a week or more I help you with errands and we miss 15 to 30 minutes of our lunch.

I feel . . . tired from rushing and disappointed that I don't get to relax at lunch.

I want . . . to stop being a taxi service for you during my lunch hour.

The "I want" seemed a bit harsh and attacking, so Annie changed it to: "Let's eat on our own if either of us have errands."

Recall a problematic situation in your own life. As an exercise in thinking on your feet, try mentally composing an assertive message:

I think . . . (just the facts)

I feel . . . ("I statements")

I want . . . (specific behavior change)

Now keep practicing. Think of at least five to ten situations where you'd like to be more assertive. As you recall each one, pretend you are really there and have to make some response. Quickly go over the three parts of your assertive statement, then say it out loud. Listen to how it sounds. Is it blaming? Is your request specific enough? Are you saying clearly what you want? Are you criticizing the other person's motives or feelings? Correct what doesn't sound right and try saying it again.

5. *Assertive Body Language*

The fifth step in assertiveness training is to develop assertive body language. Practice with the mirror will help you follow these five basic rules:

1. Maintain direct eye contact.

2. Maintain an erect body posture.

3. Speak clearly, audibly, and firmly.

4. Don't whine or use an apologetic tone of voice.

5. Make use of gestures and facial expression for emphasis.

6. *Learning How To Listen*

The sixth step of assertiveness training involves learning how to listen. As you practice using your LADDER in real life situations, you will find that sometimes you need to deal with an issue that is important to the other person before he or she will be able to focus on what you have to say. This is especially true when what you want directly conflicts with long unspoken and unmet needs of the listener. Example: "You say you want an hour of silence when you first get home from work? Well, I haven't said this before, because you're working so hard, but I'm ready to tear out my hair after spending the day with the kids. I have needs too, you know." At this point, it might be wise to practice assertive listening.

In listening assertively, you focus your attention on the other person so that you can accurately hear the speaker's opinions, feelings, and wishes. Assertive listening involves three steps:

1. *Prepare.* Become aware of your own feelings and needs. Are you ready to listen? Are you sure that the other person is really ready to speak?

2. *Listen and clarify.* Giving your full attention to the other person, listen to the speaker's perspective, feelings, and wants. If you are uncertain about one of these three elements, ask the speaker to clarify with more information. Examples: "I'm not quite sure how you view the situation . . . could you say more about it?" "How do you feel about this?" "I don't understand what you want . . . could you be more specific?"

3. *Acknowledge.* Communicate to the other person that you heard the speaker's position. For example, "I hear you don't want to take on this new project because you're feeling overwhelmed with your current responsibilities and want to catch up." Another way to acknowledge the other person's feelings is to share your own about what has been said: "I'm feeling overwhelmed too, and I feel terrible about having to ask you to do more work."

Assertive listening and assertive expressing go together. Here is a sequence in which both people use assertive listening and expressing skills to solve a problem. John is unhappy about the way Carmen communicates her needs to him.

John: Is this a good time to talk about something that's bugging me a little? (Arrange)

Carmen: Okay.

John: Yesterday you told me you were feeling cut off and kind of abandoned by me. (Define) I felt like I was doing something horrible to you. I felt very wrong, but totally confused about exactly what I was doing. (Describe feeling) Rather than making general complaints like that, could you say what I'm not doing that you need, or what I could change? (Express request) I think I could be a lot more responsive that way. (Reinforce)

Carmen: What was it you needed more information about? (Clarify)

John: What you needed me to do, at that moment, to feel closer.

Carmen: Okay, so what you're saying is that my talking about my feelings without making any specific requests for change leaves you feeling confused and responsible. (Acknowledge)

John: Right.

Carmen: Well, sometimes I'm just telling you how I feel. I don't know why I feel that way or what to do about it. Telling you is an attempt to open the discussion. (Redefining problem)

John: I see. So you really aren't sure what I could do at that point. (Acknowledge) How about just saying you aren't sure and asking what *we* could do about it together? Making it we instead of me would help a lot on my end. (New request)

Carmen: That sounds right. I like it.

Notice that Carmen clarifies and acknowledges before attempting any further explanation of the problem from her point of view. Then, in a non-blaming way, she says why she can't go along with John's request. John, in turn, acknowledges what Carmen has said. He then uses this new information to make a second proposal that works better for Carmen.

Here's the rub. You can't always expect the other person to play by the rules. There are times when you'll have to express and listen assertively in the face of defensive or hostile reactions. Consider the case of Hal and Sara.

Sara: I have a problem with the cash projections, can we talk? (Arrange)

Hal: Whatever.

Sara: Currently you're only running them out to the next three months, and I can't see how sales, inventory, and costs are going to interact six-eight months down the line. (Define) I'm getting pretty nervous about the big reprinting bills because we don't know if the money will be there. (Describe feeling) Could you run out the cash projection at least six months? (Express request) I think we'd all breathe easier. (Reinforce)

Hal: Forget it, Sara. There's no time. I haven't got the bodies in my department to do stuff like that. Take a Valium and cool off.

Sara: How much extra work would it take? (Clarify)

Hal: (loudly) Forget it, Sara. Forget it, okay?

Sara: I hear you. You're overworked and haven't the staff to take on anything extra. (Acknowledge) But I'm wondering how many extra hours of work are involved? (Clarify)

Hal: At least twenty. Keep pushing, Sara. I'm up to here with everybody's demands.

Sara: I hear how stressed you are. (Acknowledge) If once a month I got a twenty hour bookkeeper from the pool for you, could you handle it? (New request)

Hal: Probably, Sara. Let me see the body first.

In the face of sarcasm and anger, Sara continues to clarify and acknowledge until she understands Hal's problem. She doesn't get sidetracked by hostile resistance. She keeps working to understand Hal's stresses and needs so she can make a new, more acceptable proposal.

7. *Arriving at a Workable Compromise*

The seventh step of assertiveness training is learning to arrive at a "workable compromise."

When two people's interests are in dire conflict, a fair compromise that totally satisfies both parties is difficult, if not impossible, to achieve. Instead, look for a workable compromise you both can live with, at least for a while. Although a compromise may naturally emerge in your discussion, sometimes you might need to make a list of all the alternative solutions you can think of. Cross off the ones which are not mutually acceptable. Finally, decide on a compromise you can both live with. This brainstorming process is most effective if you let your imaginations run wild while generating ideas. It's best to agree to review a workable compromise in a specified length of time like a month. At that time, you can examine the results of your changed behavior. If you aren't both sufficiently satisfied, you can renegotiate.

Typical compromise solutions include:

- My way this time, your way next time

- Part of what I want with part of what you want

- Meeting halfway

- If you'll do _____ for me, I'll do _____ for you

- We'll do this one my way, but we'll do _____ your way

- We'll try my way this time, and if you don't like it you can veto it next time

- My way when I'm doing it, your way when you're doing it

If you feel resistant to brainstorming and making lists of alternatives, try this simpler approach. When a person doesn't want to give you what you want, ask for a counterproposal. If the counterproposal isn't acceptable to you, make a new one of your own. But first do a little assertive listening to uncover the other person's feelings and needs in the situation. Keep going back and forth with counterproposals until something works for both of you.

A second route to compromise is to ask this question: "What would you need from me to feel okay doing this my way?" The answer may surprise you and offer solutions you never thought of.

8. Avoiding Manipulation

The eighth and final step to becoming an assertive person is learning how to avoid manipulation. Inevitably, you will encounter blocking gambits from those who seek to ignore your assertive requests. The following techniques are proven ways of overcoming the standard blocking gambits.

Broken Record. When you find that you are dealing with someone who won't take no for an answer or refuses to grant you a reasonable request, you can carefully choose a concise sentence to use as your broken record and say it over and over again. You could say to your insistent four-year-old, "Jeff, I am not going to give you any more candy." You might say to the aggressive used-car salesman, "I am not going to buy a car today; I'm just looking." You might say to the uncooperative store clerk, "I want you to give me back my money for this defective radio." Briefly acknowledge that you have heard the other person's point, and then calmly repeat your Broken Record without getting sidetracked by irrelevant issues. "Yes, but . . . Yes, I know, but my point is . . . I agree, but . . . Yes, but I was saying . . . Right, but I'm still not interested."

Content-to-Process Shift. Shift the focus of the discussion from the topic to an analysis of what is going on between the two of you. ("We're getting off the point now." "We've been derailed into talking about old issues." "You appear to be angry with me.")

Defusing. Ignore the content of someone's anger, and put off further discussion until he has calmed down. ("I can see that you are very upset and angry right now. Let's discuss it later this afternoon.")

Assertive Delay. Put off a response to a challenging statement until you are calm, and able to deal with it appropriately. ("Yes . . . very interesting point . . . I'll have to reserve judgment on that . . . I don't want to talk about it at this time.")

Assertive Agreement. Acknowledge criticism with which you agree. You don't need to give an explanation unless you wish to. ("You're right. I did botch the Sudswell account." "Thanks for pointing out that I was smiling when I was trying to say no to that salesman. No wonder I couldn't get rid of him." "You're right, boss, I am half an hour late . . . my car broke down.")

Clouding. When someone is putting you down as a person, acknowledge something in the criticism with which you can agree, and ignore the rest. Agree in part: "You're right. I am late with the report." *Agree in the probability:* "You may be right that I am often late." *Agree in the principle* (agreeing with the logic without agreeing with the premise). "If I were late as often as you say, it certainly would be a problem." When clouding, rephrase the critic's words so that you can honestly concur. By giving the appearance of agreeing without promising to change, you soon deplete the critic of any reason to criticize you.

Assertive Inquiry. Prompt criticism in order to find out what is really bothering the other person. ("I understand you don't like the way I chaired the meeting last night. What is it about it that bothered you? What is it about me that you feel is pushy? What is it about my speaking out that bothers you?")

It is helpful to prepare yourself against a number of typical blocking gambits that will be used to attack and derail your assertive requests. Some of the most troublesome blocking gambits include:

Laughing it off. Your assertion is responded to with a joke. (*Only three weeks late? I've got to work on being less punctual!*) Use the Content to Process Shift (*Humor is getting us off the point.*) and the Broken Record (*Yes, but . . .*)

Accusing Gambit. You are blamed for the problem. (*You're always so late cooking dinner, I'm too tired to do the dishes afterward.*) Use Clouding (*That may be so, but you are still breaking your commitment.*) or simply disagree (*8:00 is not too late for the dishes.*)

The Beat-up. Your assertion is responded to with a personal attack, such as, "Who are you to worry about being interrupted, you're the biggest loudmouth around here." The best strategies to use are Assertive Irony (*Thank you*) in conjunction with the Broken Record or Defusing (*I can see you're angry right now, let's talk about it after the meeting.*)

Delaying Gambit. Your assertion is met with, "Not now, I'm too tired" or "Another time, maybe." Use the Broken Record, or insist on setting a specific time when the problem can be discussed.

Why Gambit. Every assertive statement is blocked with a series of "why" questions, such as, "Why do you feel that way . . . I still don't know why you don't want to go . . . why did you change your mind?" The best response is to use the Content-to-Process Shift. (*Why isn't the point. The issue is that I'm not willing to go tonight.*) or the Broken Record.

Self-Pity Gambit. Your assertion is met with tears and the covert message that you are being sadistic. Try to keep going through your script using Assertive Agreement. (*I know this is causing you pain, but I need to get this resolved.*)

Quibbling. The other person wants to debate with you about the legitimacy of what you feel, or the magnitude of the problem, and so on. Use the Content-to-Process Shift (*We're quibbling now, and have gotten off the main concern*) with the assertion of your right to feel the way you do.

Threats. You are threatened with statements like, "If you keep harping at me like this, you're going to need another boyfriend." Use Assertive Inquiry (*What is it about my requests that bother you?*) as well as Content-to-Process Shift (*This seems to be a threat.*) or Defusing.

Denial. You are told, "I didn't do that" or "You've really misinterpreted me." Assert what you have observed and experienced, and use Clouding. (*It may seem that way to you, but I've observed . . .*)

Further Reading

Alberti, Robert E., and Emmons, Michael. *Your Perfect Right.* rev. ed. San Luis Obispo, California: Impact Press, 1974.

Bach, George, and Goldberg, Herb. *Creative Aggression.* New York: Doubleday, 1974.

Bower, S. A., and Bower, G. H. *Asserting Your Self.* Reading, Massachusetts: Addison-Wesley, 1976.

Fensterheim, Herbert, and Baer. *Don't Say Yes When You Want to Say No.* New York: David McKay, 1975.

Jakubowski-Spector, P. "Facilitating the Growth of Women Through Assertive Training." *The Counseling Psychologist.* 1973, 4, 75–86.

Lazarus, A. "Behavior Rehearsal vs. Non-directive Therapy vs. Advice in Effecting Behavior Change." *Behavioral Research and Therapy.* 1966, 4, 209–12.

Phelps, Stanlee, and Austin, Nancy. *The Assertive Woman.* San Luis Obispo, California: Impact Press, 1975.

Smith, Manuel J. *When I Say No, I Feel Guilty.* New York: The Dial Press, 1975.

Wolpe, J. *Psychotherapy by Reciprocal Inhibition.* Stanford, California: Stanford University Press, 1958.

13

Time Management

Time can be thought of as an endless series of decisions—small and large—that gradually change the shape of your life. Inappropriate decisions produce frustration, lowered self esteem and stress. They result in the six symptoms of poor time management:

1. Rushing.

2. Chronic vacillation between unpleasant alternatives.

3. Fatigue or listlessness with many slack hours of non-productive activity.

4. Constantly missed deadlines.

5. Insufficient time for rest or personal relationships.

6. The sense of being overwhelmed by demands and details, and having to do what you don't want to do most of the time.

Time management techniques for relieving these symptoms have been developed by management consultants and efficiency experts who teach busy people to streamline their lives. Alan Lakein, who wrote *How to Get Control of Your Time and Your Life,* sees himself as a "time planning and life goals consultant." Many therapists such as Harold Greenwald (*Direct Decision Therapy*) have also contributed to time management theory by developing techniques for facing and clarifying decision-making.

All methods of time management can be reduced to three steps: 1. You can establish priorities that highlight your most important goals, and that allow you to base your decisions on what's important and what's not. 2. You can create time by realistic scheduling and the elimination of low priority tasks. 3. You can learn to make basic decisions.

Symptom Effectiveness

Effective time management has been used in minimizing deadline anxiety, avoidance anxiety and job fatigue.

Time for Mastery

The initial assessment of how you spend your time takes three days. Prioritizing goals and activities takes one day. The *habit* of effective time management may take from three weeks to six months to integrate into your life.

Instructions

Before examining the three steps to effective time management, it will be useful to explore how you really spend your time. An easy way to do this is to divide up your day into three segments:

1. From waking up through lunch
2. From the end of lunch through dinner
3. From the end of dinner until going to sleep

Carry a small notebook with you, and at the end of each segment (after lunch, after dinner, in bed just before sleep) write down every activity you engaged in. Note the amount of time each one took. The total amount of time for all activities should be fairly close to the total number of hours you were awake.

Unless you are particularly interested in improving time utilization at work, simply describe work activity as socializing, routine tasks, low priority work, productive work, meetings and telephone calls.

Keep this time inventory for three days. At the end of three days, note the total amount of time spent in each of the following categories. If you wish, you can divide by three to get the average daily time for each activity. You can also order the categories from the most to the least time consuming to get a rough picture of your current priorities.

Categories of Activity	Total Time (divide by three to get the average daily time spent)
At work:	
Socializing	_____
Routine tasks	_____
Low priority work	_____
Productive work	_____
Meetings	_____
Telephone calls	_____

Categories of Activity	Total Time (divide by three to get the average daily time spent)

Not at work:
Telephone calls   _____
Conversation (face to face)   _____
Television   _____
Hobbies   _____
Reading   _____
Sports (jogging, tennis, etc.)   _____
Civic activities, clubs   _____
Other recreation   _____
Travel for errands   _____
Commuting   _____
Shopping   _____
Household chores and maintenance   _____
Childcare and supervision   _____
Personal hygiene, grooming, dressing   _____
Sexual activities   _____
Daydreaming   _____
Drinking   _____
Cooking   _____
Eating   _____
Naps   _____
Night sleep   _____

Other:

_____   _____
_____   _____
_____   _____

You should modify or add categories to suit yourself. You might wish to distinguish between conversation at home with intimates and talk at social gatherings, or distinguish between shopping for pleasure and shopping for necessities. You might want to break down household chores into several categories. The important thing is to separate and examine categories of time use, and then determine if you want to spend more or less time engaged in each of these activities.

A radio public affairs interviewer, who was always late, kept the following record on the first day of her three-day time assessment:

Activity	Time
Waking through lunch:	
Lying in bed trying to get up	20 min
Shower	20 min
Dress, makeup	25 min
Cook breakfast	15 min
Eat breakfast (read paper)	30 min
Phone call	15 min
Commute	45 min
Routine tasks	30 min
Daydreaming	5 min
Socializing	20 min
Meeting (non-mandatory)	1 hr
Productive work	40 min
Lunch	1½ hr
After lunch through dinner:	
Productive work	1½ hr
Phone	30 min
Daydreaming	5 min
Phone	10 min
Phone	10 min
Daydreaming	5 min
Low priority work	50 min
Socializing	15 min
Commute	50 min
Shopping	45 min
Phone	10 min
Phone	15 min
Neighbor visits	30 min
Phone (work related)	25 min
Phone (work related)	15 min
Cook (while reading paper)	1 hr 15 min
Eat meal with wine	45 min
After dinner to retiring:	
Phone	10 min
Phone	20 min
Television	1 hr
Preparing for bed	30 min
Reading novel	15 min

Later, when reviewing her activities, and adding up these times for her category list, she was amazed to find that on this day she had spent four hours and 15 minutes either preparing food or eating it. She had spent an hour and 50 minutes on the phone at home, as well as nearly an hour on the phone at work: two and a half hours in total! She also became aware that a half hour had been wasted in the morning with extra time in bed and a long shower. When analyzing her work patterns, it was now obvious that her most productive hours were at midday—interrupted right in the middle with lunch!

Using data from her daily logs and her categories of activities list, she made the following decisions:

1. Limit most work-related phone conversations to five minutes.

2. Make breakfasts that don't require cooking. Cut lunch to one hour. Cut dinner preparation to 45 minutes.

3. Get up at the alarm and limit shower to ten minutes.

4. Eliminate television. Go to bed and get up one half hour earlier to avoid rushing on work mornings.

5. Eat a late lunch to take advantage of most productive working hours: 11:00 to 2:00.

Setting Priorities

Having made your own time inventory, you can begin to compare your current use of time to important goals. You might facilitate this by imagining yourself very old and aware that your days are numbered. What did you want to accomplish in your life, what are you most proud of, what might you most regret? Limber up your imagination and put anything down that comes to mind. Don't think about it or analyze it—if something occurs to you, write it down. Distill what you have written into your long-range goals.

Second, make a list of your one-year goals that stand a reasonable chance of being accomplished. Finally put down all your goals for the coming month, including work priorities, improvement schemes, recreational activities, etc.

You have created three lists of goals: long, medium and short range. Each list can be prioritized by deciding which are the top, middle and bottom drawer items:

1. Top drawer: those items ranked most essential, most desired.

2. Middle drawer: those items which could be put off for awhile, but which are still important.

3. Bottom drawer: those items which could easily be put off indefinitely with no harm done.

Once your lists are prioritized, combine them by choosing two top drawer items from each list that you would like to begin work on. You will have six top drawer items that represent your currently most desired goals.

Goal Planner

Rank as T, M or B
(Top, Middle or Bottom drawer items)

Lifetime goals

_____

_____

_____

_____

One-year goals

_____

_____

_____

_____

One-month goals

_____

_____

_____

_____

Pick two top drawer goals from each category and enter them here. These are the goals you will begin to work on.

_____

_____

_____

_____

_____

Example

A speech therapist listed the following for his top six goals:

T-1 Buy a house (one-year)

T-2 Write pamphlet on newest behavior modification technique with stutterers (Part of lifetime goal to make written contributions to his field).

T-3 Home visits to observe the interaction of particular children with their families and record speech patterns in natural environment (one-month).

T-4 Take wife out to candlelight dinner once a week (one-month).

T-5 Tennis lessons with wife (part of one-year goal to become mixed doubles partners).

T-6 Investigate ways of starting a summer camp for children with speech pathologies (part of lifetime goal to make humanitarian efforts).

Breaking Priorities Down Into Manageable Steps

Now it is time to break down the six top drawer items into manageable steps. Using our example of the speech therapist, writing a pamphlet might at first seem an awesome task, one that might be put off indefinitely. However, by reducing it to simple steps, it becomes much more attractive and realistic:

1. Go to the library this Saturday afternoon and photocopy all pertinent articles on therapy techniques with stutterers.

2. Read and underline articles during lunch next two weeks.

3. Assemble review of the literature by end of month.

4. Write first draft outlining directions for the newest technique on Thursday evenings when wife is at night school for the next month.

You have six goals to work on. They are your top priorities. Give them a month. Next month you will make a new list. Some goals will remain top drawer, others will drop off. Always, the goals will be accompanied by a list of specific, easy to accomplish steps. Set aside a certain time period each day to work on your top drawer goals. Emphasize results rather than activity. Try to accomplish one step toward your goal each day, no matter how small.

If you are a very busy person, or one who finds it hard to keep focused on top drawer items, you will need a daily "to-do" list. The to-do list includes everything you would like to accomplish that day. Each item is rated top, middle or bottom. If you find yourself doing a bottom drawer item and some of the tops aren't yet finished, you can be almost certain that you are wasting your time. Work your way down:

When the top items are completed, get to the middle drawer tasks. Only when everything else is done should you permit your time to be taken with the bottom drawer. You'll find that it is often possible to just ignore the bottom items. They may never be missed. In making and following your to-do list, it is useful to be aware of the 80-20 rule. 80 percent of the value will come from only 20 percent of the items.

It's easy sometimes to let top drawer goals slip to the back of your mind, and say, "Not today. I'll get to it after I get the house cleaned up." One solution to this tendency is to make signs describing your six current top drawer goals and post them conspicuously around the house or office. Every time you look at them you'll be reminded of your priorities.

Making Time

There are four "must" rules and nine optional rules for making time. The four must rules are as follows:

1. Learn to say, "no." Unless it's your boss who asks, keep away from commitments that force you to spend time on bottom drawer items. Be prepared to say, "I don't have the time." If you have trouble saying no, see the chapter on assertiveness training.

2. Banish bottom drawer items, unless you have completed all higher priority items for the day. The definition of bottom drawer items is that they can wait.

3. Build time into your schedule for interruptions, unforeseen problems, unscheduled events, etc. You can avoid rushing by making reasonable time estimates for activities, and then adding on a little extra time for the inevitable snafus.

4. Set aside several periods each day for quiet time. Arrange it so that you will only be interrupted in an emergency. Focus on deep relaxation using any of the techniques you've found useful in this workbook.

These are the nine "optional" rules for making time. Check three of them that would be most helpful to you. Begin the habit of following the rules you have marked right now.

☐ 1. Keep a list of short five-minute tasks that you can do any time you are waiting or are "between things."

☐ 2. Learn to do two things at once: Organize an important letter in your mind while driving to work, plan dinner while vacuuming.

☐ 3. Delegate bottom drawer tasks. Give them to your children, your secretary, your housecleaner, your mother-in-law.

☐ 4. Get up a half hour or an hour earlier.

☐ 5. Television is a huge time-killer. If you watch, make an agreement with yourself to write a one-sentence summary of each commerical.

☐ 6. When you have a top drawer item to do, block off your escape routes:
- Schedule daydreaming for a latter time.
- Stop socializing.
- Put away the books.
- Put away tiny, unimportant tasks.
- Don't run out for ice cream or other sudden indulgences.
- Forget the errands you could probably do more efficiently later.

☐ 7. Cut off non-productive activities as soon as possible (e.g. socializing on the phone when top drawer items are begging to be done).

☐ 8. Throw away all the mail you possibly can. Scan it once and toss it.

☐ 9. Stop perfectionism. Just get it done. Everyone makes mistakes.

Making Decisions

Decisions are made constantly, over and over. Every minute of your life you are making decisions. Even if you decide not to decide, it is a decision. If you let yourself daydream for five minutes, that is a decision. The important choices in life are usually composed of one or two early, "original" decisions, and hundreds of little decisions thereafter. For example, you might have decided early in life never to suffer embarrassment, and that decision has been supported by choices to procrastinate or relinquish any task in which you might fail or look foolish.

Many people have great difficulty making *any* decision. This is usually because they were blamed and criticized for choices they made as children. They decided very early to leave the decision making to others. The difficulty is that other people don't know exactly what you want or need, and usually aren't worrying much about it. Even though the early decision not to decide made sense at the time, it becomes a liability later on as you develop into a helpless adult. Tracing back to the point of that initial decision can be the first step in remaking it. Awareness can help you see that decision at work in your life every day, and you can begin to discard it.

Here is a list of original decisions that may lie behind your choice to procrastinate now:

1. Not to suffer more than a minimum amount of pain.

2. Not to ever become really tired, or work too hard.

3. Everything should be easy.

4. Nothing should be easy, but should be earned with hard work.

5. Never to hurt anybody.

6. Never to feel guilty, angry or competitive.

7. To be punished for pleasure.

8. To be liked and accepted by everybody.

9. Always to be taken care of.

Personalize this list by adding your own original decisions. To find out what they are, think of things you characteristically avoid or put off. How did that get started? When was the first time you noticed the avoidance? What basic attitudes values or beliefs influence the avoidance? What important person in your past is associated with the early decision to put off this particular kind of task, experience or challenge?

In *Direct Decision Therapy,* Harold Greenwald suggests these rules for overcoming an original decision:

1. State clearly the current conflict: You would like to change or decide to do something, but find it very difficult.

2. Examine the past ("original") decision that helped to create this conflict.

3. Look at the context of the original choice that lies behind your current reluctance to decide. How did the rewards and punishments in your world then influence you to make the original decision?

4. Examine the alternatives to your original decision, and the habitual way you have carried it out over the years.

5. Choose a new alternative and decide to put it into practice. Resolve the current conflict by using the new alternative.

6. Reward yourself each time you make a decision based on the new alternative.

If you have difficulty tracing back to and overcoming your original decision, there is no reason for despair. Here are eight specific ways to overcome procrastination now. It is sufficient that you know what you want to do, and that you realize that you will pay later for not deciding to act now. Check three of these rules that will be most useful to you and put them into effect right now:

☐ 1. Recognize the unpleasantness. The right decision is often a little more difficult than the wrong one, or none at all. Really face the prospect of how unpleasant the right decision may be. Now examine the greater unpleasantness of putting it off or doing it the easy way. Look squarely at the cost and risks of delay. Use this information to create enthusiasm for getting something done that results in less overall unpleasantness.

☐ 2. Examine the payoffs for not deciding or taking the easy way. For example, you may not be as anxious if you procrastinate. You won't call attention to yourself or have to face the possibility of failure. Also examine the advantages of avoiding whatever changes might follow from the decision. You might have to face up to the difficult task of revising your self concept upward. You might have to give up your depression, or the secondary gain of attention that you get from chronic unhappiness.

☐ 3. Join your resistance. Exaggerate and intensify whatever you are doing that is putting off the decision to begin a task. If you are staring at yourself in the bathroom mirror in the morning instead of getting to work, draw it out. Really study all your pores, go over each quadrant of your face minutely. Keep it up until you are really bored, and getting to work seems much more attractive.

☐ 4. Take responsibility for each delay. You are the one wasting your own precious time. Make a list of each procrastination or escape activity and note how long it took.

☐ 5. Decide everything *now,* and include in the decision when you will set aside all escapes to begin the task.

☐ 6. Use these guidelines to instantly resolve unimportant decisions:
   • Pick north or west over south or east.
   • Pick right rather than left.
   • Pick the smoothest.
   • Pick it if it has green, if it is heavier, etc.
   • Pick the one with the most letters.
   • Choose it if it's to be done earlier rather than later.
   • Choose the closest, or the one that takes the least time.
   • Pick the one that comes first in the alphabet.

☐ 7. Con yourself with lead-in tasks. Let yourself into the cold water gradually with a small but related task. If you have to mow the lawn, decide to go as far as filling the gas tank on the mower, and wheeling it out to the edge of the lawn.

☐ 8. Finish things. Avoid beginning a new task until you have completed a predecided segment of your current task. The experience of finishing something is one of the greatest rewards in decision making.

Further Reading

Assagioli, Roberto. *The Act of Will.* New York: The Viking Press, 1973.

Greenwald, Harold. *Direct Decision Therapy.* San Diego, California: EDITS, 1973.

Lakein, Alan. *How to Get Control of Your Time and Your Life.* New York: Signet, 1973.

14

Job Stress Management

The classic symptoms of job burnout include pessimism, increased dissatisfaction, absenteeism, and inefficiency at work. While you may not be on the verge of job burn-out, you are probably one of the growing majority of Americans who report that their job causes them stress. A 1985 study conducted by the National Center for Health Statistics found that more than half of the workers surveyed experienced "a lot" to "moderate" stress in their jobs in the last two weeks. Job stress accounts for a tremendous amount of personal misery and billions of dollars lost annually in productivity, wages, and medical bills. Americans are waking up to the fact that job stress management makes personal and financial sense.

What Causes Job Burnout?

Every job includes some built-in difficulties to which the worker is paid to adjust. But job difficulties alone do not cause burnout. Rather, it is the worker's lack of control over his job situation that leads to uncertainty, frustration, reduced motivation, and eventually burnout. For example, you can become demoralized because you are unable to meet the impossible expectations of your boss, because you can't get the support of your co-workers, because you are inadequately trained, or because no matter how well you do your efforts are not recognized.

Even minor factors beyond your control can have a stressful impact. Consider the many unexpected interruptions in the course of your day: special meetings, phone calls, people dropping in, and equipment breakdown. Think about having to "go through channels" and deal with bureaucratic red tape. Think about the faulty air conditioning system or the constant din of machines, elevator music, and voices. Even your daily commute can add to your accumulated stress for the day.

It is a common error to associate only excessive stress with lowered productivity. As early as 1908, Robert Yerkes and John Dodson pointed out that the symptoms of stress underload are quite similar to those of stress overload: reduced efficiency, irritability, a sense of time pressure, diminished motivation, poor judgment, and accidents. We all have a unique "performance zone" within which we experience manageable stress that stimulates our energy, motivation, decision making, and productivity.

In summary, burnout is not simply caused by too much stress in your job. If your job made no demands on you, you would be bored. Job stress management, like stress management in general, involves finding the right types and amounts of challenge to stimulate your interest and performance without overloading you. It also requires managing those distressing areas of your job that are inevitable. Finally, it includes balancing leisure and work-related activities so that they complement one another. Job stress management is a dynamic process over which you can exercise your personal control.

Symptom Effectiveness

Job stress management is effective in increasing your sense of control in the work setting. Increased feelings of control can improve job-related symptoms of guilt, depression, anxiety, and low self-esteem. Job stress management can also reduce job-related psychosomatic symptoms such as insomnia, ulcers, headaches, eating disorders, and lowered immunity to infection.

Time for Mastery

The initial assessment of your job stressors and your response to them can be completed in one day. Learning how to respond more effectively to job stress will take at least a month. The habit of effective job stress management may take from two months to a year to integrate into your daily life.

Ten Steps Toward Managing Your Job Stress

Step 1. Identify Your Symptoms of Job Stress

Instructions: Rate each of the following items in terms of how often the symptom is true for you during the last three months.

0 = Never
1 = Occasionally
2 = Somewhat often
3 = Frequently
4 = Almost always

_____   1. I feel little enthusiasm for doing my job.

_____   2. I feel tired even with adequate sleep.

_____   3. I feel frustrated in carrying out my responsibilities at work.

_____   4. I am moody, irritable, or impatient over small inconveniences.

_____   5. I want to withdraw from the constant demands on my time and energy.

_____ 6. I feel negative, futile, or depressed about my job.

_____ 7. My decision-making ability seems less than usual.

_____ 8. I think that I am not as efficient as I should be.

_____ 9. The quality of my work is less than it should be.

_____ 10. I feel physically, emotionally or spiritually depleted.

_____ 11. My resistance to illness is lowered.

_____ 12. My interest in sex is lowered.

_____ 13. I am eating more or less, drinking more coffee, tea, or sodas, smoking more cigarettes, or using more alcohol or drugs in order to cope with my job.

_____ 14. I am feeling emotionally callous about the problems and needs of others.

_____ 15. My communication with my boss, co-workers, friends, or family seems strained.

_____ 16. I am forgetful.

_____ 17. I am having difficulty concentrating.

_____ 18. I am easily bored.

_____ 19. I feel a sense of dissatisfaction, of something wrong or missing.

_____ 20. When I ask myself why I get up and go to work, the only answer that occurs is "my paycheck."

If you scored 0 to 25, you are probably coping adequately with the stress of your job. If you scored 26 to 40, you are suffering from job stress and would be wise to take preventative action. If you scored 41 to 55, you need to take preventative action to avoid job burnout. If you scored 56 to 80, you are burning out and must develop a comprehensive job stress management plan.

Step. 2 Identify the Sources of Your Job Stress

Instructions: Rate your experience in your job during the past year, using the following 5-point scale:

0 = Never
1 = Occasionally
2 = Somewhat often
3 = Frequently
4 = Almost always

Lack of Control

_____ 1. I lack the authority to carry out certain responsibilities.

_____ 2. I feel trapped in a situation without any real options.

_____ 3. I am unable to influence decisions that affect me.

_____ 4. There are a lot of requirements that get in the way of my doing certain tasks.

_____ 5. I can't solve the problems assigned to me.

_____ Subtotal

Information Gap

_____ 6. I am unsure about the responsibilities of my job.

_____ 7. I don't have enough information to carry out certain tasks.

_____ 8. I am underqualified for certain tasks I'm expected to do.

_____ 9. Others I work with are not clear about what I do.

_____ 10. I don't understand the criteria used to evaluate my performance.

_____ Subtotal

Cause and Effect

_____ 11. There is no relationship between how I perform and how I am rated.

_____ 12. I sense that popularity and politics are more important than performance.

_____ 13. I don't know what my supervisor thinks of my performance.

_____ 14. I don't know what I am doing right and what I am doing wrong.

_____ 15. There is no relationship between how I perform and how I am treated.

_____ Subtotal

Conflict

_____ 16. I am expected to satisfy conflicting needs.

_____ 17. I disagree with co-workers.

_____ 18. I disagree with my supervisor.

_____ 19. I am caught in the middle.

_____ 20. I can't get what I need to get the job done.

_____ Subtotal

Blocked Career

_____ 21. I feel pessimistic about opportunities for advancement or growth in my job.

_____ 22. My supervisor or boss is critical.

_____ 23. I feel unaccepted by the people I work with.

_____ 24. My good work is not noticed or appreciated.

_____ 25. My progress on the job seems less than it could be.

_____ Subtotal

Alienation

_____ 26. I experience little meaning in my work.

_____ 27. I feel unsupported by my co-workers or boss.

_____ 28. My values seem at odds with those of the management.

_____ 29. The organization seems insensitive to my individuality.

_____ 30. I find I cannot be myself at work because I feel different from my co-workers.

_____ Subtotal

Overload

_____ 31. I have too much to do and too little time in which to do it.

_____ 32. I take on new responsibilities without letting go of any of the old ones.

_____ 33. My job seems to interfere with my personal life.

_____ 34. I must work on my own time (during breaks, lunch, at home, and so on.)

_____ 35. The size of my workload interferes with how well I do it.

_____ Subtotal

Underload

_____ 36. I have too little to do.

_____ 37. I feel overqualified for the work I actually do.

_____ 38. My work is not challenging.

_____ 39. Most of my work is very routine.

_____ 40. I miss contact with people in my job.

_____ Subtotal

Environment

_____ 41. I find my work environment unpleasant.

_____ 42. I lack the privacy I need to concentrate on my work.

_____ 43. Some aspects of my environment seem hazardous.

_____ 44. I have too much or too little contact with people.

_____ 45. I have to deal with many little hassles.

_____ Subtotal

Value Conflict

_____ 46. I must do things that are against my better judgement.

_____ 47. I must make compromises in my values.

_____ 48. My family and friends do not respect what I do.

_____ 49. I observe my co-workers doing things that I don't approve of.

_____ 50. The organization that I work for pressures employees to do things that are unethical or unsafe.

_____ Subtotal

_____ Grand total

If your score is over 100, you have more than an average number of job stressors. If your score is 130 or higher, the number of job stressors is unusually high. Identify the categories in which you scored 12 or more. In addition to dealing with your specific major stressors, you will want to give consideration to these general areas.

Step 3. Identify How You Respond to Your Specific Job Stressors

What are your specific job stressors and how do you tend to respond to them? In addition to referring to your responses on the job stress inventory, reflect back over your recent experiences at work. In the far left hand column, list your specific stressors. For each stressful item, write down your feelings when it occurs, what you say to yourself about it, and what you do in response to it.

For example, Patty, a computer programmer, wrote down the specific stressors in her job and her response to them in the following shorthand manner:

Your Job Stressor	Your Feelings	Your Thoughts	Your Behavior
Programming	Bored, numb	"Non-stop programming makes Patty a dull girl."	Plodding, inefficient; eat sweets, drink coffee
Deadlines	Anxious	"I'll never make it!"	Work faster and longer; mistakes
Meetings	Annoyed, impatient	"What a waste, I've got work to do."	Critical, resistant to suggestions
Vague supervisor	Insecure, confused, annoyed	"What does it take to please this jerk?"	Guess what he wants; complain
Chatty co-worker	Angry	"Why does he keep interrupting me? He's so inconsiderate!"	Respond politely and return to my own work
Uncooperative secretary	Angry, frustrated, dissatisfied	"She's lazy, slow, and utterly useless."	Refuse to talk to her
No privacy	Annoyed	"Hard to focus."	Tense my muscles; neck and backache
Terminal	Strained, tired	"I wish I didn't have to do this."	Eye strain, headache
Down time	Frustrated, refreshed	"Damn, I lost it!"	Eat, drink coffee, socialize
No raise	Angry, frustrated	"I deserve better than this!"	Complain bitterly

Exercise: List your specific stressors and how you respond to them. Use as little or much detail as you need.

Your *Job Stressor*	*Your* *Feelings*	*Your* *Thoughts*	*Your* *Behavior*
_____	_____	_____	_____
_____	_____	_____	_____
_____	_____	_____	_____
_____	_____	_____	_____
_____	_____	_____	_____
_____	_____	_____	_____
_____	_____	_____	_____
_____	_____	_____	_____
_____	_____	_____	_____
_____	_____	_____	_____
_____	_____	_____	_____
_____	_____	_____	_____
_____	_____	_____	_____

Now that you have written out your specific job stressors and how you typically respond to them, review your list and see if any patterns emerge. When Patty did this, she noticed the following patterns:

1. I respond to boredom and frustration by eating and drinking coffee.

2. Working at a computer terminal for long periods of time and having to concentrate in spite of a lack of privacy causes me to have a variety of physical and emotional symptoms of stress.

3. I waste time because I'm not assertive enough to ask questions of my supervisor, say no to my office mate, or firmly request secretarial support.

4. I tend to be highly critical of myself, others, and my environment, but rarely do anything constructive to improve my situation. I can see why I feel chronically irritated and tense at work.

In looking over your list of specific job stressors and your responses to them, what patterns did you pick out?

1. _____
   _____
   _____

2. _____
   _____
   _____

3. _____
   _____
   _____

4. _____
   _____
   _____

Step 4. Set Goals To Respond More Effectively to Your Job Stressors

Now that you have identified your patterns of stress, you can begin to formulate a more effective plan for responding to the stressors that you can anticipate. Maybe you can avoid some of them all together. Perhaps you can be better prepared for them when they happen. The name of the game is taking more control. And this is where you begin to do it.

You will probably want to make changes in one or more of these general areas:

1. Change the external stressor (quit the job, assertively tell the boss not to overload you, take regular breaks, reorganize your time).

2. Change your thoughts (turn off the job when you go home, alter your perfectionist attitude, stop assuming that you are responsible for others' problems).

3. Change physically (relax, exercise, eat properly, get sufficient sleep).

When you are designing goals for yourself, remember the following guidelines. Useful goals are generally:

- Specific

- Observable

- Achievable within a certain time frame

- Broken down into small intermediate steps

- Compatible with long-term goals
- Written down in simple self-contract form
- Reevaluated at specified iintervals
- Rewarded when achieved

Example: Patty decided to set a new, more effective response to each of her four stress patterns as a goal for herself. She wrote out the following self-contract:

I, Patty Bowers, agree to change the following four old patterns of responding to stress as follows:

Patterns 1 and 2. Rather than eating or drinking coffee when I am bored or frustrated, I will take regular breaks once an hour in which I either do a brief relaxation exercise or get up and walk around and talk to people. I'll take advantage of flex time and go to an aerobics class three days a week and run personal errands two days a week in the middle of the day. I will eat three nutritious meals, rather than snack on junk.

Pattern 3. I will take a one-day workshop on Assertiveness Training and ask my supervisor more questions until I am sure I know what he wants. I also will tell my co-worker not to interrupt me with small talk, other than when I get up and walk around. I will assertively ask the secretary for help.

Pattern 4. I will take each one of my critical thoughts and turn them into constructive action thoughts. For instance, rather than saying about meetings, "What a waste, I have work to do," I could say, "Whew, a break from programming! What constructive contribution can I make here?"

I will revaluate my progress for each goal on a weekly basis. I plan to spend a weekend at a local hot springs as a reward for changing these four patterns for one month.

(*Signed,*) Patty Bowers

If it would increase your motivation, make this contract with a friend or co-worker. Then report back weekly on your progress toward each goal.

Exercise: Write out goals to modify a few of your responses to specific stressors in your life in the form of a self-contract.

I, _____ , agree to:

1. _____
   _____
   _____
   _____

2. _____
   _____
   _____
   _____

3. _____
   _____
   _____
   _____

I will monitor my progress every _____ (*length of time*).

I will reward myself with _____ .

Step 5. Motivate Yourself

Create specific rewards for every goal you establish:

- Give yourself one point for each relaxation break you take. 25 points means a new dress or car radio.

- You'll buy that book you've wanted to read after clarifying with your boss some of his expectations.

- You'll rent that spicy new murder mystery after you tell John not to interrupt you when you're writing.

- You'll call Rebekah for a little chat after you write that memo requesting flex time.

- After you've requested a limit on the number of cases you're expected to take, you'll call Art and invite him to dinner at Walker's.

- You'll assign one dollar toward a shopping spree for each stress-producing thought you catch and change (see step 6).

Here's a way of motivating stress reducing activities that you normally feel too rushed to do. Sometimes a work-related task that you enjoy has no immediate pay-off, so you postpone it and focus your attention on tasks that have immediate deadlines. Such was the case with Marty who kept putting off writing a professional article he had outlined two years earlier. Administrative responsibilities swallowed up his time. He decided to deal with the problem by setting aside half an hour each morning to work on his article before letting himself tackle the demands of the day. He used the motivating power of immediate deadlines to prompt him to accomplish something fun and rewarding.

Step 6. Change Your Thinking

Job stress occurs because your thoughts trigger a painful emotional reaction. There are three generic thoughts that do you in:

1. I've got to do _____(a certain task)_____ (perfectly) (on time) (so my boss will be pleased) or (something painful) will happen.

2. They're doing this to me and it's not fair.

3. I'm trapped here.

Thought 1 makes you anxious, thought 2 triggers anger, and thought 3 generates depression. You can do something about these thoughts and the job stress they create. Right now, list the things you tell yourself about your job that fit into each of the above three categories.

Category 1

_____

_____

_____

_____

_____

Category 2

_____

_____

_____

_____

_____

Category 3

_____

_____

_____

_____

_____

Here's how you cope with these stress producing thoughts.

1. Make a *realistic appraisal* of what exactly will happen if the task isn't on time, flawless, or totally pleasing to your boss. A realistic appraisal means looking at what has happened to yourself and others in the past when tasks such as this were late, had errors, and so on. Realistic also means being specific. It's time to get rid of that vague sense of doom. Exactly what is your boss likely to say to you? What, if anything, is likely to happen to you?

Now complete this sentence: "If _____ isn't (*perfect*) (*on time*) (*totally acceptable*), the boss' response will likely be _____. I can handle it."

Mentally repeat this coping statement each time you catch yourself catastrophizing about vague and dire consequences. Note: If you have no idea how your boss would respond, ask him. "If I'm a day late with the Crocker report, will that be a problem?"

2. There's absolutely no good that can come from blaming anybody for your job stress. Blaming maintains your sense of being stuck and helpless. You see yourself as a victim who has no alternatives and has lost the power of choice. Blaming triggers anger and stress hormones such as noradrenalin that deplete your energy and over the long run damage your health.

Reread the chapter on Refuting Irrational Ideas: "The conditions for things or people to be otherwise than they are don't exist. . . . Things are what they are because of a long series of causal events." Saying to yourself that your boss or the company president *should* act differently is like saying Nixon should never have authorized Watergate. The conditions necessary for Nixon to be fearful and obsessed with secrecy existed, the means and opportunity existed. His values, needs, ambitions, advisors, and personal history all pushed him toward the break-in.

No one is *supposed* to take care of or protect you on this job. They are all busy taking care of and protecting themselves. This is natural. This is the inescapable fact of working life. So what can you say to yourself to avoid chronic blaming and anger?

The first thing you can do is ask yourself this question: "What steps can I take to change the conditions I don't like?" If you can't think of any way to change the job, you have two rational choices. You must either adapt to and accept the conditions or look for another job.

The second coping statement you can make is as follows: "_____ is acting exactly as he should. The conditions necessary for him to act this way (*his needs, available coping strategies to meet those needs, past successes and failures, fears, attitudes toward our relationship*) all exist, therefore he did _____ (*to*) (*with*) me."

3. You are not trapped. You may have difficult choices, but you aren't trapped. Right now the pain of this job seems less than the pain associated with other available choices. Is this really true? Here's a chance to list your options for change. What specific steps could you take to change a major stress producer on your job?

_____

_____

What would you risk in attempting that change?

_____

_____

What steps could you take to change jobs altogether?

_____

_____

What would you risk in attempting that change? (See Step 10, "Knowing when to Quit," for help in exploring these fears.)

_____

_____

Rather than "I'm trapped," the more accurate thing to say to yourself is: "I *choose* to stay with the current conditions on this job because right now it seems less painful than _____ (*the steps to change*). I may choose differently in the future."

Step 7: Deal With Your Boss

Since one of the primary sources of job stress is ambiguity about what is expected of you, the time has come for a conference with your boss. Here are some suggested questions to use during the interview. The main thing you want to do is to get enough information so you no longer have to mind-read his or her reactions.

1. What is expected of me in my position?

2. Where is this organization going and how do I fit into the plan in the near and long-term future?

3. How am I doing? What are my strengths? What areas do I need to improve?

4. What additional skills or education do I need to progress?

5. What happens if something goes wrong? What can I expect from you if a problem develops?

6. If I continue my current level of performance, what can I expect?

If your boss is a clear, straightforward communicator, the above discussion may significantly reduce your job stress. But if your boss is indirect, irascible, or highly demanding, you have more work to do. You'll have to learn what motivates him or her and how to use that to your beneffit.

Look beneath the surface of your boss's actions to understand what motivates him. Does your boss have a difficult boss, a miserable home life, or does your boss also find you impossible? Is he just marking time until he retires, and thus views any new ideas as unnecessary or threatening? Is he a guy who needs to be liked, and therefore always says nice things about you but fails to give constructive criticism? Is he is the silent type who never lets you know what he expects? Does he lack management skills? Is he buried under his own heavy workload? Or is it something else? Is he a slave driver who was raised to expect perfection of himself and others? If your boss insists on always being right and criticizes any idea that is not his own, he may be suffering from low self-esteem and secretly crave recognition and approval.

You can often use your knowledge of what motivates your boss to get what you want. For example, with a critical boss you can satisfy some of his need for recognition by praising his successes. You can have a candid talk with him about how his put-downs make you feel and how you need positive feedback as well as constructive criticism. If your boss is a perfectionistic slave driver, it would take some of the pressure off of him if certain decision-making responsibilities were shifted to a committee or delegated down. One powerful, yet relatively low risk way to give a slave driver feedback is in the form of a questionnaire filled out by all his employees. If your boss is the silent type, you may need to confront him regarding his expectations of you in the job.

Exercise: Describe what is difficult about your boss's behavior:

_____

_____

_____

Describe what you think motivates his behavior:

_____

_____

_____

Describe how you might use your understanding of what motivates him to anticipate his next move and deal with him more effectively:

_____

_____

_____

Changing your boss is unlikely; changing yourself is the easiest way to improve your relationship with him. Through trial and error, you can develop strategies for effectively influencing your boss. Perhaps you will look for common ground upon which to build your relationship. Maybe you will decide to support your boss on points that are important to him and confront him only on the points that are vital to you, and only when he is in a good mood.

Step 8. When in Conflict, Negotiate

Whether you disagree with your boss regarding your salary or with your co-workers about who is going to get the coffee, you need to present your position and negotiate a compromise you all can live with.

Read the chapter in this workbook on Assertiveness Training for a more in depth understanding of how to express your opinions, feelings, and wants as you negotiate for change. The following is a brief four-step model for you to follow when you want to discuss specific problems with your supervisor or co-workers with the aim of arriving at a mutually acceptable outcome.

1. State the problem (what you perceive to be the cause of your stress).
2. State how it makes you feel.
3. State how it affects your productivity and motivation.
4. State win-win solutions (both sides of the conflict get something positive from your solution).

For example, Randy, a creative high school teacher, was refused compensation for the time he spent developing new courses.

Randy told his boss, "Ever since I realized I wouldn't receive money for my course development work, my enthusiasm for teaching has deteriorated. I think my students have gained tremendously from my special classes. They're now suffering as a result of my lost motivation. It's important to me and the school to continue creating new classes and to be compensated in some way. Since the money isn't available, I would be satisfied if I could take one class period each day for a semester to develop my new class."

The principal's response was, "I can't spare you a period every day, but I would agree to three hours a week." Randy accepted this workable compromise.

Exercise: Write out a script to negotiate a win-win solution to a job related conflict or problem, using the following four-part model.

1. State a work related problem:

_____

_____

2. State how it makes you feel:

_____

_____

3. State how it affects your motivation and productivity:

_____

_____

4. State a win-win solution:

_____

_____

Step 9. Pace and Balance Yourself

Do you pace yourself at work? If you are a sprinter, you can afford to throw everything you've got into the race. This is because at the end of a fast short run you know you have plenty of time to recover from your intense effort. Most jobs, however, require you to be more like a marathon runner who must pace himself in order to get across the finish line in a timely manner without collapsing. Like the marathon runner, you need to maintain a certain detachment from the immediate demands of your job so that you will remember to reserve enough energy to deal with what you anticipate down the road as well as any surprises.

Here are eight tips for pacing and balancing yourself.

1. Pay attention to your natural rhythm to determine when you tend to perform optimally and schedule your most difficult tasks for then.

2. Try to set up your day so you shift back and forth between pleasant and more difficult tasks. After something tough, make an effort to schedule something you enjoy.

3. Schedule inviolate periods of time into your day for work-related tasks that are pleasurable, even though not terribly productive. Try to do this even when you feel rushed.

4. Take advantage of your coffee breaks and lunches to do things that will reverse the stress response. For example, go to a quiet place and do a relaxation exercise. A ten-minute brisk walk will give you as much energy as a cup of coffee. A light conversation with your co-workers will release tension and may be just what you need to get a fresh perspective on a problem that was weighing you down.

5. If you are fortunate enough to have a flexible schedule, consider taking a long break in the middle of the day to do aerobic exercise, a relaxation exercise, or personal errands.

6. Take mini-breaks throughout your day to reduce or prevent symptoms of tension and stress. These breaks never take more than a few minutes and pay for themselves in terms of increased mental alertness and productivity. See the Brief Combination Techniques chapter for exercises appropriate to short breaks.

7. Choose leisure activities that balance the unique stresses of your job.

If your job requires	*Consider a complementary leisure activity such as:*
Much sitting or mental concentration	Aerobic exercise
Mindless repetition	Intellectually challenging hobbies and interests
A controlled environment	Hiking in nature; adventure
Boring tasks or no recognition	Competitive or achievement-oriented activities
Responding to people demands	Solitary activities
Dealing with conflicts	Peaceful activities
Working alone	Social activities

8. Carefully plan the timing and type of vacations that you take to maximize their recuperative effects.

Step 10. Know When To Quit

After making a genuine effort to modify your own thinking, behavior, and work conditions, you may find that your job is still dissatisfying. It may be that you are just not suited to your job. Ask yourself whether the price you are paying emotionally is worth the material benefits. Visualize yourself continuing in the same manner for another five years. Will your job make you a stronger, happier person in five years or a weaker, more miserable person? Your time is precious. Is this how you want to spend it?

Exercise: Describe your ideal job. Include your job title, your job responsibilities, your boss, your co-workers, your environment, and the management.

_____

_____

_____

_____

_____

_____

_____

_____

_____

_____

_____

_____

Although you may have yearned to quit for years, you probably have several fears that stand in the way of making your move. Perhaps you think that you are too old or too young, too inexperienced or over-qualified, the wrong sex, or that you interview poorly, or there aren't any jobs that you want out there, or the economy is going to hell and you're lucky just to be employed.

Exercise: List your fears about leaving your job:

_____

_____

_____

_____

_____

_____

Each one of your fears is a barrier that stands between you and finding your ideal job. Turn each one of your fears into a goal designed to get around the barrier. For example, if the fear is that you are too old, your goal statement might be: "I will talk to someone my age who has a job like my ideal one and find out if age really makes a difference." If your fear is that you will do poorly in an interview, your goal statement could be, "I will take an interview class and improve my skills."

Now your turn:

My fear: _____

My goal statement: _____

_____

_____

My fear: _____

My goal statement: _____

_____

_____

My fear: _____

My goal statement: _____

_____

_____

Carefully explore your alternatives. Looking at your options can either make you realize how good you have it or motivate you to plan for change.

Further Reading

Davis, Martha. "Job Stress Management," *Relax: The Stress Reduction System*. Richmond, CA: Synapse Software Corporation, 1984. (Parts of this chapter were duplicated with the permission of the author.)

Kemper, Donald, Giuffre, Jim, and Drabinski, Gene. *Pathways: A Success Guide for a Healthy Life*. Boise, Idaho: Healthwise, Inc., 1985.

Pelletier, Kenneth R. *Healthy People in Unhealthy Places: Stress and Fitness at Work*. New York, NY: Delacorte Press/Seymour Lawrence, 1984.

Potter, Beverly A. *Preventing Job Burnout: Transforming Work Pressures Into Productivity*. Los Altos, CA: Crisp Publications, Inc., 1987.

Veninga, Robert L., and Spradley, James P. *The Work/Stress Connection: How To Cope With Job Burnout*. Boston, Mass.: Little, Brown, and Company, 1981.

15

Brief Combination Techniques

The relaxation exercises presented in this chapter are based on the work of many different therapists. They are creative blends of some of the techniques you have already learned about in this book. Learning several brief combination techniques can greatly benefit you for three reasons. First, when you put two or more relaxation approaches together, the combination can have a *synergistic* effect. This means that the sum relaxation effect of the combined techniques is far greater than what you would achieve if you did each relaxation procedure individually. As you experiment with the material presented in this chapter, you'll learn which techniques are best at activating each other and combining for the most powerful effect. The second reason that combination techniques are often more powerful is because the sequence is set up to draw you deeper into the relaxation experience. Each technique builds progressively upon the one before. For example, the relaxation you experience from visualizing a pleasant beach scene is more profound if you precede the visualization with some deep breathing. And if you follow the deep breathing and the beach scene with autogenic themes of heaviness and warmth, you have a sequence of techniques that build one upon the other toward a deeper relaxation response. The third advantage to using the combination techniques presented in this chapter is their brevity. You can easily do any of these combination sequences during a ten-minute coffee break. Any time you have a few minutes to spare, they can help you center yourself and regain a sense of calmness.

The combination techniques presented here are merely suggestions. While each one has been tested and proven useful, feel free to be inventive. Try your own unique combinations. Experiment with a different sequence. Since you are a unique person with unique needs and patterns of responses, it is important that you add, delete, and modify until you have a brief relaxation sequence that really works for you.

Symptom Effectiveness

The brief combination techniques presented here have been proven effective in the treatment of fight or flight symptoms and stress-induced physiological disorders. They are particularly helpful when stress is work-related and requires brief but frequent booster sessions during the day to cope with mounting tensions.

Time for Mastery

If you have mastered the component techniques presented in earlier chapters of the book, these combination approaches can be immediately and effectively applied. Otherwise, allow one to two weeks to successfully use these combined approaches.

Instructions

1. *Stretch and Relax*

A. Take a big stretch. Tighten your arms and pull them back so that you stretch your chest and shoulders. Stretch and tighten your legs at the same time by first pulling your toes up toward you and then pushing them out straight.

B. Place one hand on your abdomen, just above your belt. Inhale slowly and deeply through your nose into your abdomen. Push up your hand as much as feels comfortable. Take four more deep breaths using the same procedure.

C. Suspend a pencil by its point over a desk or table or the floor. Tell yourself that when you are deeply relaxed the pencil will drop. The sound of the dropping pencil will be your signal to enter a healing, five-minute trance. (If you wish to omit the pencil, proceed with step C from here.) Close your eyes and say to yourself the key word or phrase that you have learned in self-hypnosis. Tell yourself that you will become more and more relaxed with each number as you count backwards from ten to zero. After the countdown, repeat to yourself these four phrases, over and over, in any order: "I am drifting deeper and deeper, deeper and deeper . . . I am more and more drowsy, peaceful, and calm . . . I am drifting and drowsy, drowsy and drifting . . . I am drifting down, down, down, into total relaxation." If your pencil has not already dropped by this time, let it go deliberately and remind yourself that you will now enjoy five minutes of peaceful self-hypnosis.

D. While in trance, visit your special place and enjoy the uniquely relaxing qualities of that environment. Really experience the sights, sounds, and sensations of your special place. When it feels that you've been there long enough, count back up from one to ten. Suggest that you are becoming more and more alert, refreshed, and wide awake as you count up.

2. *Autogenic Breathing*

A. Begin by taking slow, deep breaths as described in 1B. Become aware of the growing feeling of relaxation as each deep breath expands your diaphragm.

B. Visualize a beach. See the waves rolling up the sand, the seagulls wheeling over head, a few puffs of fleecy clouds. Hear the roar of waves, and then the quiet. Hear the alternating roar, quiet, roar, quiet. Over the ocean sound you can hear the seagulls calling. Now feel the warm sand. Imagine it covering your body, warm and heavy. Really feel the weight of the sand on your arms and legs. Feel surrounded by warmth and comfort.

C. While visualizing the sand, continue to breathe as deeply as feels comfortable. Notice the rhythm of your breath. As you breathe in, say the word "warm" to yourself. Try to feel the warmth of the sand around your body. As you breathe out, say the word "heavy." Experience the weight of the sand on your limbs. Continue your deep breathing, thinking "warm" as you inhale and "heavy" as you exhale. Continue for at least five minutes. (Note: If after a time you feel more comfortable shifting to shallower breathing, let yourself do so.)

3. *Stop and Breathe*

A. Whenever you notice disturbing or anxiety-provoking thoughts, internally shout "stop" to yourself (see the chapter on thought stopping). Imagine hearing a voice with a great deal of sharpness and authority. If shouting "stop" to yourself doesn't interrupt the flow of thoughts, put a rubber band around your wrist and snap it as you shout "stop."

B. Shift your attention to your breathing. Begin taking slow, deep breaths into your belly. Place a hand over your abdomen to make sure it is expanding with each breath.

C. Now start counting your breaths. As you exhale, count one. As you exhale again, count two. Keep counting up to four. Each time you reach four, start over again at one. Try to keep your mind as empty as possible as you focus on counting each breath. Continue the procedure until you feel relaxed and repeat each time anxiety-provoking thoughts occur.

4. *Changing Channels*

A. Utilize the same thought-stopping procedure described in 3A above.

B. As soon as you have interrupted the stressful cognition, use a prerehearsed visualization to block the return of any unwanted thoughts. Make sure the visualization is something you can elicit easily without struggle. Use an exciting sexual fantasy, images of success from some important achievement, scenes from an anticipated vacation, or images of your special place. The common thread of all these suggestions is to see yourself doing something that feels really good, something you picture easily. (Helpful hint: try visualizing scenes you already use for daydreaming.)

C. If visualization doesn't work, try these alternatives: turn on the radio, put a favorite tape in your walkman, go out for a jog or some other strenuous aerobic exercise, start counting things (each Chevrolet you see, each person wearing a hat, how many families have children on your block), pick up a book or magazine, even sing or whistle. What matters is that the activity be arresting enough to divert attention away from stressful thoughts for a time.

D. Use a coping mantra. This is a reminder that you're basically safe and okay and can handle any stress that comes along. Some coping mantras are general affirmations such as "I am well . . . I am safe and calm . . . I trust my ability to cope . . . I am surrounded by support and love . . . I can relax my body and my mind . . . I can plan and decide later, now I'll relax." Other mantras require the development of a coping statement about a specific situation: "These are just stomach cramps and I'm not going to worry about them . . . Tests show my heart is strong and healthy . . . This is the same old neck pain, it always passes . . . I can always get a loan . . . I can set limits, I'll just tell her no . . . I can ask for help with _____ . . . I can make mistakes . . . I don't have to finish everything on time . . . I can disappoint _____ sometimes and we'll still love one another . . . I have a plan I can implement tomorrow . . . These are just fight or flight symptoms, they'll pass soon . . . I did the best I could, we'll see what happens." Use your coping mantra whenever the stressful thought threatens to take hold again. Repeat your mantra as often as necessary.

5. I Am Grateful

This exercise is particularly helpful as the day is wearing on and your sense of stress and frustration is rising. It is also an excellent sequence for relaxing and putting yourself in a pleasant frame of mind before you drift off to sleep.

A. Use the short form for progressive muscle relaxation outlined in the progressive relaxation chapter. (1. Curl fists, tighten biceps. 2. Wrinkle forehead, face like a walnut. 3. Arch back, take a deep breath. 4. Pull feet back, curl toes while tightening calves, thighs, buttocks.)

B. Reflect back over your day so far and select three things for which you feel grateful. These do not have to be major events. For example, you may be grateful for the warm shower you took this morning, a co-worker helping you, your child giving you a hug and telling you he loves you, a lovely sunrise, and so on. Take a moment to relive and enjoy these experiences.

C. Continue to think back over your day. Recall three things you did that you feel good about. Remember, these don't have to be major feats. For example, you may feel good about saying no to something you really didn't want to do, taking time for yourself to exercise or relax, or being supportive to someone you like. Take a moment to reexperience those positive moments.

6. *Deep Affirmation*

A. Put your hand over your abdomen and begin taking slow deep breaths as described in 1B.

B. Close your eyes and continue to breathe deeply as you scan your body for tension. Start with your toes and move up your body. Notice any tension in your calves, thighs, and buttocks. Explore areas of tension in your back, abdomen, or chest muscles. Notice your shoulders and neck, your jaw, cheeks, and forehead. Check for tension in your biceps, forearms, and hands. Whenever you discover a tense area, exaggerate the tension slightly so that you can become aware of it. Notice exactly which muscles in your body are tense and then say to yourself, "I am tensing my _____ . . . I am hurting myself . . . I am creating tension in my body . . . I will let go of that tension starting now."

C. Use the self-hypnosis exercise outlined in 1C.

D. Select an affirmation to use while in trance. The following is a list of suggested affirmations reprinted from *Visualization for Change* by Patrick Fanning.

I can relax at will.
Tension is draining from my muscles.
I'm filled with peace, calm, and serenity.
I can turn my tension down like the volume on a radio.
Relaxation floods my body like healing, golden light.
I am in touch with my peaceful center.
I can look inward and find peace.
Relaxation is always within my grasp.

When you have relaxed long enough, count back up from one to ten. Suggest as you count that you are feeling more and more refreshed, alert, and wide awake.

7. *The Tension Cutter*

A. Take four deep breaths as described in 1B.

B. Close your eyes. Visualize your tension by giving it a color or a shape. Now change the shape and color of your tension. Make it bigger or smaller, lighter or darker. Now see yourself picking it up. Look at it in your hands, toss it up and down once or twice like it was a ball. Now see yourself rearing back in slow motion to throw your tension away. Go ahead and throw it. See it slowly leave your hand and move further and further away. Watch until it disappears out of your awareness.

C. Now imagine your body filled with lights. See red lights for tension and blue lights for relaxation. Imagine the lights changing from red to blue in all the tension areas of your body. Be aware of any physical sensation you experience while you change to the blue light of relaxation. See all the lights in your body as blue and see that color blue becoming darker and darker. Feel yourself relaxing further with each shade of blue you experience.

D. Now it's time for a mini-vacation. Here are two itineraries.

Vacation 1. Picture yourself in a forest. The light is bright in places and mottled in others. You feel safe and comfortable, taking a long pleasant walk. The air around you is cool and refreshing. You enjoy the bright spots of sunshine on the ground where the sun has filtered down through the leaves. You are walking barefoot. The leaves and moss feel soft and cool on your feet. You hear the bird sounds and the soft rustle of wind through the trees. The sounds make you happy and comfortable. As you walk your muscles feel more and more loose, heavy and relaxed. The forest carpet of leaves and moss feels so comfortable that you want to lie down and close your eyes to rest. Now you see a small stream making a soft, bubbly noise. And next to the stream is a patch of tall, soft grass, lit and warmed by sunlight. It's a lovely place to rest and you sink down to your knees and roll gently over onto the soft, warm grass. You hear the bubbling stream, the birds' song, and the gentle wind. You are so deeply relaxed that every part of your body from your toes to the top of your head is loose and heavy.

Vacation 2. Picture yourself alone in a beach house with a view of the sea. The first rays of sun light up the wall of your bedroom as you sink deeper into the warm, soft bed. You take a deep breath and notice how relaxed your muscles are. Outside you hear the sounds of seagulls and the rhythmic crashing of the waves. The waves roll in and out, in and out. Each wave makes you more and more deeply relaxed. In and out, in and out. Drowsy, heavy and calm. You can feel the cool salt air coming through the open window and you roll over to see the sand and the waves and the blue sky. You take deep breaths of the air and the relaxation deepens with each breath. You feel safe and yet very free, unhurried, aware that the day ahead is full of possibilities.

Use these examples as a model to create your own mini-vacations.

8. Breath Counting

A. Preselect a brief affirmation (see the list in 6D) or coping mantra (see the list in 4D). Try to make sure that the affirmation or coping reminder is no longer than seven or eight words. Make up a statement that feels right for you and your unique situation.

B. To begin the relaxation process, use the short form of progressive muscle relaxation found in 5A and the progressive relaxation chapter.

C. Take four deep breaths as described in 1B.

D. Now let your breathing go back to a normal rate. Focus on each breath, and as you exhale count the breath. When you get to the fourth breath, instead of counting four, say your affirmation or coping mantra. Here's a sample of what you might do. As you exhale you count one, two, three, "I can make mistakes and be okay," one, two, three, "I can make mistakes and be okay," and so on.

9. *Taking Control*

A. Get comfortable, close your eyes, and begin noticing your breathing. Try to notice each breath and nothing else. As you exhale, say to yourself the word "one." Keep saying "one" with each exhalation.

B. When you feel sufficiently relaxed, turn your attention from your breathing to a situation you find stressful or difficult. See yourself handling that stressful situation successfully, confidently. See yourself saying and doing the appropriate thing to succeed. See yourself smiling, standing or sitting erectly. Now visualize yourself hesitating or making a small error, uncertain for a moment. But then you go on, confidently finishing the task, looking satisfied. You remind yourself, "I can handle this, I'm in control."

10. *Accepting Yourself*

A. Use the body scanning procedure described in 6B.

B. Continue to relax by doing several minutes of autogenic breathing as described in 2C.

C. When you feel deeply relaxed, make these suggestions to yourself: "I let go of shoulds . . . I accept myself for all my humanness . . . I breathe, I feel, I do the best I can." Rewrite this mantra in any way that feels more authentic or true for you. Anything will work, as long as it carries the basic message that you accept yourself.

16

Recording Your Own Relaxation Tape

One of the best ways to develop a complete relaxation regime is to make your own audio tape. A tape of twelve to twenty minutes can become a "relaxation workout" that incorporates many of the important techniques described in this book.

There are many relaxation tapes on the market, including five that are recommended for use with this book. But there are advantages to making your own. First, you can delete segments that don't work for you while retaining and emphasizing techniques that you find particularly effective. Second, you can combine as many or as few relaxation techniques as you want for a long, medium, or short relaxation workout. Third, you can be creative. You can develop your own unique approach, create special relaxation or coping mantras, or visualize images that you find uniquely peaceful or calming. Fourth, using your own voice can make the tape feel especially intimate and friendly. Finally, you may use any accompanying music or sound effects that you wish, or leave the background entirely silent.

Relaxation tapes are also a big help when you're feeling passive, when you want to be told what to do. It's a lot easier to put on a tape and follow instructions than it is to figure out each step of a relaxation procedure yourself.

Symptom Effectiveness

Tapes can be effective for almost any symptom of stress or stress-related illness. A taped relaxation procedure can be especially helpful when you are low in energy or motivation. If you commit yourself to play the tape at specific times during the day, you are more likely to follow your relaxation program consistently.

Time for Mastery

You will probably need to make several relaxation tapes before your voice and phrasing and the techniques you've selected feel right to you. Let yourself experiment. Over the course of a week, you should be able to develop a tape that works sufficiently well for you to get real benefit. From then on, you may periodically change the tape, rewriting, adding, and deleting certain parts as ideas occur to you. Make an effort to listen to your tape at least twice a day, morning and evening.

Instructions

The first thing to work on is your voice. Speak at normal volume, in a flat, almost monotonous tone. An uninflected voice on the tape will help keep your focus inward so that you can pay attention to your body and the exercise rather than to any distracting qualities of the voice. Speak slowly. Give yourself time to actually take a deep breath, tense or relax your arms, or form a visualization. Rushing through a relaxation tape defeats its purpose. When you wish to give special emphasis to an important word or instruction, simply say the words slower, drawing out the vowel sounds. "Your muscles are looose and relaxed . . . take a deeeep breath . . . your forehead is smoooooth as silk."

Many people enjoy hearing music in the background of a relaxation tape. There are two problems with adding your own musical background. First, you can't stop recording in order to fix mistakes. If you do, the background music will skip each time you stop the tape. Second, few rooms are acoustically suited for recording music. Your selection is apt to sound tinny or have a slight echo effect. But if music is important to you, go ahead and experiment. Try moving your microphone closer or farther away from the speaker; try different volumes for the music. If you enjoy New Age music, artists such as George Winston, Will Ackerman, Shadowfax, Steve Halpern, and Andreas Vollenweider can provide a very peaceful background. If you prefer classical music, the following pieces have been recommended by the Institute for Music and Imagery (Box 173, Fort Townsend, WA 94368).

Composer	Title
Respighi	Fountains of Rome
	"The Fountain of Valle Giulia at Dawn"
	"The Villa Medici Fountain at Sunset"
Debussy	Danses Sacred and Profane
Bach	Passacaglia and Fugue in C
Pachelbel	Canon in D
Hadyn	Cello Concerto in C: Adagio
Glinka	Life of the Tsar: Susanin Aria
Sibelius	Swan of Tuonela
Boccherini	Cello Concerto in B: Adagio

Mantras and Affirmations

When you relax, you're in a suggestible state. Listening to your tape is an ideal time to remind yourself of important affirmations, coping strategies, and new attitudes that you are striving to remember. These affirmations and reminders may change daily. On the other hand, you may want to repeat an important basic truth each time you listen to the tape so that it gradually finds its way into your subconscious beliefs.

Here are some examples of helpful affirmations that you may wish to use while listening to the tape.

> Each day I become more and more relaxed.
> I accept my body, every feeling, every sensation.
> I can relax away stress.
> I breathe deeply and calmly when I feel stress.
> I can be direct and clear with my boss.
> I am expressing my needs and feelings to my wife.
> I am responsible for making myself feel good.
> My stomach is loose and calm.
> The knots in my shoulders are dissolving.
> I am loving and good.
> I can stop unloving thoughts.
> I will succeed in my physics course.
> Whenever I feel stress, I'll fill my body with peaceful light.

Affirmations can involve specific relaxation instructions, suggestions for behavioral change, imagery for healing, suggestions for improved self-esteem, mantras for success, reminders for attitudinal change, and assertions that everything, in the end, will turn out okay. If you want to change something, write an affirmation that will remind you to do so. Make the affirmation positive, and be certain it describes exactly what you want to achieve.

Mantras and affirmations work best if they are combined with an image, a mental picture of the change you want to create. If you want your stomach to be loose and calm, see braided strands untwisting. If you wish to express your needs and feelings to your wife, see yourself talking to her intimately and earnestly. If you wish to succeed in the physics course, see the report card with a B + or an A.

Constructing Your Relaxation Tape

The relaxation script below is divided into sections. Each section is a discrete component which can be included or deleted from your tape. Read through the entire script first and mark the sections that feel appropriate to include. Over the next few weeks you may rerecord your tape several times, adding or subtracting sections as you learn more about what works best for you.

Relaxation Script

Deep Breathing. Close your eyes. Put your hand over your abdomen (just above the belt). Take a deep breath, way down into your belly. (Pause.) Let go and hear the air whoosh out through your lips. (Pause.) And when you're ready, take another deep breath. You can feel your belly rise slowly as the air comes in. Let it out with a whooshing sound, like the wind, as you blow through your lips. Each breath leaves you more and more relaxed. Each breath purifies and relaxes your whole body and mind. Take another deep breath down into your belly. Feel your belly push out. As you relax, the air goes gently out your lips. Imagine with your next deep breath that clean, pure, white air is coming in through the soles of your feet. See it spread throughout your whole body, collecting the debris of tension and stress. The air gets darker as it takes the stress and tension from your body. Imagine the dark air being expelled through your lips, your whole body clean and fresh and relaxed. Now take a deep purifying breath and feel it cleaning your body of stress and tension. See the tension leaving your body with the breath. Relax and enjoy the feeling of peace and calm that has spread throughout your body with each deep breath. Imagine one more breath coming in through the soles of your feet, pure and white. It is removing the last bit of tension from your body. As you exhale you feel your body clean and relaxed, deeply relaxed.

Counting Your Breath. Now let your breathing slow down and become automatic. Each breath continues to relax you. You are breathing quietly, peacefully. You're breathing in an easy and natural way. Each time you exhale, say silently to yourself, "one." Continue to breathe in and out, saying "one" each time you exhale. Whenever thoughts or perceptions take your attention away from your breathing, let go of them and return to saying "one." Breathe naturally, calmly, saying "one" as you exhale. (Leave one to two minutes blank on the tape to really enjoy this exercise.)

Progressive Relaxation. Now, while keeping the rest of your body relaxed, clench your right fist, tighter and tighter. (Pause five seconds). Now relax. Notice the contrast between a tight muscle and a loose one. Notice a pleasant sort of burning that occurs when the muscle relaxes. Now try to relax your arm even more. Let the chair hold your arm up as you let go of the last bit of muscular tension. Now tighten your left fist, tighter and tighter. (Pause five seconds.) Relax and enjoy the feeling of looseness in your left arm. Really give yourself a chance to feel a difference between tension and relaxation. (Pause.)

Now bend your elbows and tense your biceps. Tense them as much as you can and observe the feeling of tautness. (Pause five seconds.) Relax, straighten out your arms. Let the relaxation develop and feel the difference. (Pause.)

Now turn your attention to your head and wrinkle up your forehead as tight as you can. (Pause five seconds.) Now relax and smooth it out. Let yourself imagine your entire forehead and scalp becoming smooth and relaxed. (Pause.) Now frown and notice the strain spreading throughout your forehead. Feel the tension and the tightness. (Pause.) Now let go, allow your brow to become smooth again. Notice the difference between tension and relaxation in your forehead. (Pause.) Now clench your jaw, bite hard, and notice the tension throughout your jaw. (Pause five seconds.) Relax your jaw. When the jaw is relaxed, your lips will begin to part. Really feel and appreciate the contrast between tension and relaxation in your jaw. Notice how it feels to relax your lips and tongue.

Now shrug your shoulders. Keep the tension as you hunch your head down between your shoulders. (Pause five seconds.) Relax. Drop your shoulders and feel the relaxation spreading through your neck, throat and shoulders. Pure relaxation, deeper and deeper. Feel how loose and easy your neck feels balanced on your shoulders.

Give your entire body a chance to relax. Feel the comfort and the heaviness. Take a deep breath and let if fill your abdomen. (Pause.) Now exhale, letting the air out with a whooshing sound. Continue relaxing, letting your breath come freely and gently. Now, tighten your stomach and hold. Note the tension. (Pause five seconds.) Relax. Place your hand on your stomach. Breathe deeply into your belly, pushing your hand up. Hold. (Pause.) And relax. Feel the contrast with the tension as the air rushes out.

Now concentrate on your back. Arch it very slightly, without straining. Focus on the tension in your lower back. Feel the tension. (Pause.) And then relax. Imagine loosening the lower back and pelvic muscles, feel yourself sinking deeper into the chair or bed. Focus on letting go of all the tension in the muscles of your lower back and pelvis and abdomen. Feel yourself sinking heavier and heavier into the chair or bed as your abdomen and back relax more and more deeply. (Pause.)

Now tighten your buttocks and thighs. Hold the tension and notice how it feels. (Pause five seconds.) Relax and notice the contrast between tension and looseness. Really experience what it feels like to relax your buttocks and thighs. (Pause.) Now curl your toes downward, making your calves tense. Study the tension. (Pause five seconds.) Relax. Feel and enjoy the relaxation. (Pause.) Now bend your toes toward your face, creating tension in your shins. (Pause five seconds.) Relax again, enjoying the feeling of peace and heaviness that spreads everywhere in your legs.

Feel the heaviness in your body as the relaxation deepens. Feel yourself heavier and heavier, more and more deeply relaxed. More and more heavy, peaceful and calm.

Body Awareness. Now you can scan your body for any last bit of tension. Let your arms become heavy and relaxed. Heavier and heavier, more and more deeply relaxed. Your arms are heavy, heavy, letting go of the last bit of muscle tension. More and more deeply relaxed. Heavy and relaxed. Your arms are becoming more and more deeply relaxed. Letting go, letting go of all muscle tension. And now your face too can relax. Your forehead becomes smooth as silk, smooth and relaxed, letting go of all the tension and the worry. Smooth and relaxed. Your cheeks become smooth and relaxed, completely free of tension. Your cheeks and forehead are smooth and relaxed. And your jaw too lets go of the last bit of tension. Your jaw hangs loose and relaxed, loose and relaxed. Your tongue and lips are relaxed. And as your jaw becomes completely loose and relaxed, your lips begin to part, very slightly. They begin to part as you let go of the last bit of muscle tension. Your jaw is loose and relaxed. Your neck and shoulders can now let go. Your shoulders droop and relax, droop and relax. Your neck is loose and easy. Your neck and shoulders are relaxed, you feel safe and calm. Your shoulders droop and you let go of the last bit of muscular tension. Now you can take another deep breath, way down into your belly. Your belly pushes up as you inhale. (Pause.) Let go now, making the whooshing noise with your lips. Feel the relaxation spread throughout your abdomen and chest and back.

Take another deep breath, and as you do feel the air relax your chest and abdomen and back. Exhale with a whooshing noise, and feel the last bit of muscular tension leave your lower body. (Pause.) Now focus on your legs. Let them become heavier and heavier, more and more deeply relaxed. Heavier and heavier, letting go of the last bit of muscular tension. Letting go, letting go of tension, more and more deely relaxed as your legs become heavier and heavier. You can imagine your legs as lead pipes, so heavy and relaxed. Now you feel a relaxation throughout your entire body. Every cell is relaxed, calm, and quiet. Your legs and arms are heavy and relaxed, your face is smooth and relaxed, your jaw hangs loosely, loosely. Your neck and shoulders are relaxed, your shoulders droop and relax. Take another deep breath. (Pause.) As you do your entire body will be filled with peace, calm, and relaxation.

Special Place. Now imagine a place where you feel peaceful, calm, and relaxed. A place where you are secure and safe. See whether it is outdoors or indoors, whether it is a place from your past or your present or a place you've never really seen. This is your special place, a retreat and a haven. You're going there now. You can see the shapes and colors of your special place. You see every detail like a picture. (Pause.) And now you can begin to hear the sounds of your special place. You can see and hear. (Pause.) And now you are able to feel your special place. You feel the temperature and you feel the textures of your special place. You can feel it against your skin. You feel bathed in peace and a deep sense of contentment in your special place. Take a deep breath as you let the peace and tranquility of your special place spread throughout your entire body. Enjoy your place for a while. Let it nourish and relax you. (Pause one to two minutes.)

Autogenics Theme. Take a deep breath, way down into your belly. As you breathe in, say the word "warm" to yourself. And as you breathe out, say the word "heavy." (Pause.) Take another deep breath and think to yourself, "warm." (Pause.) Let it go and think, "heavy." Now breathe deeply, at your own pace, thinking "warm" on the in-breath and "heavy" on the out-breath. Feel the warmth and heaviness in your arms and your legs. And with each breath let the feeling spread throughout your entire body, relaxing every muscle as you feel more and more heavy, warm, and relaxed. (Pause 90 seconds.)

Coping Imagery. Notice the feeling of peace and relaxation. Imagine carrying this feeling into your everyday life. See yourself confident, relaxed, talking calmly. See yourself smiling with friends, co-workers, family. Your manner is easy as you state your needs and concerns. You see yourself standing comfortably and calmly with your boss, with people you barely know, with strangers. You see yourself smiling and enjoying the conversation. You are able to speak what is in your mind. You say what you feel and think clearly, in such a way that you are appreciated and understood. Your posture is relaxed yet straight. You feel strong and capable.

Affirmation. Now is the time to remember your affirmation. Say it to yourself slowly while focusing on any accompanying imagery. Give yourself time to let your affirmation really sink in, repeating as often as feels appropriate. (Pause 20 seconds.)

Anchoring. Now feel the relaxation in every part of your body. Notice the feeling of heaviness and peace in your arms and your legs. Feel the looseness in your jaw, the relaxation in your neck and shoulders. Take a deep breath, and as you exhale the last bit of tension will leave your body. (Pause.) Experience the feeling of being completely at rest. Now, while staying very aware of what relaxation feels like in your body, place your right hand over your left wrist. Grasp your wrist gently, but firmly. Whenever you hold your wrist in this way it will be your cue to relax. Any time you hold your left wrist with your right hand you will recover the deep feelings of relaxation you have right now. Take a deep breath. Feel it cleansing and refreshing your body. Feel the healing energy of relaxation flowing through your arms and throughout your body. When you link your hand and wrist, it completes a circuit so the healing energy flows freely and reaches every part of your body. From now on, whenever you wish to relax, you will hold your left wrist with your right hand.

Using Your Tape

Now it's time to try out your tape. As you experiment by including or omitting different segments, you will discover which procedures work best for you. You may want to try writing some of your own and including them on the tape. Certain breathing exercises, visualizations, or meditation procedures may be more effective for you than some of the techniques on this sample script. The only rule to follow is: Do what works.

"Do what works" applies not just to the omission or inclusion of techniques. It means that you should order the techniques in any sequence that feels good to you, experiment with your voice and inflection, and try recordings of wind chimes, waterfalls, babbling brooks, or any other background noises or sound effects that seem appropriate.

Buying Tapes

If you prefer relaxation tapes based on a single specific technique, the following tapes were made to accompany this book and can be ordered from New Harbinger Publications: Progressive Relaxation and Breathing; Body Awareness and Imagination; Autogenics and Meditation; Self-Hypnosis; and Thought Stopping.

17

Biofeedback

In a sense, all the other chapters in this book have talked about getting feedback from your body—learning what makes you tense and developing inner controls for handling stress. Biofeedback is the use of instrumentation to become aware of processes in your body that you usually don't notice, and to help bring them under voluntary control. Biofeedback machines give you immediate information about your own biological conditions: muscle tension, skin surface temperature, brain wave activity, skin conductivity (sweating), blood pressure and heart rate.

Each of your body systems affects how you experience relaxation. If your muscles are relaxed and your skin temperature is warm, that doesn't mean you are completely stress-free. Your heart rate might still be high, an EEG might show high brain wave activity. Biofeedback helps you find out which components of your nervous system are and are not relaxed. It can enhance your awareness of what total relaxation feels like for you.

Biofeedback is often used as a supplement to many of the stress reduction exercises in this book. For example, if you learn deep breathing and autogenics in order to relax, biofeedback can then be useful to tell you just how relaxed your muscles are and how much you can lower your heart beats-per-minute, as well as give feedback about how your exercises affect other systems.

After the instrumentation has helped you develop the ability to read tension in your various body systems, you can continue without a machine. The goal is to learn to lower muscle tension, or blood pressure, or to increase hand temperature whenever you need to counteract a stressful situation. You can identify subtle early signs of arousal and self-correct before you become really stressed. If you catch the arousal pattern at its earliest point, it's easier to reverse the direction of stress build-up.

Is biofeedback for you? If you are suffering symptoms of stress, it can be a very powerful treatment tool. However, if you assume that biofeedback machines can magically erase tension from your body, you may end up very frustrated. That's because there are basically two steps in relaxation: first identifying when and where the tension is inside your body, and then letting go of it. The first step alone brings very little relief. You can become aware of stress cues inside your body via biofeedback, but you must also learn ways of letting go of physical tension. That means finding stress reduction techniques that work for you.

The clinical application of biofeedback was pioneered by Alyce and Elmer Green of the Menninger Foundation in the late 1960s. Many other researchers have followed the Greens in exploring this promising treatment approach. By providing an objective measurement of bodily functions, biofeedback has given credibility to the whole field of stress reduction. Biofeedback instruments are accepted as being accurate, and are particularly useful because they tell you *immediately* that there is tension in your body.

Symptom Effectiveness

The Biofeedback Institute of San Francisco reports that the following symptoms can be treated with biofeedback:

Tension headache	Epilepsy
Migraine	Anxiety
Hypertension	Phobic reactions
Insomnia	Asthma
Spastic colon	Stuttering
Muscle spasm/pain	Teeth grinding

How Biofeedback Works

Barbara Brown, noted researcher and writer in the area of biofeedback, defines it as "the process or technique for learning voluntary control over automatic reflex-regulated body functions." You have two nervous systems. The voluntary or somatic nervous system controls the nerve cells and fibers serving the skeletal muscles. These are the muscles employed in deliberate or consciously controlled movement, such as leg, arm or hand movement.

The second nervous system is called the involuntary or autonomic nervous system. This system regulates the heart, blood vessels, stomach, endocrine glands and all functions which have traditionally been considered outside of your control. Biofeedback technology has now given you the ability to tune into and regulate these functions.

Biofeedback instruments monitor selected body systems that can be picked up by electrodes and transformed into visual or auditory signals. Any internal change instantly triggers an external signal, such as a sound, a flickering light, or readings on a meter. When you are hooked up to the biofeedback equipment, you can see or hear (or both) the continuous monitoring of your selected body functions. Biofeedback training allows you to take this information about your body states and use it to modify or change them. You will be able to apply your increased awareness of tension to your daily life. Soon you can say, "I am aware of feeling tension now and I need to _____."

In this chapter we discuss the five main ways that biofeedback measures important body functions. Although these five standard modalities are the ones most commonly used, biofeedback principles and practice allow any physiological function to be measured and trained: gut tonus, acid and enzyme secretion, sexual response, blood pressure, cardiac functions, and so on. Eventually the ability to monitor any physiological function in the laboratory will be made available for clinical use.

Electromyogram (EMG) Training

The EMG machine monitors skeletal muscle tension, which is part of the voluntary nervous system. Almost any muscle can be monitored, but the following three muscles are most commonly used:

1. *Frontalis*. The muscle in your forehead that makes you frown and tightens when you are worried or under pressure.

2. *Masseter*. The muscle that tightens your jaw and stays clenched when you are frustrated or angry.

3. *Trapezius*. The muscle that hunches your shoulders and tightens when you are alarmed or chronically anxious.

These muscles are chosen because they typically respond to stress and can be measured without much interference from other muscles. They are a good starting point from which muscle relaxation training can be generalized.

EMG Training is done by placing two sensors (electrodes) at a convenient distance from each other on the skin over the appropriate muscle. A third electrode is placed on a neutral tissue (such as over a bone) to serve as an electrical reference point.

The EMG is the biofeedback instrument most frequently used. It has been successfully employed to treat muscular tension, insomnia, anxiety and psychosomatic disorders such as asthma, hypertension, ulcers, colitis and menstrual distress. EMG training has proven to be highly effective with tension headaches.

Thermograph (Temperature) Training

The thermograph monitors minute fluctuations in body temperature. These are measured by monitoring finger, hand or foot temperature. A sensor (heat sensitive semiconductor in an epoxy bead) is usually attached to the middle or little finger of your dominant hand, or to your foot.

The themograph is important because your skin temperature goes down when you are anxious. The lowered temperature is due to peripheral vasoconstriction, reduced blood flow to the tiny capillaries that nourish your skin. Changes in blood flow are regulated by the autonomic nervous system, which responds to stress (sympathetic arousal) by taking blood from the skin and sending it to the skeletal muscles. It is accordingly believed that voluntarily raising skin temperature will produce an anti-stress effect.

Temperature training has been very successful with migraine headaches and vascular problems often associated with cold hands and feet. Controlling body temperature is one way of monitoring and controlling the whole autonomic nervous system. The ability to raise the temperature of your hands appears to be a good indicator of whether the autonomic nervous system is relaxed. When the autonomic nervous system is relaxed, headaches usually subside or can be prevented from occurring. The thermograph and the EMG machine are often used together to monitor tension in both nervous systems.

Galvanic Skin Response (GSR) Training

A feedback dermograph measures the electrical conductance or electrical potential in your skin. This instrument can monitor tiny changes in the concentration of salt and water in your sweat gland ducts. An imperceptible electric current is run through your skin. As the sweat glands become more active, the machine registers your skin's increased ability to conduct electricity. Some feedback dermographs also measure electrical potential in your skin. The natural metabolism of cells produces a slight voltage (actually millivolts) which varies as sweat gland activity varies. The lower the measurable voltage, the less there is of sweat gland activity. Historically, the GSR has been used in lie detectors as a measure of emotional arousal.

The sympathetic branch of your autonomic nervous system controls sweating. By monitoring the activity of your sweat glands, GSR training helps you gain control over your autonomic nervous system. It is often used in the treatment of hyperhydrosis (excessive sweating), phobia, and anxiety states. GSR training usually takes place in conjunction with EMG and temperature training.

Electroencephalogram (EEG) Training

EEG training is a method of monitoring brain waves. Brain waves have been classified into four states: beta (wide awake and thinking), alpha (associated with a state of calm relaxation), theta (deep reverie or light sleep) and delta (deep sleep). The EEG equipment lets you know which brain wave state you are in. EEG training is used in the treatment of insomnia.

Alpha Training was popular for several years as a way of teaching people to relax. You are trained to become aware of a subjective state that is associated with relaxation (alpha) and eventually learn to duplicate the feelings that go along with this state. Unfortunately, alpha training has been exploited by overzealous entrepreneurs. It is now less often used by professional biofeedback trainers who have found that people can achieve the alpha state without necessarily relaxing other body systems. Alpha training alone is not effective with insomnia or epilepsy, as previously thought, and should only be used in conjunction with other biofeedback modalities.

Researchers have recently developed a new EEG machine called a neuroanalyzer. It has been suggested that certain kinds of electrical activity in the sensory motor strip (the part of the brain controlling motor activity) are better indicators of relaxation. The Neuroanalyzer monitors and feeds back the sensory motor rhythm. The idea is to shape your brain wave activity so that you have:

1. less beta activity (problem-solving mode)
2. less delta activity (total sleep)
3. more sensory motor rhythm intensity
4. less muscle tension

Research has suggested that sensory motor rhythm feedback has been shown to be clinically effective with insomnia and epilepsy.

Heart Rate Training

The heart rate monitor measures beats-per-minute and gives immediate feedback on how relaxation efforts are affecting heart rate. Your heart rate changes in response to stress and speeds up when fight-or-flight messages are sent from the autonomic nervous system. A lowered heart rate is an important component of the relaxation response.

There are also biofeedback machines that give readings of blood pressure. People using these machines can find out which thoughts and attitudes raise or lower their blood pressure. They can also observe the effect of relaxation exercises on blood pressure.

Home Trainers

The biofeedback industry has begun to develop inexpensive monitoring equipment for home use. Some people have bought machines that measure only temperature, only heart rate, or only alpha activity. The problem is that these give feedback on a single system. The more systems you measure, the better your awareness is of what it takes for *you* to get relaxed. Just lowering your heart rate or just raising skin temperature usually isn't enough for total relaxation. At the very least you should be measuring skin temperature, skin conductivity, and heart rate.

Levels of quality in home training equipment vary. There are, for example, wrist watches that measure heart beats-per-minute and inexpensive temperature monitors such as heat sensitive dots that change color. Some companies have developed hand-held GSR trainers. These gadgets provide a gross measure of certain body activities. Unfortunately, there is usually interference from systems unrelated to the system you want to measure. Measures are broadly calibrated and not very accurate. Heat sensitive dots, for example, usually indicate gross temperature changes (2.5 degrees). A sophisticated thermograph will measure a fluctuation of 100th of a degree.

Some companies made moderately expensive home trainer components and systems. A complete system should have a GSR, thermograph and EMG trainer. You should also pick up an inexpensive pulse monitor.

The EMG is the most expensive of the home trainer components (but also the easiest to learn). If you can't afford one, be certain to at least acquire GSR, temperature and heart rate components. EEG machines are not available for home training. Alpha home trainers are rarely used now. They are so inaccurate that they don't effectively

Clockwise from upper left: An array of sophisticated biofeedback instruments for use in a clinical setting. A wristwatch that monitors and displays your pulse rate. Portable myograph, dermograph, feedback thermometer, and digital analyzer for use as home trainers. "Biodots"—small circles of microencapsulated liquid crystals that change color as your skin temperature changes—are interesting but not very sensitive. The same liquid crystal principle applied to a ring.

Photos courtesy of Autogenic Systems, Inc., Prime Microelectronic Instruments, Inc., Futurehealth, and Medical Device Corp.

train you to relax. A sophisticated machine is needed to measure brain waves, and alpha trainers simply don't do the job. Furthermore, alpha is harder to learn than EMG or GSR training. You often get alpha waves as a side effect of reaching criteria on these other systems, so an alpha trainer is superfluous.

If you own a personal computer, you may already have the heart of a personal biofeedback system. The latest home training systems consist of temperature, GSR and other sensors that plug into your personal computer. The readings are interpreted and displayed on the screen by a special program.

You can teach yourself to relax with home trainers, but always use them in conjunction with other relaxation techniques. In general, working with a professional will probably be more effective than practicing biofeedback at home. He or she will have high quality equipment and will be trained at overcoming roadblocks that might otherwise interrupt your progress.

To get a directory of certified biofeedback practitioners in your area, write to:

Association for Applied Psychophysiology & Biofeedback
10200 W. 44th Ave
Suite 304
Wheat Ridge, CO 80033
(303) 422–8436

Also at the same address and phone number is the Biofeedback Certification Institute of America. The association maintains a membership list and maintains a registry of biofeedback practitioners it certifies. Most large cities now have a Biofeedback Institute that trains professionals and provides biofeedback training for individuals wishing to pursue this technique. Most large universities also have biofeedback training available.

The following companies specialize in the manufacture of biofeedback equipment:

Thought Technology Ltd.
RR 1
Route 9 North
Box 380
West Chazy, NY 12992
1–(800) 361–3651

Thought Technology Ltd.
2180 Belgrave Ave.
Montreal, Quebec
Canada H4A 2L8
(513) 489–8251

Autogenic Systems
1350 South Kostner Avenue
Chicago, IL 60623
(312) 522–7777

Davicon
79 Second Ave
Burlington, MA 01803
(617) 229–2800

J&J Enterprises
22797 Holgar Court, N.E.
Poulsbo, WA 98370
(206) 779-3853

The Stens Corporation
6451 Oakwood Drive
Oakland, CA 94611
(415) 339-9053
(213) 389-6223
1 (800) 25-STENS outside CA

Biofeedback Research Institute, Inc.
6399 Wilshire Boulevard
Suite 1010
Los Angeles, CA 90048
(213) 933-9451

Self Regulation Systems, Inc.
14770 NE 95th Street
Redmond, WA 98052
(206) 882-1101
(800) 345-5642

Biofeedback Study Center of New York
55 East 9th Street
New York, NY 10003
(212) 673-4710

Biofeedback International
14189 Old Cazadero Rd
PO Box 308
Guerneville, CA 95446
(707) 869-3970
(800) 528-0100 Nationwide
(800) 528-0400

Further Reading

Brown, Barbara. *New Mind, New Body, Biofeedback: New Directions for the Mind.* New York: Harper & Row, 1974.

Brown, Barbara. *Stress and the Art of Biofeedback.* New York: Harper and Row, 1977.

Karlins, Marvin and Andrews, Lewis M. *Biofeedback: Turning on the Powers of Your Mind.* New York: J. B. Lippincott, 1972.

Lamott, Kenneth. *Escape From Stress.* New York: G. P. Putnam Sons, 1975.

Sterman, M. B. "Biofeedback and Epilepsy." *Human Nature,* May, 1978, 50-7.

18

Nutrition

You need 40 to 60 nutrients to stay healthy. Without the right balance of these nutrients you could be suffering from chronic, subclinical malnutrition and not even know it. Because it's subclinical, you don't feel any identifiable symptoms; and because it's chronic, the symptoms you do have may feel "normal."

When you are under stress your need for all nutrients increases, especially your need for calcium and the B vitamins. Conversely, a poor diet contributes to a poor reaction to stress. For example, a diet low in milk and leafy vegetables can lead to a calcium deficiency. Then, when your tense muscles produce a high level of lactic acid, there isn't enough calcium to counteract it. You feel more fatigued, anxious, and irritable than you would if you were eating a more balanced diet. For many people who have trouble sleeping, the answer is not a sleeping pill, but spinach, milk, and relaxation exercises.

This chapter will help you identify where your diet is deficient or where your eating habits are contributing to high levels of stress. You can learn to make changes in your diet that will help rather than hurt you in coping with stress.

There is no ideal diet that is best for everyone. People's needs differ according to age, sex, body size, physical activity, heredity, and conditions such as allergies or pregnancy. You need patience and a willingness to experiment in order to discover the diet that is right for you.

Symptom Effectiveness

A good diet can directly control or prevent high blood pressure, indigestion, ulcers, constipation, obesity, diabetes, and dental caries. Eating properly can also help to reduce depression, irritability, anxiety, headaches, fatigue, and insomnia.

Time for Mastery

You can make important changes in your diet immediately and begin noticing the effects in a matter of days. It will take three to six months to firmly establish the habits of good nutrition.

Instructions

Use the following Food Diary to record your eating habits for three days. The areas in which your average daily consumption varies the most from the ideal are the areas in which you can make the greatest improvement in what you eat.

Food Diary For three days, keep track of how many servings your have of each of these food categories. For each category, divide the total servings by three to get your daily average for the period. Compare your eating pattern to the ideal.					
	Day One Servings	Day Two Servings	Day Three Servings	Average Servings per day	Ideal Servings per day
Vegetables and Fruits serving = ½ cup, 1 apple, 1 orange, medium potato					4
Bread and Cereals serving = 1 slice bread, ¾ cup cereal					4
Milk, cheese, yogurt serving = 1 cup milk, 1 medium slice cheese					2–4
Meat, poultry, fish, eggs and beans, nuts serving = 3 oz. lean meat, two eggs, 1¼ cup cooked beans, 4 Tb. peanut butter, ¾ cup nuts					2
Alcohol serving = 1 beer, 1 glass of wine or cocktail					0–1
Fats and Sweets serving = 1 candy bar, 2 Tb. salad dressing, 1 cup ice cream, 1 order french fries					0
Caffeine serving = 1 cup coffee or black tea					0

Ten Steps to Good Nutrition

These ten steps are listed in order of their importance for the average adult American. If you follow all ten faithfully, you will have an exemplary diet that will be far superior to the average daily fare. If you are not able to make such sweeping changes in your eating habits, at least attempt to follow the first four or five steps.

If you have a disease such as diabetes, a special condition such as extensive allergies, or if you are pregnant or a nursing mother, consult a health professional to make sure you are meeting your special nutritional needs. Discuss with him or her the dietary changes you would like to make.

1. Eat a variety of foods.

The 40 to 60 nutrients you need to stay healthy include vitamins and minerals, as well as amino acids from proteins, essential fatty acids from vegetable oils and animal fats, and sources of energy from carbohydrates, proteins, and fats.

Most foods contain more than one nutrient. For example, milk provides proteins, fats, sugars, riboflavin, other B vitamins, vitamin A, calcium, and phosphorus. However, no single food supplies all the essential nutrients in the amounts that you need. For example, milk contains very little iron or vitamin C. That's why you should eat a variety of foods to assure an adequate diet. The greater the variety, the less likely you are to develop either a deficiency or an excess of any single nutrient. Variety also reduces your likelihood of being exposed to excessive amounts of contaminants in any single food item.

The best way to assure variety is to select foods each day from each of these major groups:

Vegetables and fruits	4 servings
Bread, cereal and grain products	4 servings
Milk, cheese, yogurt	2 servings (3 or 4 servings for teens, pregnant women and nursing mothers)
Meat, poultry, fish, eggs, beans, peas	2 servings

2. Maintain Ideal Weight

Obesity is associated with high blood pressure, increased levels of blood fats and cholesterol, and the most common type of diabetes. All of these in turn are associated with increased risk of heart attack and stroke. Being overweight puts stress on your body, interferes with your ability to cope with environmental stresses, and in our slim-conscious society threatens your self-esteem.

The following table shows acceptable weight ranges for most adults. Your ideal weight is probably within the range for your sex and height. If you have been obese since childhood you may find it difficult to reach or to maintain your weight within the acceptable range. Generally speaking, your weight should not exceed what it was when you were 20 to 25 years old.

Weight chart for persons twenty years and older

Men

HEIGHT (without shoes)	WEIGHT (without clothing) Normal range	Obesity level*
5'3"	118-141	169
5'4"	122-145	174
5'5"	126-149	179
5'6"	130-155	186
5'7"	134-161	193
5'8"	139-166	199
5'9"	143-170	204
5'10"	147-174	209
5'11"	150-178	214
6'0"	154-183	220
6'1"	158-188	226
6'2"	162-192	230
6'3"	165-195	234

Women

5'0"	100-118	142
5'1"	104-121	145
5'2"	107-125	150
5'3"	110-128	154
5'4"	113-132	158
5'5"	116-135	162
5'6"	120-139	167
5'7"	123-142	170
5'8"	126-146	175
5'9"	130-151	181
5'10"	133-156	187
5'11"	137-161	193
6'0"	141-166	199

*A weight above 20% of upper normal is generally considered the obesity level.
Adapted from: U.S. Department of Agriculture, Home and Garden Bulletin No. 74.

It isn't very well understood why some people can eat more than others and still maintain normal weight. However, one thing is definite: to lose weight, you must take in fewer calories than you burn. This means that you must either select foods containing fewer calories or you must increase your activity, or both.

If you want to figure out exactly how many calories you should consume to lose a pound a week, here are the mathematics of weight loss: there are 3,500 calories in a pound of body fat. To lose that pound, you will have to burn 3,500 more calories than you consume. Dividing by seven gives 500 calories that you must burn each day, over and above what you consume, in order to lose that pound of fat in a week. Thus, if you normally burn 1,700 calories a day, you should eat 1,200 calories a day to lose a pound a week.

Tune into calories by browsing through one of the many calorie charts available today. You may be surprised at what you find. For instance, not all fruits and vegetables are low in calories—an avocado contains nearly 400 calories. A cup of raisins may contain 240 calories, while a cup of unbuttered popcorn may only contain 90 calories. And bread and potatoes are not the villains you may think. The average slice of bread contains only about 65 calories and a medium potato contains only 90 calories.

The best diet plan is the simplest:

- Eat a variety of foods.

- Cut down on fat and fatty foods, sugar and sweets, and alcohol.

- Exercise (see the chapter on exercise in this book).

If you have an "uncontrollable" appetite, there are some things you can do to bring it under control or trick it into subsiding:

- Start each meal with a filling, low calorie appetizer such as clear broth, celery sticks, or a small salad with low-fat dressing.

- Curb between meal hunger pangs with cold drinks of water or sparkling water with lemon juice.

- A half hour before mealtime, eat a little carbohydrate food such as two soda crackers, a small glass of tomato juice, or half a grapefruit. This will make you feel less hungry at the main meal.

- Use vegetables to provide low-calorie bulk in a meal.

It's best to lose weight gradually at a rate of one to two pounds per week. A gradual reduction is safer than a crash diet, and you are more likely to keep the weight off. Long-term weight maintenance depends on acquiring new habits of eating and exercise. The resumption of old, bad eating habits is why crash diets usually fail. To improve your eating habits, consider adopting some of these suggestions:

Eat slowly. It takes approximately twenty minutes after food reaches your stomach for your brain to get the message that food has been eaten. Allowing at least twenty minutes to eat a meal will allow you to feel full after a reasonable amount of food. Try taking a five minute break in the middle of a meal. Pay more attention to the taste, smell, and texture of your food. Try to be the last person to finish each course of a meal. Cut your food into smaller bites, and put your fork down between bites or between every second bite.

Eat regularly. Plan to eat every three to five hours to avoid extreme hunger and binge eating.

When you're bored: Instead of eating, engage in some other pleasurable activity such as a hobby, a walk, or a special project. Get out of the house more often, even if it means finding a school course to attend or some community activities. When hunger and boredom strike, call up a supportive friend.

When you're angry: Instead of eating, get your feelings down on paper or tell them to the person you're angry with. Call a friend. If you must bite something, chew sugarless gum.

When you're tired: Instead of eating, go to bed. Take a relaxing bath or shower. Drink water or sparkling water with lemon juice. Get some fresh air and exercise to perk yourself up.

When you're anxious: Engage in physical activity or other enjoyable pastimes. Deal with the problem that is causing the anxiety. Divert your attention by thinking about something pleasant.

Eat smaller portions. This starts in the grocery store. Buy less, prepare less, put less on your plate. Keep the serving dishes off the table to avoid seconds. When clearing the table, don't nibble leftovers off others' plates. Don't let your problem foods such as chocolate, cookies, or potato chips even enter the house.

Eat when you're eating. Don't read, watch TV, listen to music, or do anything else while eating. When you are eating, concentrate on eating so that you are aware of how much you are eating.

3. Avoid Fats

Fat is an essential nutrient, but Americans eat too much of it. We get 45% of our calories from fat, whereas a healthy diet should contain only about 30% fat.

There are three kinds of fat. Saturated fat is solid at room temperature (meat fat, butter, heavy cream). Unsaturated or monosaturated fat is liquid at room temperature but solidifies when chilled (olive oil, the oils in avocados and cashews). Polyunsaturated fats remain liquid even when chilled (corn oil, safflower oil).

There is much controversy surrounding the connection between fats, blood cholesterol levels, blood pressure, and heart disease. The traditional, and still most widely accepted theory, is that saturated fats tend to elevate the level of cholesterol in your blood. High levels of cholesterol are associated with high rates of heart disease. Therefore, the first fats to reduce in your diet are the saturated ones: those in fatty meats, butter, whole milk, and ice cream.

The following chart will help you identify the foods you eat that contain fat, and what kinds of fats they contain.

High in polyunsaturated fats	High in monounsaturated fats	High in saturated fats
Safflower oil	Peanut oil	Meat: Beef, lamb, pork, pork products such as luncheon meats, sausages
Corn oil	Olive oil	Chicken fat
Walnuts	Olives	Meat drippings
Soynuts	Avocados	Lard
Sunflower seeds	Almonds	Hydrogenated shortening
Sesame seeds	Pecans	Coconut oil
Products made with the above	Cashews	Palm oil
	Peanuts	Butter
Moderate in polyunsaturated fats	Brazil nuts	Whole milk
Soybean oil		Whole milk cheese
Cottonseed oil		Cream: sweet and sour
Margarine		Ice cream
Commercial salad dressings (most)		Ice milk
Mayonnaise		Chocolate
		Coconut
		Products made with the above, such as most cakes, pastry, cookies, gravy, nondairy creamers, sauces, and many snack foods

People vary widely in their ability to tolerate a high fat intake without elevating their cholesterol level. The only way to be sure that you aren't consuming too much fat is to have a series of blood tests that measure cholesterol level. Two facts are certain, however: if you smoke or have high blood pressure, restricting your fat intake is essential.

4. Eat More Whole Foods

Whole foods for good nutrition include raw or lightly steamed vegetables, fruits, whole grains and cereals, brown rice, beans, dried peas, nuts, and seeds. These are complex carbohydrate foods that contain a complex mix of starch, fiber, sugar, vitamins, and minerals.

Simple carbohydrate foods to avoid are white flour, white rice, refined sugar, sugar-coated cereals, processed fruit products, and over-cooked vegetables. They are foods in which milling, refining, processing, and cooking have removed much of the fiber, vitamins, minerals, and starch, leaving a little starch and a lot of sugar. They are higher in calories and lower in nutrients than the whole foods from which they are made. "Enrichment" of flour and rice means that a few B vitamins are put back in, but falls quite short of restoring the nutrient mix that was destroyed in processing.

By choosing complex over simple carbohydrates you will be increasing your intake of dietary fibers such as cellulose from brain husks, lignin from vegetables, and pectin from fruits. Although most of this "roughage" is not absorbed by your body, it is important to digestion. Fiber has a laxative effect, resulting in softer, bulkier stools and more rapid elimination of wastes.

There is good evidence that a high fiber diet helps control weight by absorbing excess fats, and reduces your risk of diverticulosis and colon cancer. Many experts recommend supplementing your fiber intake by taking three to five tablespoons of wheat bran daily—either in a glass of water or sprinkled over other foods at one meal. If you choose to take bran, start slowly with only one tablespoon a day, because a sudden large increase in your fiber intake may result in gas pains, flatulence, and diarrhea.

5. Avoid Sugar

Americans get 25% of their calories from sugar in various forms, consuming an average of 160 pounds of sugar per year per adult. Sugar is a highly refined simple carbohydrate with no starch, fiber, vitamins, or minerals at all. It provides nothing nutritionally but calories.

Avoiding sugar is especially important if you are under stress and are one of the three out of five people who are pre-diabetic or pre-hypoglycemic. You may be extremely sensitive to changes in your blood sugar level. When you eat foods high in refined sugar, your blood sugar level shoots up, giving you a little boost of energy and perhaps a restless feeling. The sudden sugar increase stimulates your pancreas to produce insulin, which counteracts the sugar in your blood. Three out of five people have pancreases that overreact, producing too much insulin, which depresses the blood sugar level to a point much lower than before. The low blood sugar level produces hypoglycemic symptoms: dizziness, irritability, depression, tremor, nausea, anxiety, and hunger pangs that may prompt you to have another sweet treat. If you add environmental or emotional stresses to this vicious circle, you can mount an emotional rollercoaster that is hard to get off, and sugar is one of the fuels that keeps it going.

To avoid excess sugar:

- Use less of all sugars, including white sugar, brown sugar, raw sugar, honey, and syrups.

- Eat less of foods containing these sugars, such as candy, soft drinks, ice cream, cakes, cookies.

- Select fresh fruits or fruits canned without sugar or with light syrup rather than heavy syrup.

- Read food labels for clues on sugar content. If the names sucrose, glucose, maltose, dextrose, lactose, fructose, or syrups appear first, then there is a large amount of sugar.

6. Avoid Sodium

Table salt contains 40% sodium. Sodium is also present in many processed foods, condiments, sauces, pickled foods, salty snacks, and sandwich meats. Baking soda, baking powder, monosodium glutamate (MSG), soft drinks, and many medications such as antacids contain sodium.

Sodium is an essential mineral, but adults in the United States take in about 10 times more than they need. No more than five grams per day should be consumed. The major hazard of excessive sodium is for persons who have high blood pressure. Hypertensive patients consume much more sodium than those with normal blood pressure.

To avoid too much sodium:

- Learn to enjoy the unsalted flavors of foods.

- Cook with only small amounts of added salt.

- Add little or no salt at the table.

- Limit your intake of salty foods such as potato chips, pretzels, salted nuts, and popcorn, condiments like soy sauce or steak sauce, cheese, pickled foods, and cured meats.

- Read food labels carefully and pass up those listing salt or sodium early in the list of ingredients.

7. Avoid Alcohol

Alcohol is high in calories and low in other nutrients. It depletes your system of the B vitamins, which are important in helping you cope with stress.

If you are going to drink, stick to one or two glasses of beer or wine a day.

8. Avoid Caffeine

Coffee, black tea, chocolate, and colas are high in caffeine. Caffeine is a stimulant that chemically induces a "fight or flight" response in your body and depletes it of vitamin B. If you are having trouble coping with stress already, caffeine will make matters worse.

9. Take Vitamin and Mineral Supplements

Vitamins and minerals are organic and elemental substances that are contained in food, are essential to health, and are either not synthesized by your body, or are not synthesized in adequate amounts by your body.

When you are under stress you require more of all vitamins and minerals, especially the B vitamins. Deficiencies in the B vitamins, Vitamin C, and calcium/magnesium have been linked to stress-related symptoms such as insomnia, irritability, depression, and fatigue.

No single micronutrient is most important. They all work together. E helps linoleic acid, linoleic acid helps D, D helps phosphorus, phosphorus helps calcium, calcium helps C, and so on. Thus, taking massive doses of one vitamin will not give you an optimum benefit if you are deficient in other vitamins and minerals.

Nutritionists disagree about the need for supplementation of vitamins and minerals. Some say that a good diet supplies all the vitamins and minerals you need. Others say that today's supermarket foods are so nutritionally inadequate that you would have to eat three times the food your grandparents ate to get the same nutrients they did. Those who favor supplementation cite these facts about modern food:

- White flour, white rice, and white sugar are stripped of essential nutrients.

- Supermarket vegetables are bred for appearance and durability, grown in mineral-depleted soils, contaminated with pesticides, picked before they're ripe, and held in cold storage or frozen—all of which lowers their nutritional value.

- Feedlot beef, pork, and lamb and "chicken factory" poultry and eggs are low in nutrients.

- Salt, preservatives, and colorings in processed foods lower their food value.

- Chlorinated water interferes with the absorption of vitamin E.

- Drugs such as aspirin, nicotine, caffeine, and toxins from environmental pollution all deplete your body of vitamins and minerals or interfere with your body's ability to absorb them.

Given that you have decided to take vitamins and minerals, the question is how much of each? Again, there is controversy. The Federal Drug Administration and the Food and Nutrition Board of the National Research Council have come out with "RDA's" — Recommended Daily (or Dietary) Allowances for most vitamins and minerals. These recommendations tend to be on the low side, perhaps because some of the scientists who created the RDA's are consultants to food and drug companies, or hold academic chairs funded by these companies. Companies favor low RDA's because they make their food and drug products appear to be more nutritious.

The other side of the "how much" argument is represented by independent researchers such as Linus Pauling, who often recommend much larger doses than the RDA's. One of the reasons they give for these "megadoses" is that there is a great difference between the minimum amount of a nutrient required to prevent the clinical symptoms of disease, and the optimum amount of that nutrient necessary to maintain vibrant good health and resistance to disease.

A reasonable regimen of supplements might be a tablet with a balanced "stress formula" of vitamins A, E, D, C, and the B complex. Then take extra A, C, and calcium/magnesium. One of the most common stress formulas is suggested by Adele Davis in *Let's Get Well*. It includes a high protein diet supplemented by:

500 milligrams Vitamin C
100 milligrams pantothenic acid
2 milligrams each of vitamins B_2 and B_6

When you are acutely ill, Davis suggests taking these amounts with each meal, between each meal, and every three hours during the night if awake. During mild illnesses or periods of high stress, she suggests taking half these amounts six times daily, in conjunction with a daily multivitamin tablet containing vitamins A, D, and E, and a diet high in milk, liver, fresh vegetables, and wheat germ.

The following chart will help you in comparing labels of vitamins and designing your own program of supplementation. It's important not to take arbitrary megadoses of vitamins and minerals. Some can be harmful and most are only optimally effective in the correct proportion to each other. For example, calcium and magnesium must be kept in a two-to-one ratio, and your need for potassium is directly related to your intake of sodium — the more salt you consume, the more potassium you need to counteract it.

Megadoses of minerals are usually prescribed after laboratory analysis of a hair sample has indicated a specific deficiency.

When shopping for vitamins, you'll notice that some are derived from natural sources and some are synthetic. It makes sense to choose the natural sources, since they undoubtedly contain traces of important nutrients that have not yet been identified. However, it is difficult and expensive to extract some vitamins from natural sources, and this is reflected in their price. The answer is to buy the most naturally-derived vitamins that you can reasonably afford.

	RDA—Recommended Daily Allowance for adults to prevent disease	Typical daily mega-dose for adults to promote optimal health
Vitamin A	5,000 units	25,000 units*
Vitamin E	30 I.U.	400 I.U. for women
		800 I.U. for men
Vitamin D	400 units	800 units*
Vitamin C (Ascorbic acid)	60 mg.	2–10 grams (at the first hint of a cold of flu, take your normal daily dose every 3 hours for 24 hours or until you develop diarrhea)
Vitamin B_1 (Thiamine)	1.5 mg.	75 mg.
Vitamin B_2 (Riboflavin)	1.7 mg.	75 mg.
Vitamin B_3 (Niacin)	20 mg.	75 mg.
Vitamin B_6 (Pyridoxine)	2 mg.	200 mg.
Pantothenic acid	10 mg.	100 mg.
Folic acid	400 mcg.	
Vitamin B_{12}	6 mcg.	75 mg.
Biotin	150 mcg.	
Calcium	1,000 mg.	3 grams
Magnesium	350 mg.	1.5 gms.
Zinc	15 mg.	60 mg.
Manganese	**	100 mg.
Iron	10 mg. (20 mg. if there is blood loss from menstruation)	100 mg.*
Iodine	160 mcg.	40 mg.*
Chromium	1 mg.	1.5 mg.
Selenium	50 mcg.	300 mcg.*
Potassium	**	2 grams
Copper	25 mcg.	

* Toxic in high doses. Discontinue Vitamin A and resume it at a lower dose if you experience chapped lips or headaches; lower dose of iodine if you experience headaches or worsened acne; lower dose of selenium if your experience nausea, vomiting, a metallic taste, or a garlic-like breath odor.

** Essential in human nutrition, but no U.S. RDA has been established.

If you want to increase your intake of natural vitamins and minerals more economically, you can eat these foods:

- Brewer's yeast (vitamin B complex, protein) two or three tablespoons daily. Never use yeast intended for baking.

- Cod liver oil, plain, not fortified (vitamins A, F, and D), one teaspoon daily.

- Raw wheat germ (vitamin E, B complex, protein, minerals, enzymes) three to five tablespoons daily. Make sure it's fresh, with a sweet taste. Rancid wheat germ has a bitter, tangy aftertaste.

- Rose hips, powder or tablets (vitamin C, bioflavinoids, enzymes). Take the equivalent of 200 mg. vitamin C or more daily.

- Wheat germ oil (vitamin E, unsaturated fatty acids) two to three teaspoons daily.

- Bone meal, powder or tablets (minerals) two teaspoons or ten tablets daily. Lacto vegetarians can use calcium lactate.

- Kelp (iodine, minerals, trace elements) two to five tablets daily. Use kelp granules on salads as a salt substitute.

- Lecithin, granules or liquid (inositol, choline, lecithin) one tablespoon daily.

- Whey powder (lactose, minerals, iron, B vitamins) two tablespoons daily.

10. Eat Frequent, Calm Meals

Frequent, small meals—four or five a day—are better than two or three large meals, especially if you are under stress. Frequent eating avoids the stresses associated with the hunger state and maintains a more constant blood sugar level to avoid hypoglycemic symptoms.

Take time for meals. Eat slowly and enjoy the natural relaxation that comes from nutritious foods eaten in peaceful surroundings.

Further Reading

Corbin, Cheryl. *Nutrition.* New York: Holt, Rinehart and Winston, 1980.

Davis, Adele. *Let's Eat Right to Keep Fit.* New York: Harcourt, Brace, & World, 1954.

Davis, Adele. *Let's Get Well.* New York: Harcourt, Brace,Jovanovich, 1965.

Dietary Goals for the United States. Second Edition, Select Committee on Nutrition and Human Needs, U.S. Senate. Washington, D.C.: U.S. Govt. Print. Off., 1977.

Kunin, Richard A. *Mega-Nutrition: The New Prescription for Maximum Health, Energy, and Longevity.* New York: McGraw Hill, 1980.

Lappe, F. M. *Diet for a Small Planet.* New York: Ballantine Books, 1971.

Recommended Dietary Allowances. Washington, D.C.: National Academy of Sciences, 1979.

19

Exercise

Exercise is one of the simplest and most effective means of stress reduction. Vigorous physical exertion is the natural outlet for the body when it is in the "fight or flight" state of arousal. After exercise your body returns to its normal equilibrium and you feel relaxed and refreshed.

You have the same need for exercise as your primitive ancestors, whose hunting and gathering lifestyle required walking and running several miles every day. If you live the kind of sedentary lifestyle that has developed since the industrial revolution, you're probably not getting the exercise you need. Only one out of four modern city-dwellers gets enough exercise. This widespread physical inactivity is a major contributor to coronary heart disease, obesity, joint and spinal disc disease, fatigue, muscular tension, and depression.

Aerobic Exercise

There are two broad categories of exercise: aerobic exercise and low intensity exercises. Aerobic exercise involves sustained, rhythmic activity of the large muscle groups, especially the legs. Popular aerobic exercises are running, jogging, brisk walking, swimming, bicycling, and dancing. Aerobic exercise uses up lots of oxygen. This increased demand for oxygen is met by an increased heart rate, stroke volume, and respiratory rate, and a relaxation of the small blood vessels to allow more oxygen-carrying blood to reach the muscles.

The goal of aerobic exercise is to produce a "training effect" that will gradually strengthen your cardiovascular system and increase your stamina. To produce this training effect you need to exercise three days a week. Each day your heart rate should reach the aerobic range appropriate for your age and remain at that rate for twenty minutes. Exercising below your aerobic heart rate will not produce the training effect, and exercising consistently above your aerobic heart rate could put too much strain on your heart.

Low Intensity Exercise

Low intensity exercise is not vigorous or prolonged enough to produce the training effect. It can be used to increase muscle strength and flexibility and joint mobility. However, it does not provide much benefit to your cardiovascular system. If you are very sedentary or in poor physical condition, low intensity exercise will help prepare you for aerobic exercise with minimum risk of a cardiovascular accident.

You probably get more low intensity exercise than you realize, since it includes such activities as slow walking, house cleaning, shopping, office duties, and light gardening. To find out how much low intensity exercise you get, you can use a pedometer. This is a device which clips to your clothing and measures the number of miles you walk or run. It must be adjusted to your walking stride. Wear it for one week, removing it when you do aerobic exercies, and record how far you have walked at the end of each day. If you walk less than 2½ miles per day, you are considered an inactive person, and you should begin your exercise program slowly.

In addition to everyday activities such as walking, there are three kinds of low intensity exercise to choose from:

Calisthenics are stretching exercises that improve the flexibility of all your major muscle groups. They help older people maintain joint mobility. They also help prevent injury when integrated into an aerobic exercise program in the warming up and cooling down periods. The greatest attraction to these limbering-up exercises is their convenience. You need no special clothing or equipment. Weather is irrelevant because you can do them indoors at any time. Typical calisthenics include toe-touching, sit-ups, and knee-bends.

Isotonics involve the contraction of muscles against a resistant object with movement. Weight lifting is the most popular form of isotonic exercise. For younger people, bigger muscles can mean more power, endurance, and speed. For older people, isotonic exercises help tone muscles which are important in protecting joints.

Isometrics require the contraction of muscles against resistance, without movement. For example, you can push your two hands together at chest level, or push against a wall or doorjamb. Isometrics do not make muscles larger, but they do increase strength.

Symptom Effectiveness

Regular and adequate exercise is the obvious choice for increasing muscular strength, endurance, and flexibility. It is also an excellent way to relieve chronic muscular tension and associated muscle spasms, tics and tremors. Provided you combine it with proper diet, exercise will help you lose weight by burning up calories and suppressing appetite.

A program of regular aerobic exercise such as running improves your cardiovascular efficiency and your metabolism. Your heart is strengthened and enlarged, your blood vessels become more elastic, your oxygen utilization becomes more efficient, your resting pulse rate is lowered, and your level of blood fats like triglycerides and cholesterol is likely to be lowered. All this means less chance of high blood pressure, arteriosclerosis, heart attack, or stroke.

The greater flexibility and better posture gained through exercise can relieve lower back pain. Improved metabolism can relieve indigestion and chronic constipation.

Exercise will fight both chronic fatigue and insomnia. Immediately afer exercise you will feel refreshed and alert rather than fatigued. A few hours later the natural, long term relaxing effects of exercise will help you sleep.

Research is just beginning to explain why exercise is effective in reducing general anxiety and depression. Fifteen to twenty minutes of vigorous exercise stimulates both the secretion of neurochemicals called catecholamines into your brain, and the release of endorphins into your blood. Depressed people are often deficient in catecholamines. Endorphins are natural pain killers and mood elevators.

Exercise, especially in a competitive sport, is a good outlet for stressful emotions such as anger and irritability.

Contraindications

Abruptly starting a strenuous program of aerobic exercise could bring on a fatal heart attack if you are not used to the exertion. Begin slowly with low intensity exercises such as walking and easy calisthenics if you lead a sedentary lifestyle, are somewhat overweight, eat a great deal of fatty or salty foods, or smoke.

Don't start any program of exercise without seeing a doctor for a complete physical examination if you are over thirty, obese (20% over ideal weight), or have high blood pressure, arterial narrowing, or high levels of blood cholesterol. Most doctors recommend a stress electrocardiogram if you are over 40.

Once you have begun your exercise program, see a doctor if you develop heart palpitations, dizziness, chest pain, or extreme difficulty getting your breath.

Instructions

Keep a daily diary to discover times in your schedule when you can increase low intensity exercise. Make a note in the diary every time you have a chance to walk at least ten minutes. Also note how you block yourself from getting more exercise with "good reasons."

Daily Diary

Time   **Opportunity to exercise**   **Reasons to exercise or not**

Example

Angela, a 32-year-old administrative assistant, kept the following diary on a typical day:

Time	Opportunity to Exercise	Reasons to exercise or not
7:45	Let dog out to run in yard.	"I'm running late, so I can't walk the dog this morning."
8:15	Drive to work	"It's too far to walk, and my bike has a flat."
10:00	Drive with friend to special conference 3 blocks away.	"I would have walked, but I couldn't very well say 'no' to a friend offering a ride."
12:00	Drive to lunch	"I want to save time. Besides, it looks like rain."
1:00	Make calls to people who work on different floors of same building.	"It's more efficient to phone."
3:00	Walk to Post Office	"I need to stretch my legs."
5:00	Collapse on sofa at home	"I could go jogging, but I'm exhausted and I'm too out of shape since gaining 5 lbs. at Christmas."
7:30	Back on the sofa	"I could walk the dog, but it's dark and this isn't a safe neighborhood. Also, I have a headache. Maybe tomorrow . . ."

The reasons you give yourself for not exercising are powerful—they have been successful in depriving you of one of your basic needs. Facing up to them is an essential step in overcoming an inactive lifestyle. Before you attempt to refute your reasons, consider the following suggestions:

You may think that you do not have time to exercise. You say to yourself: "I'm running late; I have more important things that must be done first; my busy schedule requires that I be as efficient as possible; I know I should exercise, but my obligations just won't let me." If this sounds familiar, exercise is near the bottom of your list of priorities. Substitute all your "I can't" statements with "I choose not to." If exercise is really important, you will create a space for it in your life. Remember that as a busy person, exercise is an essential outlet for your daily pressures. Without exercise, you will become increasingly tense, out of shape, and low on physical energy. Your ability to cope with the stresses of your busy life will be jeopardized.

Even though you recognize the advantages of exercise, you may persist in a sedentary lifestyle because you believe that exercise is for the young and athletic. You may see yourself as too mature or out of shape to engage in an activity that would make you sweat, look silly, or allow others to see how uncoordinated or out of shape you are. Such beliefs will make it hard for you to initiate an exercise program on your own. You should take a class, join a group, or get together with a friend who already exercises regularly. Others will soon show you that exercise is for all ages and shapes.

There are many fears associated with exercise. Fear of a heart attack is one of the most common. You need have no fear if you get a physical exam first and start slow under a doctor's supervision. You may be afraid of injuring yourself. In this case, books, classes, and experienced people can provide you with information about how to exercise safely, what to expect as you progress, and how to cope with any difficulties you encounter.

If you are a woman, you may not have received much support for vigorous exercise. Adjectives such as weak, passive, and fragile, so long associated with femininity, do not precede nouns such as sprinter, basketball player, or swimmer. Even today, the mass media often portrays women as delicate, helpless maidens waiting to be rescued by strong, active, successful men. Here are a few facts that might interest you: Almost all women can do aerobic exercise while menstruating. About one-third of the women competing in a recent Olympiad had their period. Your reproductive organs are better protected than a man's. An athletic woman is likely to have fewer complications during pregnancy and childbirth than those who are nonathletic. Even after having children, women have won medals and set new athletic records. Exercise can be helpful in reducing tension and aches and pains during menopause. Weight lifting will not cause you to develop bulky muscles; it will help you become stronger, perform better in certain sports, and improve your figure. If you experience fatigue for reasons you cannot easily explain, you may have an iron deficiency, which can easily be rectified by eating iron-rich foods or taking an iron supplement.

Return to your **Daily Diary** and examine your reasons for not exercising.

Reason	Reason Refuted or Problem Solved
Running late . . . can't walk dog	I rarely have time to walk the dog in the morning because I don't get up early enough to do it . . . I'll set the alarm 15 min. earlier and get up as soon as the alarm goes off.
Can't bike to work . . . flat tire	It is not a matter of "can't" . . . I don't want to bike to work. But I can fix the flat, so I can bike on weekends, when I do enjoy biking in the country.
Can't decline a ride from a friend to a nearby conference	I'm full of "can't's." Obviously I can say "no," but sometimes I choose not to. I'll ask my friend to walk to such meetings in the future.
Save time by driving to lunch	I have plenty of time to walk to lunch and eat in an hour.
Drive to lunch because it looks like rain	This is the dumbest excuse yet! So what if it's cloudy . . . if I'm so concerned about the weather, I'll carry an umbrella or eat in the cafeteria downstairs.
It's more efficient to phone	True, but face-to-face contact is valuable. I have time to make the rounds in person.
Too exhausted, out of shape, and overweight to jog	All signs of exercise deprivation and the very reasons I should jog.
Unsafe neighborhood after dark	I could ask my husband to walk with me, or do some indoor exercises, or join a health club, or plan my exercise for earlier in the day.
Headache	Another possible sign of exercise deprivation and stress accumulation.
Putting off till tomorrow	My favorite strategy for avoiding exercise . . . I'll go walk the dog right now!

30-50 Minute Exercise Program

This program will stretch and tone the major muscle groups in your body. For best results, do a full set of exercises daily. If you don't have time for such an ambitious

Warm Ups—5 Minutes

Arm Circling. Stand erect, with feet comfortably apart. 1. Circle your arms 10 times in one direction. 2. Circle them 10 times in the other direction.

Toe touching. Sit on the floor with your feet against a wall. Keep your legs straight and knees locked throughout the exercise. Rest your hands on your knees. 1. Bend forward slowly and attempt to touch the wall with your fingertips. When you have bent over as far as possible, hold this position for 5 seconds. 2. Return to starting position and relax for 3 seconds. 3. Do 3 to 5 repetitions.

Muscle Conditioning—12 to 20 Minutes

These calisthenic and isotonic exercises will increase the muscular strength and endurance of all the major muscles in your body. If you feel sore after the first day of practicing these exercises, skip a day and then start again at a reduced number of repetitions until the soreness disappears.

Major Muscle Groups:

EASY

Lie on back, palms on floor, legs straight, feet together. 1. Bring knees to chest, heels as close to buttocks as possible, keep legs together. 2. Stretch legs up until they are at right angles to the floor, with toes together and pointed. 3. Return to 1. 4. Return to starting position. Begin with 4 repetitions.

Abdominal

schedule, exercise every other day. If you have to choose between the calisthenics or aerobics, do the aerobic exercises. Whenever you exercise, do the warm up stretches first to avoid putting too much sudden stress on your body.

Achilles' tendon stretch. Stand facing a wall with your feet 2 to 4 feet from it. Place your palms flat against the wall at shoulder level. Your trunk and legs remain straight and your heels remain on the ground throughout this exercise. 1. Gradually bend your arms until you feel stress in your achilles' tendons and calves. Hold this position 10 seconds. 2. Return to starting position and rest for 5 seconds. 3. Do 3 to 5 repetitions. Note: You can increase the stress on your tendons by moving your feet further from the wall and bending your arms more.

Jumping jacks. Stand erect with your feet together. 1. Jump off both feet at once, spreading them a little more than a shoulder width apart and landing on your toes. As you jump, swing arms sideways and clap them over your head. 2. Return to starting position. 3. Do 30 jumps in about 30 seconds.

Depending on your body type and experience, some muscle groups may be more powerful than others. The charts below provide progressively more difficult exercises for four main muscle groups. Select the appropriate difficulty level for each of the four grups, and then increase the number of repetitions as you grow stronger. Generally speaking, you should start with the recommended number of repetitions. Then add two repetitions each week for a month. If you feel comfortable at the end of the month, go on to the next difficulty level.

Intermediate

Lie on back with knees bent at angle of 45 to 90 degrees. Interlace fingers behind head. 1. Tucking chin into chest, curl forward into sitting position until elbows touch knees. 2. Return to starting position. Begin with 16 repetitions. Begin slowly and gradually increase pace.

Advanced

Lie on back, knees bent, calves resting on chair, fingers interlaced behind head. 1. Tucking chin into chest, curl forward into sitting position. Hold for 3 seconds. 2. Return to starting position. Begin with 10 repetitions.

Major Muscle Groups

Trunk

EASY

Stand erect, arms at sides, feet shoulder length apart, legs always straight. 1. Raise one arm over your head to the side. Keeping abdomen tucked in, chest high, and pelvis firm, continue to bend your arm and trunk to the side until you feel stress in your waist. Hold this position for 4 seconds. 2. Return to starting position. Repeat on other side. Begin with 4 repetitions.

Stand with feet comfortably apart, with hands on hips. 1. Bend knees to half squat position as you swing arms forward with palms down. 2. Return to starting position. Begin with 10 repetitions.

Thighs, hips, buttocks, lower back

Intermediate

Stand with feet a shoulder width apart. Interlace fingers behind neck. Always keep legs straight and elbows back. 1. Bend forward to waist level. 2. Twist trunk to one side. 3. Twist trunk to other side. 4. Return to starting position. Begin with 10 repetitions.

Advanced

Stand with feet a shoulder width apart and hands on hips. 1. Bend forward from waist as far as possible. 2. Twist clock-wise from the waist. 3. Continue clock-wise until you are bending backward from the waist. 4. Continue clock-wise to the side. 5. Return to starting position. Begin with 8 repetitions.

Lie on back with knees bent in angle of 45 to 90 degrees. Arms at sides with palms down. 1. Raise hips off floor as high as possible, keeping feet and shoulders on floor. Tighten buttocks and abdomen and hold for 5 seconds. Gradually increase this hold to 10 seconds. 2. Return to starting position. Begin with 8 repetitions.

Squat with hands on floor. Extend left leg to rear. Right knee is inside right elbow. 1. Simultaneously reverse position of feet. 2. Reverse feet position again, returning to starting position. Begin with 10 repetitions.

Major Muscle Groups

EASY

Stand with feet a shoulder width apart, head up, buttocks and abdomen tucked in. Extend arms at shoulders. 1. Palms up, rotate arms backwards 12 times, beginning with small circles. Gradually increase the size of the circles until you are rotating in as large circles as possible. 2. Relax your arms. Repeat with palms turned down and rotating forward. Begin with 2 repetitions. Moderate pace.

Arms, shoulders, chest for women

Place hands about a shoulder width apart on the edge of a sturdy object. Move your feet back until your legs and back are in a straight line, your body supported by your feet and hands. Always keep head up. 1. Bend arms at elbow, lowering your body until your chest touches edge. 2. Push up, straightening arms, and returning to starting position. Begin with 10 repetitions.

Arms, shoulders, chest for men

INTERMEDIATE

Stand in doorway, feet together, palms against door frame at shoulder height. 1. Press as hard as you can against frame, tucking in chin and buttocks. Hold for 6 seconds. 2. Relax arms. Begin with 3 repetitions.

Keeping feet together, squat down and put palms on floor. Hands will be inside knees about a shoulder width apart. Thrust legs backward into leaning position. 1. Keeping body and legs straight, bend elbows until chest touches ground. 2. Return to leaning starting position by straightening arms. Begin with 10 repetitions.

ADVANCED

Same as men's beginning level for arms, shoulders, and chest.

Stand with feet together, arms at sides, head up. 1. Squat down, placing palms on floor about a shoulder width apart. Arms inside knees. 2. Thrust legs back into front leaning position. 3. Lower body until chest touches floor by bending arms. 4. Raise to front-leaning position. 5. Touch chest to floor. 6. Raise to front-leaning position. 7. Return to squatting position. 8. Return to starting position. Begin with 8 repetitions.

Aerobic Exercise—20 Minutes

The simplest, most readily available form of aerobic exercise is brisk walking, jogging or running. Therefore in this section, a walking and jogging program will be used to illustrate the basic principles of aerobic exercise. You can apply these principles to other aerobic forms of exercise such as swimming, bicycling, cross-country skiing, rowing, or jumping rope.

As you jog, your large skeletal muscles rhythmically tense and relax, stimulating the blood flow through your vascular system, heart, and lungs. In order to benefit from aerobic exercise, your heart must beat at 70% of its maximum rate for at least 20 minutes. This places a moderate stress on your heart which gradually will improve its efficiency. The maximum heart rate is the fastest that your heart can beat when you exercise. The following table shows the estimated heart rates for different age groups:

Estimated Heart Rates per Minute for Average Man or Woman by Age Group

| | | EXERCISE LEVEL | | | |
Age Group	Maximum Heart Rate	80% Maximum Heart Rate	70% Maximum Heart Rate	60% Maximum Heart Rate	50% Maximum Heart Rate
18-29	203-191	162-153	142-134	122-115	101-95
30-39	190-181	152-145	133-127	113-108	95-90
40-49	180-171	144-137	126-120	107-102	90-85
50-59	170-161	136-129	119-113	101-96	85-80
60-69	160-151	128-121	112-106	95-90	80-75
70-79	150-141	120-113	105-99	89-84	75-70

To determine your heart rate for one minute, simply take your pulse for ten seconds and then multiply this number by six. Practice taking your pulse while sitting quietly. Wear a watch with a sweep-second hand on your left arm. Turn the palm of your right hand toward you. Put the tips of your left hand on your right wrist. Locate on your right wrist the bone down from the thumb. Move about 1/8 inch from that bone, and press firmly. You will feel your pulse. Your resting pulse may range from 40 to 100 beats per minute, and still be normal. Most healthy men have a resting pulse between 70 and 84 beats per minute. Most healthy women's resting pulses range between 75 and 85 beats per minute.

If you are out of shape, brisk walking may push your pulse over the 70% of the maximum heart rate for your age group. But as your cardiorespiratory system becomes conditioned, you will have to exert more effort (walk or jog faster) to attain that 70%.

Here are three simple tests that you can do to determine how fast you should walk or jog in order to achieve the 70%:

1. Walk five minutes at a comfortable pace. Take your pulse immediately, because the rate falls off rapidly. If it is about 50% of the maximum heart rate for your age group (see the above table), go on to the next test. If it is already above the 70% level, continue to walk at this pace every other day until it falls below that level. Then go on to the next test. And if you have not already had a recent physical exam, have one soon.

2. Walk five minutes at a vigorous pace. Again, take your pulse immediately. If it is about 60% of maximum, go on to the next test. If your pulse is over the 70% maximum, continue at this pace. Take five minute walks every other day until your pulse falls below the 70% level. Then go on to the next test.

3. Alternate one minute of slow jogging with one minute of brisk walking for five minutes, and then take your pulse. If it is above the 70% of maximum heart rate for your age group, continue to alternate one minute of jogging with one minute of brisk walking every other day until it falls below that level. Then you are ready to proceed on your own. If your pulse rate on this test was below 70% of maximum, you can begin a combination of brisk walking and slow jogging for a minimum of twenty minutes every other day. You will gradually spend more time jogging or even running in order to stay at the 70% of maximum rate. A good rule of thumb is to continue to jog until you feel winded, and then slow to a brisk walk for a minute. You should be able to carry on a conversation while you are jogging. If you can't, you're going too fast! You will have to check your pulse frequently until you find a pace that will keep your pulse at about 70% of maximum for at least twenty minutes. Then you can let your mind wander. The distance you run and the number of minutes it takes you to run a mile is irrelevant. However, you may enjoy measuring your progress occasionally by timing yourself on a quarter mile track.

Cool Down—5 Minutes

Always end your exercise sessions with five minutes of slow walking. Take exaggerated, long steps, stretching your legs. Let your arms dangle loosely and shake your hands. Rotate your head around on your neck a few times in one direction and then in the other direction.

Establishing Goals

Examine your daily diary to determine ways to increase the amount of low intensity and aerobic exercise you get during your day. Express these opportunities in terms of two-week goals. Make your goals realistic, taking into account your current exercise level, available resources, time limitations, and personal interests. Be conservative in setting goals that you can comfortably accomplish.

Two-Week Goals

	Low intensity (miles walked)	Muscle conditioning (minutes)	Aerobics (minutes)
Monday			
Tuesday			
Wednesday			
Thursday			
Friday			
Saturday			
Sunday			
Monday			
Tuesday			
Wednesday			
Thursday			
Friday			
Saturday			
Sunday			

_____
signature

At the end of two weeks, examine your progress. Use your experience in accomplishing or falling short of your goals to devise another set of two-week goals. Keep up this cycle until you have established the habit of regular exercise.

Keeping At It

There are two major obstacles to overcome in undertaking an exercise program: getting started and keeping at it. If you have followed the instructions in the preceding sections, you have jumped the first hurdle. The second hurdle may be more difficult. The following suggestions will help you keep at your exercise program until it becomes as automatic as eating or sleeping:

1. *Gradualism* is the key. Start small. Never overdo. If you get sick, very sore, or exhausted, you have over-exerted yourself. Exercise is fun, not torture.

2. *Keep records* of your daily and weekly progress. Check your weight and blood pressure monthly.

3. *Congratualte yourself* for accomplishing what you set as your two-week goals. Give yourself small rewards such as dinner out, an evening at the movies, or a new pair of running shoes.

4. *Focus on the rewards* of exercise. Notice how you feel relaxed, energized, refreshed, and how your concentration and sleep have improved.

5. *Post your goals* where you can see them around the house or office every day. Put up some pictures of yourself or others doing your favorite exercise. Put up mottos or statements of encouragement.

6. *Visualize success.* See yourself as already having attained the benefits of exercise. See yourself as slender, dancing gracefully, or running down a country lane looking radiant and healthy.

7. *Get support* from your family and friends by telling them about your goals. Enlist members of your family or friends in your exercise program. Join an exercise class, running club, or fitness center. Participate in group activities like races.

To Avoid Injury

1. Use proper equipment and clothing, especially shoes.

2. Allow five to ten minutes to warm up for aerobic exercises, and three to five minutes to cool down.

3. Do not exercise when ill.

4. Stop exercise if you have any unusual, unexplainable symptoms.

5. Don't exercise until at least two hours after a large meal and don't eat until one hour after exercising.

6. Avoid smoking, especially after exercising.

7. Avoid cold or very hot showers and baths before or after exercising.

8. Avoid any type of extreme temperature change while perspiring after exercise.

9. Avoid all-out efforts in which you risk heart attack or other injury.

10. Use your common sense in deciding when and where to exercise. For example, don't jog in a sparsely populated park at dusk, or run on busy city streets crossed by railroad tracks and littered with broken glass.

Further Reading

Anderson, J.L. and Cohen, M., *The West Point Fitness and Diet Book*. New York: Avon Books, 1978.

Brems, M. *Swim for Fitness*. San Francisco: Chronicle Books, 1979.

Cooper, K.H. *The Aerobic Way*. New York: M. Evans and Company, 1977.

Counsilman, J. *The Science of Swimming*. Englewood Cliffs, N.J.: Prentice-Hall, 1968.

Farquhar, J.W. *The American Way of Life Need Not Be Hazardous to Your Health*. New York: W.W. Norton, 1978.

Fixx, J.F. *Jim Fixx's Second Book of Running*. New York: Random House, 1980.

Cale, B. *The Wonderful World of Walking*. New York: William Morrow, 1979.

Gould, D. *Tennis Everyone,* Third ed. Palo Alto, California: Mayfield, 1978.

Kostrubala, T. *The Joy of Running*. New York: Pocket Books, 1976.

Smith, D.L. and Gaston, E.A. *Get Fit with Bicycling*. Emmaus, Pennsylvania: Rodale Press, 1979.

Sorenson, J. *Aerobic Dancing*. New York: Rawson Way, 1979.

Thomas, G.S. *Exercise and Health: Evidence and Implications*. New York: Oelger, Shlager, Gunn & Hain, 1981.

Ullyot, J. *Women's Running*. Mountain View, California: World Publications, 1976.

Wood, P.D. *Run to Health*. New York: Charter, 1980.

Wiener, H.S. *Total Swimming*. New York: Simon and Schuster, 1980.

20

When It Doesn't Come Easy — Getting Unstuck

This book has covered many techniques to reduce stress and tension. Essentially they provide alternatives to our old stressful habits. You may have found that just practicing the new skills and observing the positive effects has caused you to give up the old habits. For instance, you may have found that practicing slow, deep breaths rather than short, constricted breaths results in a relaxed sense of well being. This positive feedback from your body may have provided ample motivation for you to give up your old anxiety provoking shallow breathing habit. However, if you are like most people, at some point you probably encountered some difficulty in exchanging old familiar habits for new ones. This chapter takes a look at why old habits are hard to part with, even when they are obviously contributing to your stress. It also offers some suggestions for how to deal with your own resistance to change.

If you find yourself skipping an exercise session you have contracted with yourself to do, or are aware that you are just going through the motions of the exercises, ask yourself some of the following questions:

1. Why am I doing these exercises?

2. Are these reasons really important to me?

3. What am I doing or would I like to be doing instead of these exercises?

4. Is this alternative activity more important to me than my doing the exercises?

5. Can I schedule my life so that I can do the exercises *and* this alternative activity?

6. If I do not want to do the exercises now, exactly when and where will I do them next?

7. What would I have to give up if I succeeded with my exercises?

8. What would I have to confront if I succeeded with my exercises?

Taking Responsibility for Your Decisions

It is difficult to learn new habits on your own, especially when, at least at first, the rewards for your efforts may be minimal. When distractions occur, decide whether you want to be detoured or your want to continue on your chosen route. If you decide to take the detour, do so with full awareness, after weighing the pros and cons. Before going off on the detour, make an appointment with yourself for when and where you are next going to do your exercises. In this way you are taking responsibility for your decision. In addition, you are less likely to feel bad about yourself for not following through on your original plan, if that is your conscious choice.

Questioning Your Excuses May Prove Enlightening

When you slack off on your exercises, it if often illuminating to examine the reasons you tell yourself this is happening. Typical reasons are: "I'm too busy today," "I'm too tired," "Missing once won't hurt," "David needs my help," "This isn't working," "This is boring," "I feel relaxed and unstressed today, so I don't need to exercise," or "I feel too bad today to do exercises." These excuses are seductive because they are partially true. That is, you may really feel very busy or tired, somebody may want your help, and missing one session probably won't hurt. The part that isn't true is the implication that because you are busy or tired or someone needs your help, you cannot do the exercise sessions. A more truthful statement would be, "I am tired. I could do the exercises, but I choose not to," or "I could do my exercises, but I choose to help David rather than do them." The important point here is that you take responsibility for your decision to choose one activity over another, rather than pretend that you are the passive victim of circumstances such as your fatigue, David's demands or other priorities that keep you busy.

You may find yourself repeatedly using the same reason or similar reasons for not doing your exercises. A common theme with many variations is: "I'm indispensable. Things won't get done without me and may even fall apart," For example, one very bright, middle-aged housewife and mother could rarely find time to do her exercises because her house work was never done. She believed that she could not take time out for herself or the pile of chores would grow rapidly into an unassailable mountain. After years of doing continuous housework with no time set aside to relax, she was run down, depressed, anxious, having migraines and lower back pain, and getting work done at a fraction of her previous rate. Her perfectionistic belief that she had to do all of her work before she had a right to relax had caused a gradual depletion of her energy. The result was inevitable physical and emotional signs of stress.

The excuses you give yourself for not doing your exercises are likely to be the same ones that you have used for years to keep yourself locked into a stressful situation. These excuses are based on faulty premises. For example, the middle-aged woman mentioned above believed erroneously that she had no right to relax until all her work was done. But the work of a housewife and mother is never done, therefore she could never relax. Furthermore, she had overlooked her innate right (and some would call it her obligation) to relax and replenish her vital store of energy. This woman had defined her priorities as being "housewife first" and "me second," without taking into account the importance of relaxation and getting away from stressful activities for maintaining good mental health and physical health.

If you are an energetic person who likes to succeed, who likes to get things done yesterday, slow down your pace when learning these exercises. Enthusiasm may push you to take on many exercises at once and do the sessions for too long. You run a high risk of burning out and losing interest if you do too much too fast. Furthermore, you are likely to feel guilty for not keeping up the rigorous program you have set for yourself. Soon you will find yourself coming up with excuses to avoid exercising at all ("I'm over-extended already in many areas of my life. Why add to the burden?").

You may feel confused when you begin to experience *more* energy as a result of doing the relaxation and stress reduction exercises. Resist the temptation to pour this extra energy back into your work. Rather, use it for further rest and enjoyment.

Common Roadblocks in the Road to Relaxation

If you read this workbook without doing any of the exercises, you have reason to expect that you are only dabbling. Intellectually, you see the value of the exercises, but you somehow never get much past the stage of thinking about them; or you may actually do some of the exercises, but never apply them to everyday situations. For the dabbler, this is just another book with some interesting ideas, rather than a workbook promoting experiential learning of new ways to deal with stress.

There are some individuals who are frightened by novel experiences, and this fear becomes a roadblock to success. You might become overwhelmed by some side effect of a relaxation technique such as tingling in your arms and legs. Unfortunately, you may then stop the exercise instead of going on to find that the tingling is not harmful and goes away with time. You can get turned off by a single element of an exercise and, rather than changing the exercise to fit your needs, drop the exercise. Perhaps you don't understand a step in the instructions and rather than ad lib, you chuck the whole thing. It can be a valuable growth experience to work through these difficulties on your own.

When Symptoms Persist

Sometimes symptoms of stress persist in spite of regular relaxation and stress reduction. If you are a conscientious person, and have been practicing regularly, this is disheartening. The following are just a few of the most common reasons why this might be happening to you.

Some people are highly suggestible and begin to experience every symptom that they hear about. For example, one very tense policeman joined a relaxation group to overcome his tendency to hyperventilate when under stress. He found himself experiencing all of the physical symptoms described by the other group members: migraines, lower back pain, rapid heartbeat and so forth. These tendencies may be combatted by combining thought stopping with progressive relaxation.

A surprising number of people are attached to their symptoms, which serve a very definite purpose. For example, your headaches may get you out of interpersonal situations you want to avoid, without having to take responsbility for disappointing others. You can soon find out whether your symptoms rescue you from more unpleasant experiences by keeping a log of when you get your symptoms and the activities (or would-be activities) that surround them. If you suspect that your symptoms provide you "secondary gain" in this manner, refer to the chapter on assertiveness training. It should provide you with the incentive and the tools to be more direct in saying "no."

Your symptoms of tension may be a signal that you are not dealing effectively with something in your life and that you are covering up your feelings. For example, you may be angry with your family but not sharing this fact with them. You might be putting off talking about a particular conflict because you don't see any way of improving matters. For example, a nurse was visited every other weekend by a very spoiled stepdaughter. She agreed to the arrangement when she married, and felt trapped in the arrangement. Within three years the visits invariably produced a migraine headache. To counteract this symptom, she finally negotiated a new contract with her husband to spend Sundays on her own while he babysat.

The people around you are apt to be aware that you are withholding stressful feelings and that something is wrong. Nevertheless they cannot read your mind, and are unlikely to come to your rescue. You know best what you need. Letting others know your feelings and what you want opens the way to engaging them in helping you make a change.

Your symptom may be a way of getting taken care of when you feel that you cannot direclty ask for help or consideration. If you feel tired and have a backache, someone else may have to do the cooking and cleaning and keep the house quiet. Ask yourself when your symptoms first began. What was going on in your life that might have contributed to it? One elderly woman who had suffered from periodic colitis since childhood recalled that her abdominal cramps began when her younger twin brothers were born. She remembered that the only time her busy mother ever held her and rocked her was when she had the symptoms. She noted that she tended to get colitis only when her husbnad left her alone in the evenings.

It is possible that you have developed a symptom of an important person in your life as part of your identification with them. For example, you may not only have learned to be hard working and successful from your father, but also to deal with stress in a similar manner. Carrying your tension in your stomach, you may come to the point of getting an ulcer just like your father. Since characteristic ways of responding to stress are generally learned, ask yourself who in your family shares your same symptoms. It's often easier to learn how they are not dealing effectively with the stress in their lives than to see it in yourself. The next step is to observe and see if the same is true for you.

If you continue to have difficulty reducing the stress in your life, consider consulting a professional. You may be interested in one-on-one sessions, or in joining one of the relaxation and stress reduction groups that are becoming more and more common. Your medical doctor, company health plan or community health organization are good places to start looking for professional help.

Persistence Pays

Finally, don't give up. Your ability to relax, learn to handle stress and heal yourself is a tremendous power. Change might not always come easy—you may feel stuck in your old stressful habits—but you can do it. All it takes is patience, persistence . . . and time.

Audio Tapes Designed
To Be Used With This Book

Progressive Relaxation & Breathing, $10.95

Body Awareness & Imagination, $10.95

Autogenics & Meditation, $10.95

Self-Hypnosis, $10.95

Thought Stopping, $10.95

All tapes are written by Matthew McKay, Ph.D. and Patrick Fanning and narrated by Jerry Landis. These tapes are unique. They are not just *about* relaxation—they actually *train* you in essential relaxation skills. You don't just listen to these tapes, you experience them. You interact with them in a step-by-step process of programmed learning.

Lifetime Money Back Guarantee: If you're not completely satisfied with these tapes, you may return them at any time, for any reason, for a full refund of the purchase price.

To order, use the coupon on the following page.

Other New Harbinger Self-Help Titles

When Once Is Not Enough: Help for Obsessive Compulsives, $11.95

The New Three Minute Meditator, $9.95

Getting to Sleep, $10.95

The Relaxation & Stress Reduction Workbook, 3rd Edition, $13.95

Leader's Guide to the Relaxation & Stress Reduction Workbook, $14.95

Beyond Grief: A Guide for Recovering from the Death of a Loved One, $10.95

Thoughts & Feelings: The Art of Cognitive Stress Intervention, $12.95

Messages: The Communication Skills Book, $11.95

The Divorce Book, $10.95

Hypnosis for Change: A Manual of Proven Techniques, 2nd Edition, $11.95

The Deadly Diet: Recovering from Anorexia & Bulimia, $11.95

Self-Esteem, $11.95

The Better Way to Drink, $10.95

Chronic Pain Control Workbook, $12.50

Rekindling Desire: Bringing Your Sexual Relationship Back to Life, $10.95

Life Without Fear: Anxiety and Its Cure, $9.95

Visualization for Change, $11.95

Guideposts to Meaning: Discovering What Really Matters, $10.95

Controlling Stagefright, $10.95

Videotape: Clinical Hypnosis for Stress & Anxiety Reduction, $24.95

Starting Out Right: Essential Parenting Skills for Your Child's First Seven Years, $12.95

Big Kids: A Parent's Guide to Weight Control for Children, $10.95

Personal Peace: Transcending Your Interpersonal Limits, $10.95

My Parent's Keeper: Adult Children of the Emotionally Disturbed, $11.95

When Anger Hurts, $11.95

Free of the Shadows: Recovering from Sexual Violence, $11.95

Resolving Conflict With Others and Within Yourself, $11.95

Liftime Weight Control, $10.95

The Anxiety & Phobia Workbook, $12.95

Love and Renewal: A Couple's Guide to Commitment, $11.95

Send a check or purchase order for the titles you want, plus $1.50 for shipping and handling, to:

New Harbinger Publications
5674 Shattuck Avenue
Oakland, CA 94609

Or write for a free catalog of all our quality self-help publications.